D0894069

Also by J. Bowyer Bell

The Secret Army: The I.R.A., 1916–1970   1971
Long War: Israel and the Arabs since 1946   1969
Besieged: Seven Cities Under Attack   1966

THE MYTH
OF THE
GUERRILLA

*This book was written under the
auspices of the Center for
International Affairs, Harvard
University.*

THE MYTH
OF THE
GUERRILLA

Revolutionary Theory and Malpractice

J. Bowyer Bell

322.42
B413m

Alfred A. Knopf
New York 1971

C. L. HARDY LIBRARY
ATLANTIC CHRISTIAN COLLEGE
WILSON, N. C. 27893

THIS IS A BORZOI BOOK
PUBLISHED BY ALFRED A. KNOPF, INC.

Copyright © 1971 by J. Bowyer Bell
All rights reserved under International and Pan-American Copyright
Conventions. Published in the United States by Alfred A. Knopf, Inc.,
New York, and simultaneously in Canada by Random House of Canada
Limited, Toronto. Distributed by Random House, Inc., New York.
ISBN: 0-394-47169-5
Library of Congress Catalog Card Number: 71-154922
A portion of this book first appeared in
the April 1970 issue of *The New Middle East*.
Manufactured in the United States of America
First Edition

Dedication

This is for my four daughters,
who may in the fullness of time
live in an age where the myths
need not stress the dragons instead of the princesses:

Rebecca Lynn Waring
Virginia Byrd Snowden
Elizabeth Hill Carter
Maria Champe Storrow

JUL 18 1972

72- 7778

*War is not merely a political act,
but also a real political instrument, a continuation of political
commerce, a carrying out of the
same by other means.*

—Karl von Clausewitz

*Political power grows out of the
barrel of a gun.*

—Mao Tse-tung

Contents

Foreword

THIS WAS A BOOK that I had never intended to write but found increasingly unable to avoid as I plodded the back-roads of contemporary revolutionary activity. In recent years, I have, at what often seemed interminable length, talked with past advocates of violence, who had not always successfully but usually rationally, directed campaigns in Europe and the Middle East. Increasingly I found that many if not most of the contemporary practitioners of revolution spoke much the same language, pursued similar goals with familiar tactics but seemed to live, to act in different if parallel worlds. What had at first seemed a mutual guerrilla-language served only to confuse, for increasingly it became clear that the gap between their theory and practice, between their avowed motivation and unstated premises was major, not a result of enthusiasm or conscious policy but a difference in kind from the comfortable, rational explanations of the older revolutionaries of Cyprus or Ireland or Palestine. The new generation of active revolutionaries was somehow to me very different and increasingly disturbing. Something seemed to be wrong, and consequently I gave up haranguing my academic friends, passing journalists, and those involved and turned to the typewriter to see if I could explain if not what was wrong at least what was so clearly different about these advocates of revolution.

Essentially, a great many sincere and highly dedicated men seemed to be avid in the pursuit of guerrilla activities that, on their own terms, held little if any promise of success. By the Sixties, the way of the guerrilla had become a

fashion, copied out of context by a generation of young
political activists and seized as the most appropriate strategy in the most unlikely circumstances. The guerrilla-
revolution in the streets of Paris or the jungles of South
America has been, and is, repeatedly proposed as the inevitably successful means to secure victory—and yet the
weight of evidence indicates that such means rarely succeed. The resulting analysis of what seemed and seems
to me to be a major myth could only have been undertaken
by the cooperation of many who may now see my interest
as motivated only by a desire to maim, to mock their most
cherished aspirations by what will appear cold and irrelevant, perhaps ignorant, logic; to reduce their sacrifice to
public folly; and to twist the real world in the name of
truth. This would be most unfortunate, for in the midst of
their own all-consuming struggle a great many men mindful of my doubts have nevertheless given most generously
of their time largely for no other purpose than to act as
handmaidens to the truth.

Thus, above and beyond the traditional sources of the
printed word this book has been made possible by the
willingness of men to talk about their revolutions. Through
the toleration and, more important, with the substantial
support of the Center for International Affairs at Harvard
University, I have been able to crisscross the Middle East
and Africa several times to contact the active and to review
the past with the "retired." Coupled with this academic
grand tour have been some years of work on the Irish revolutionaries, past and present, and contacts with a variety
of other active movements in Europe and North America.
None of the over twenty movements investigated are here
listed, in part to avoid invidious distinction but mainly to
protect the innocent from responsibility for my conclusions. I have had the opportunity as well to talk with the
guardians of order—military commanders, Special Branch
detectives, administrators and intelligence officers in a
dozen or more countries—and, as in the case of the revolu-

tionaries, received a degree of cooperation beyond reasonable expectations. Although exhausting at times, the long period of what my more scientific colleagues call field research gave me the opportunity to live vicariously the life of a James Bond, questioned by security agents, lost in the Sudan desert of northwest Eritrea, followed by day watched by night in exotic places; and yet despite my dubious purpose and often during troubled times in areas of great tension, I found far less suspicion and far more understanding than my contentious subject might have warranted. In a sorely troubled world the pursuit of the truth still garners consideration and cooperation. Here I thank all those who gave aid and comfort, too much beer or too kind letters of introduction, too many hours or too many glasses of tea, and hope—assuming that this should reach their eyes—that when I pass their way again they will accept that I have written the truth as I have seen it if not the way they told it.

On a more conventional level, one of the serious problems of comparative work is the necessarily shallow grasp of many very different special examples. Few can expect to know well tribal politics in Rhodesia and Revisionist theory in Israel and the mores of Bolivian Indians, and I have been most fortunate in eliciting comment from many of my colleagues or cooperating specialists who bear not even the vaguest responsibility for my egregious errors. They have at length explained that Bolivian Indians are not sullen or that the Spanish Republicans did make use of guerrillas or that my spelling of even simple English words was appalling. My thanks to them all: Lewis Ashley, Rupert Emerson, Edward Feit, Gino Germani, Michael Handel, William Harris, Robert Jervis, Seymour Martin Lipset, Richard D. Mallon, Christopher Mitchell, Amos Perlmutter, John D. Powell, George Quester, Robert Rotburg, Gene E. Sharp, Kalvin Silvert, Ghossan Tueni, and Barton Whaley. Those more directly involved in the events of the text who were kind enough to comment remain nameless, again to limit their responsibility for the disagreeable contents. I should also like to thank Maury Feld of the Center's library for rounding up the odd book and poking holes in a few theories; Marina S. Finkelstein for editing a basically unwieldly manuscript; and my secretary Jeanette Asdourian for long hours over a hot typewriter.

And then, when I assumed that the last draft was in fact final, my editor at Knopf, Carol Brown Janeway, resorting to a campaign of guerrilla-attrition, forced extensive and significant changes, drove me to despair and again to the typewriter to apply more rigorous standards to my faulty reasoning. Much of what merit the final, final draft possesses is a result of her protracted pressure, and the remaining failings are my own.

Above all else, I owe thanks to Professor Tom Schelling, without whose perceptive eye and long toleration this would never have been written at all or as well. Too often he must have wondered why, if I were supposed to be doing one thing in one part of the world, I would turn up far afield on a strange spoor. His patience and enthusiasm may in these pages not have been amply rewarded, but he has always had the courage of my convictions—a most graceful virtue.

Finally, I should like to thank my wife, who, sealed in a Knightsbridge flat in London with our four daughters, could follow my travels only vicariously through the odd postcard and the printed rumor of attractive trouble along my scheduled route. Her patience and enthusiastic support of a husband who first seemed to commute to Central Africa on alternate weeks and then came to Cambridge to bury himself amid typescript have been without measure. But then they always have been.

J. Bowyer Bell

Center for International
Affairs, Harvard University

January 1971

PART I

Old Tactics as New Strategy: The Development of the Theory of Guerrilla-Revolution

*Without a revolutionary theory
there is no revolutionary practice.*
—V. I. LENIN

FOR A VERY SUBSTANTIAL PORTION of the history of warfare, the cluster of techniques and tactics today called guerrilla formed the central and almost only means of armed combat. With the development of complex civilizations came, of course, more complex military organizations: the Athenian navy or the Roman legions. But, despite the accelerated development of sophisticated civilizations and of consequently more organized, more elegant, and more efficient forms of warfare, the little wars of hit-and-run, ambush-and-hide, retained a significant place in the spectrum of war. This remained true even after the industrial revolution; for only the advanced could afford the new engines of war, while the undeveloped retained their old tactics.

Much of the expansion of the advanced Western societies, which wielded highly developed military technology, met the opposition of the weak, the arms of the primitive—the tactics of the guerrilla. Although the *guerrilleros*, irregular soldiers, received their title in the "little war" fought by Spain against the orthodox troops of Napoleon, other formal and orthodox armies had long been forced to suffer the attrition of irregular resistance. The Americans had turned the techniques of the Indians against the British well before the Spanish *guerrilleros* arrived on the scene. For their part, the American Indians engaged in an unsuccessful campaign of attrition which was to last from the seventeenth to the eve of the twentieth century—surely one of the most protracted of conflicts.

In the academies and in the manuals of military theory, these guerrilla-wars attracted little notice.* Most natives could be intimidated by a whiff of grape; most orthodox armies would suppress, not support, "irregular" warfare. Regular armies were intended to, and would continue to, fight regular battles. Even the "revolutionary" armies of the nineteenth and twentieth centuries sought to transform themselves as rapidly as possible into "regular" armies, albeit with different banners. In any case, the campaigns on the American frontier or in Africa or on the northwest frontier of India were peripheral to the vital military concerns of the major powers.† The security of the industrial state rested on the trained soldiers and the complicated machines of war. The potential of the guerrilla was too limited to weigh, even slightly, in the complex balance of modern war games.

The war games, if not all the wars, of the nineteenth century were played by the theorists of the major powers, the field marshals and staff generals who saw the war-board as orderly squares and orthodox armies as its pieces. Victory, essentially, would go to the large battalions. Subsequently there would be those who could find the principles of guerrilla warfare within the orthodox canon. (Earliest, perhaps, was the prophetic, if difficult of application, wisdom of the Chinese Sun Yzu of the fifth century B.C.) The French Jeune École school of naval strategy, for example, can be included because of its elaboration of the eighteenth-century *guerre de course*, which

---

* The Russians had in 1812 consciously followed the Spanish example by organizing partisan resistance; but after the defeat of Napoleon, the regular army was reluctant to give credit to the exploits of the guerrillas.

† One of the best, if not widely influential, books on the subject was Charles E. Callwell's *Small Wars: Their Principles and Practice* (London, 1899).

advised shamelessly, Attack the weak, fly from the strong.[*]
Clausewitz saw in the Spanish experience of 1808–12 a
form of people's warfare—a truly new power—introducing
a new means of defense. No matter how much practice
there had been, from Bertrand du Guesclin in the Hundred
Years' War through Roger's Rangers in America to the
Zulu Wars in Africa, until the twentieth century almost
no substantial military theorists of guerrilla-war *per se* appeared; furthermore, few "professionals" then or later dis-
tinguished the essential nature of guerrilla-warfare.

However little "theoretical" interest the guerrilla attracted, the techniques of dealing with guerrilla-tactics,
distasteful or not, took up a great deal of time. The British
became involved in a difficult, protracted war in South
Africa against the Boers, who were neither "natives" nor
"regulars." Only the persistent use of the vast resources of
the Empire, the acclimatization to Boer tactics, and the
development of the concentration camp finally brought
the war to a successful conclusion. To some degree, all the
Western imperialist powers found themselves facing irregular wars—the Spaniards in Cuba or the United States
in the Philippines—but always the campaigns remained
peripheral. Few of Clausewitz's orthodox contemporaries
or successors focused on this new means of defense—a
distant sideshow insufficiently vital to attract great
academic notice. Out of necessity, the soldiers involved on
the spot developed a body of anti-irregular techniques,
which, however, seldom drifted back to the classrooms
of the academy. Indian fighting was not taught at West
Point but in North Dakota and Arizona. When the *real* war
came in 1914 after several false starts, the intricate, highly

---

[*] As would later be the case with guerrilla-warfare, the French
were attracted by the idea of winning a cheap victory by unorthodox means over superior forces. A supplement to conventional
naval warfare, *la guerre de course* offered much but as the only
alternative to superior conventional forces failed to achieve a cheap
strategic victory, only a string of irrelevant tactical successes.

reasoned scenarios of the academy were acted out by millions of men in Western Europe.

Having welded their armies into a scene of massive, immobile slaughter, the military theorists evolved no alternative to endless attrition. Even the dispatch of a hundred thousand or so men to the European flanks remained a "sideshow." In the chaos of the Eastern front after the collapse of the Romanovs, the Germans did meet irregular and often erratic resistance; but the part played by guerrillas in the calculations of the orthodox was negligible. The innovators saw hope in the new machines, not in straggling bands on the distant edge of the war. Only in one of the sideshows, General Edmund Allenby's offensive out of Egypt against the Turkish Empire, did irregulars play a recognizable role. T. E. Lawrence and the Arab Revolt swiftly became the property of the newspapers and the public, eager for a dashing hero and a campaign without mud and stolid massacre; but the generals knew that the war had been won in the mud of the Western front, not the romantic sands of Arabia. Once the military theorists had recovered from the trauma of the war, their visions of the next and future war excluded such dashing irregulars and instead turned on the lessons of France, apparently poorly learned for so long and at such cost.

Lawrence did, however, in his *Seven Pillars of Wisdom*, give military science a sound, literate explanation of the nature of irregular war. Obviously the strategy and tactics, much less the techniques, of his desert war were not novel in the history of warfare, but for the first time there was a reasoned popular explanation of guerrilla-warfare, stressing the importance of many facets which would become truism—in particular and basically the use of protracted attrition, achieved by a variety of evasive tactics, to raise the price of occupation beyond the capacity of the Turks to continue to pay. The key was not so much in the techniques of hit-and-run, hide-and-seek, quick ambushes and long periods of somnolence, but in the erosion of the will of the stronger—a victory to be won in Turkish hearts or Turkish judgment, not over Turkish troops. Lawrence's account of the Arab Revolt did, in fact, attract considerable interest in the West, but on literary grounds. The British military establishment accepted Lawrence as a genuine hero but also thought that he was unsound, difficult, and for their purposes irrelevant. War as he described it—intangible, without front or back, drifting about like gas—was not their war. *The Seven Pillars of Wisdom* did not become a text. Instead, the more daring among them grasped at the new technology—the airplane, the tank, the submarine—as means to evade another bloody stalemate. The less daring proposed theorems of the balanced attack or massive defensive lines in depth and in concrete. When the little colonial wars began again, the best military minds of the day were devising scenarios of strategic air strikes or fully armored thrusts. During the interwar period some tactical attention was focused on the small colonial wars and expeditions and some consideration given to partisans as an adjunct to regular armies, but as always the main theme was the use of the big battalions and the new military technology. The challenge of revolution was to be met either in open battle, against a Red Army or by the exercise of internal repression to overthrow the barricades or crush a general strike. Anti-guerrilla techniques were to be used against native revolts or tribal intrusion, not against the sophisticated urban-based parties of subversion.

Until well into the twentieth century, the revolutionaries, like the professional theorists, had seldom concentrated on the potential of the guerrilla, who by nature would be a peasant—an unlikely convert to the solidarity of the urban working class, and beyond the strictures of revolutionary discipline so often thought essential. There were those with faith in the potential of the peasant but few considered the prospects of a peasant-guerrilla. The nineteenth-century prophets of revolution—the nationalists and the socialists—who sought a position at the board of nineteenth-century power games, by necessity had to seek their pieces elsewhere; and they proposed to use a variety of new modes of conflict, not simply the single guerrilla chip.

The towering revolutionary theorist Karl Marx gave to the cause of revolution a philosophy, an explanation of history, a program of action, and an outline of the future. His scientific socialism introduced into revolutionary theory an elegance and order heretofore missing in the polemics of the Left. The discipline and direction of his thought, the rigor of his analysis, the relevance of his conclusions transformed the perception of the Left. It taught the rebel not so much to be sly, to apply tactics, but to be wise, to select the appropriate strategy in light of the nature of historical reality. Marx's views on revolutionary strategy remained grounded in the class struggle and the potential of the proletariat in an insurrection. The protracted campaign of attrition waged by peasants in the countryside—the way of the guerrilla—at best was outside the mainstream of revolution.

In 1849, Marx felt that a nation fighting for liberty need not adhere to the accepted rules of warfare but could apply revolutionary methods, including use of guerrilla-bands, to overcome a stronger and better organized enemy. The theorists of the Left were involved with the techniques of revolution, achieved by insurrection, rather than with those of pure war—class war, yes, or a war of national liberation, but not the "pure" war of the academies, where two professional armies clashed in open battle. As a result, they did not propose pure military solutions to class and national problems but sought the road to power by different routes. The advocacy of the true, tactical path to power caused as many schisms in the Left as arguments over the use of such power. The nihilists and some of the anarchists, Bakunin and Nechaev, opted for terror; Louis Blanc and his followers for coups and conspirators; the syndicalists looked to the general strike; and, at first at least, Marx and Engels projected the barricade as the ultimate weapon. At very best, the techniques of the guerrilla played a minor role in much of militant thinking. In Marxism the guerrilla struggle was an aspect of revolutionary tactics, but in many of the other revolutionary theories it was ignored entirely. Marx in fact had grave doubts about the lack of centralized control, which made the guerrilla so flexible and so effective and yet left him, like the Spanish irregulars, undisciplined and uncommitted to any cause but his appetites.

> As to the guerrillas, it is evident that, having for some years figured upon the theater of sanguinary contests, taken to roving habits, freely indulged all their passions of hatred, revenge and love of plunder, they must in times of peace, form a most dangerous mob, always ready at a nod in the name of any party or principle, to step forward for him who is able to give them good pay or to afford them a pretext for plundering excursions.[1]

For Marx and the Marxists his very freedom of maneuver made the guerrilla politically suspect.

The nature of guerrilla-tactics—to fly from the strong, attack the weak, disappear into the people, and return on the morrow—were well known but did not seem intrinsically to offer much to the organization of revolution. Such tactics appeared in any case to be largely rural, as had been the case in Spain and Russia, and the future according to the socialists belonged to the proletariat: the urban exploited class that would require urban revolutionary tactics. The anarchists who sought power through violence opted for terror as well as the barricades, and although the similarity between guerrilla-tactics and terrorist tactics was apparent, the difference between guerrilla bands in the hills and conspiratorial cells in the cities was great. The revolutionaries, neither socialist nor anarchist, who wanted to create new nation states or destroy the existing ruling system often foresaw grasping power with a people's army —Garibaldi and his Red Shirts sweeping out the old with his new militia-legion. Whatever the very great differences within the ranks of revolution, the combination of a reactionary dynastic system that denied both national self-determination and self-government with the rise of a capitalist economic system that denied a decent life to the working class created a whole litany of grievances. Italy was divided into mini-kingdoms often ruled by incompetent and cruel foreigners; the workers in Manchester or Saint Petersburg were brutalized and exploited; in Prussia or Spain or Portugal there was autocracy and despotism enforced by bayonets.

There were those who felt the legitimate aspirations of the people could be achieved within the system by change, by compromise, by negotiation; but there were many others who saw no means to create a new society or a new nation except through revolution. The appropriate revolutionary means became an area of deep dispute. Even when the goal could be defined—often not the case—the proper strategy divided the militant. In Russia, the eventual site of success, the differences in the ranks of revolution were, as elsewhere, vast. Many of those disillusioned with the Populist failures to transform the Russian peasant turned to assassination as members of the Land and Freedom Movement and, later, of the People's Will. The wave of assassination, culminating in the death of Czar Alexander II, led not to the revolution but to governmental repression and the outraged criticism from more scientific revolutionaries, who felt terror was as utopian as Populism. Even within the Marxian ranks of scientific socialism there were sharp divisions between revisionist and orthodox, between Martov and Lenin, between the Jewish Bund on the outside and the Social Democratic Labor Party on the inside. And there was the competition of the Socialist

Revolutionary Party, which created a Fighting Organization to carry out renewed assassinations. All these divisions in Russia had parallels throughout Europe, and all the disputes and dissertations and dissent produced a rich lore of revolutionary analysis. And the theories often led as well to the barricades or the gun. Almost every form of political violence found advocates among the theorists and usually a place in the active practice of revolution. Kings and Presidents were assassinated, mobs racked cities, peasants rose and soldiers mutinied, barricades were built—and factories. The record of failure, of brief success, and of near-run things grew as did the body of closely reasoned revolutionary theory, but without a significant role for the guerrilla.

Then in Russia in 1918 the endurance record of the Paris Commune was surpassed and soon the revolutionaries of the world had the novel experience of digesting the lessons of victory. The Left had been inundated with success. After the October Revolution in 1917 had come the victory in the Civil War. The new Red Army had reached the suburbs of Warsaw. There had been Communist revolutions in Bavaria and Budapest. First Germany and then Italy trembled on the brink of revolution. Even the French fleet had mutinied in the Black Sea. Although the "inevitable" world revolution so close in the first years after the World War soon began to fade, the success of the revolution in Russia gave the theoreticians of insurrection ample scope for analysis. Just as Marx had been fascinated by the Spanish guerrilla-rising or the Paris Commune, which he thought with certain adjustments might serve as the template for the ultimate revolution, so Lenin had sought the key to the future in the events of the past, particularly in the Russian Revolution of 1905, a near-run thing. Lenin, more flexible than the succeeding doctrinaire Leninists, had foreseen the ultimate onslaught of the proletariat against the crumbling bastions of capital-

ism as a result of a variety of techniques and tactics, assimi-
lated by the masses through preparatory failures:

> the very fact that revolts do break out at different
> times, in different places, and are of different kinds,
> guarantees wide scope and depth to the general move-
> ment; but it is only in premature, individual, sporadic
> and therefore unsuccessful revolutionary movements
> that masses gain experience, acquire knowledge,
> gather strength, and get to know their real leaders,
> the socialist proletarians, and in this way prepare for
> the general onslaught, just as certain strikes, dem-
> onstrations, local and national, mutinies in the army,
> outbreaks among the peasants, etc., prepared for war
> for the general onslaught in 1905.[2]

Alas for the pure theorists, the events in the autumn of
1917 failed to follow Lenin's prescribed pattern.

In 1917, the long-awaited "general onslaught"—the
moment of truth when capitalism was to be overthrown by
proletariat force—never came; instead, Lenin found power
lying in the streets, picked it up, and defended his position
with an orthodox if hastily organized Red Army. The
Russian state, enfeebled by the disastrous losses of the
war, had indeed collapsed under the pressure of the strikes,
demonstrations, army mutinies and peasant outbreaks, and
a series of revolts often spontaneous and seldom instigated
by the Bolsheviks—not from a carefully orchestrated revolution. The last feeble resistance was pushed aside and
Lenin rushed in to fill the vacuum.*

The Czarist autocracy was no longer the enemy of the
new Soviet—and the proposed socialist revolution—regime, but rather the quarreling and contradictory military
forces of restoration and their foreign allies were. All the

---

* The question whether or not the October Revolution was a
coup has been a vital one for Marxist historians; but to the less
ideologically committed, Lenin clearly had minimal control over
events in October and his grasp of the possibilities owes as much
to pragmatism as theory.

analysis of revolutionary theory to grasp power had to be jettisoned as irrelevant, and an *ad hoc* revolutionary defense was created. During the war to defend the Soviet regime, a war between small mobile armies fighting across vast distances, the long periods of chaos in the countryside often engendered guerrilla bands—Red-Communist, Black-Anarchist, Green-Peasant, and White-Reactionary. These bands played a significant part in the war—and later in Soviet military doctrine—but almost no part in Soviet revolutionary ideology.

Although subsequently, with the change in revolutionary fancies, Lenin would be touted as the fountainhead of guerrilla-theory, there is almost no evidence in his vast literary production of either interest in or understanding of "guerrilla-warfare." His most quoted article, *"Partisanskya Voina"* (*Proletari;* September 30, 1906), is often translated as "Guerrilla-Warfare," whereas the contents obviously have a great deal to do with the nature of the armed struggle and next to nothing with "guerrillas." For Lenin, guerrilla (read "partisan") activities were largely two: assassination and confiscation of funds—murder and theft. When used in a scientifically prescribed revolutionary formula, these became legitimate tactics and not "the old terrorism" of Bakunin or People's Will. "It is not guerrilla action which disorganized the movement but the weakness of a party which is incapable of taking such actions under its control."[3]

At various times, under various conditions, Lenin foresaw a variety of revolutionary stages, a multitude of possible tactics; but always the stress was on party control and organization to orchestrate the class struggle, rather than on paramilitary confrontation. Much in Lenin's strategy for the revolution, as well as much in his example, sometimes not fully justified in his theoretical writing, has been of vital concern to revolutionary-guerrillas; but Lenin himself, even though he recognized that revolution might come by many roads, never saw a significant revolutionary role for the guerrilla—before October 1917 or during the Civil War or after the victory. Basically Lenin stressed the vital necessity of mobilizing the raw material of history, the masses: a process which polarized the existing society, widening the contradictions, making it impossible for the rulers to rule or the subjects to tolerate subjection. This activity, carried on by the vanguard of the proletariat and organized as the party, could be achieved by a variety of means depending on the objective conditions and reaction of the ruling class; but there was no real formula, no simple list of inevitable tactical steps, and every possibility of repeated failure.

Lenin, of course, had proposed various tactics of strife, none novel, either alone or in combination. None, alone or in combination, could guarantee success unless the prior conditions for Marxian revolution had already evolved.* Once the exploited proletariat class had fully emerged, had been organized and prepared for the moment of struggle against a capitalism declining in strength and vitality, then victory would be certain. The task of the revolutionary party was to prepare the proletariat, thereby creating the essential conditions for revolution. These conditions, which were to prove so difficult to create outside of Russia, were well known to the Left, but nowhere had the revolutionaries been able to organize a permanent victory. Briefly in certain nations the moment seemed to have come, capitalism appeared to totter, the proletariat appeared determined. Perhaps Germany would follow Bavaria, or Hungary would be won by Béla Kun, or in Italy the strikes would evolve into the final confrontation. All the revolutionary hopes were disappointed. Increasingly the various Communist parties showed considerable

---

* The Leninists' strategy was largely directed at creating political, social, and economic conditions that would permit a coup d'état not unlike that of October 1917. If these mature revolutionary conditions existed then, obviously a protracted guerrilla campaign would be unnecessary.

concern that their armed struggle should not be premature, and increasingly there was an acceptance that violence elsewhere should not endanger the existence of socialism in Russia. Many continued to hope for revolution, for the old regimes appeared exhausted by war and incapable of meeting the new revolutionary threat. Somehow the new threat relying on the old tactics and doctrines did not materialize. In Russia, Stalin increasingly concentrated on socialism in his one country and the use of revolution as a defense of the Soviet regime.

As Soviet communism, in fact if not theory, grew less revolutionary and more defensive, the only place found for the guerrilla was his inclusion in Russian war plans. The effectiveness of the guerrilla-bands during the Civil War had not gone unnoted. *The Russian Partisan Directive of 1933* outlined Soviet military doctrine for guerrilla activity in occupied areas in case of invasion. Little else was done in theory or practice until the necessity arose after the German attack in the summer of 1941. In any case, Soviet partisans were not intended to be a revolutionary force but a tightly controlled branch of the conventional army.

That the Soviets considered guerrillas as partisans, adjuncts to conventional armies, was quite in accord with conventional military thinking. Partisan-guerrillas had often been attached as auxiliaries to regular professional armies, differing from regular troops mainly in their isolation from a solid front and in their use of irregular tactics. And the irregular tactics of the partisan-guerrilla operating on his home ground had changed little during the course of human warfare. These partisan-guerrillas, poorly trained and independent in the field, were essentially units of a conventional army operating unconventionally in the classic sense at a distance from the main battle line. Once the main conventional battle had been lost, the solid front dissolved, the regular troops defeated and dispersed, the partisan-guerrilla had perforce to act independently, to accept the full responsibility for the continuation of the struggle. Most if not all of these partisan-guerrillas fought essentially defensive actions, seeking to maintain or re-create an order, a system, a nation by harassing the invader or interloper. They were partisans of restoration. Their technique was the weapon of the weak. The guer-rillas were simply the oppressed people in arms or the remnants of their former conventional defenders. Motivated by religion or patriotism or ethnic pride, unconverted to a fresh dogma but representatives of the orthodox, they fought—even when on the offensive—an essentially defensive war. To go over to the offensive against a superior foe was futile and to strike into the opponent's own territory would cut off the home base—the partisan-guerrilla would be transformed into a mobile raider in an alien land. If such a maneuver were in conjunction with the regular army's advance, then the partisan-guerrillas would be transformed into irregular, deep-penetration formations. Partisan-guerrillas, however, fought on their own ground for a victory, however distant, that would restore the past as it had been or as it should have been. Partisan-guerrillas were not revolutionaries.

In the European revolutionary world, the armed struggle was largely still seen as an insurrection, hope-fully in mature revolutionary circumstances. The workers fighting on an urban battlefield, united by class solidarity nourished by the party, would topple the capitalists not at the end of a long period of attrition after a protracted armed struggle, but in a relatively short burst of revolutionary energy. The Left thought in terms of the Paris Commune and the Winter Palace. True, the preparation for the climactic moment might be long and arduous, but to take to the streets before the party and the proletariat were ready would be foolhardy. The key is that the Left thought in terms of streets, not hillsides, and most assuredly in terms of workers, not peasants. Lenin's interest in an alliance of the proletariat of the capitalist countries with the people of the colonies and semi-colonies was neglected. And of course at the moment of confrontation all help—including perhaps that of peasant-guerrillas—would be welcome, but the united proletariat would power the revolution. The Asturias miners' revolt in Spain in 1934 and the Social-Democrats' *Schutzbund* defense of the workers' quarters in Vienna the same year—slightly premature proletarian insurrections—fit most closely into the theorists' expectations of revolutionary armed struggle. Even the Spanish Civil War, 1936–9, saw only the most limited use of guerrillas by the Republicans and then not as "revolutionaries" but as tightly controlled partisans.[4] At the same time, however, that attention in Europe was focused elsewhere, a new, coherent revolutionary doctrine divorced from the necessity of an urban-industrial base that had often preoccupied Western theorists was being elaborated in the caldron of the Chinese Civil War. There Mao Tse-tung would fuse the tactics and strategy of classical guerrilla-war with a new revolutionary theory based on the power of peasant masses, and by so doing offer to the exploited elsewhere a means to act, a means to power and pride, a means so compelling that the new doctrine would become the repository of the hopes and aspirations of the masses, would rise beyond reasoned ideas to the position of a new revolutionary myth.

On January 1, 1912, Sun Yat-sen had been sworn into office as President of the Provisional Government of the Chinese Republic at Nanking. On February 12, the last Manchu emperor abdicated and a new era of unity, stability, and justice appeared imminent. This proved to be a matter of appearance. The anarchy and corruption of the Manchus continued as China slipped largely into the control of the warlords. Fragmented, and open to foreign exploitation, within a decade the new Chinese Republic was little more than a vast collection of feuding baronies dominated by the corrupt and the cruel—a China without unity, without law or order, without a purpose or a future, a giant helpless pawn to be exploited. The revolution of 1911 had replaced the Manchu dynasty with anarchy.

Thus, since the revolution of 1911, not only has the situation of China not improved, but it has actually deteriorated at an accelerating speed. The dictatorial behavior of the warlords is worse than ever; so is the aggressive conduct of foreign powers. As China sinks deeper and deeper into the hellish existence of a semi-colony, the Chinese people, resentful and worried, are at a loss to find a way out of this debacle. Meanwhile, as the hour is late and the need is urgent, the most informed of them are thinking hard of how to bring about some new hope for China.[5]

The new hope proved to be the wrangling Kuomintang that allied with the Communists. Briefly in 1926 and 1927, the revolutionaries appeared to have succeeded. With a base in the Yangtze valley they had the desire and, perhaps, the capacity to reunite and transform China. Then in 1927 the Communists were expelled, the divided Kuomintang reunited with Chiang Kai-shek returning from abroad. With the seat of government at Nanking, the Kuomintang sought to unite China and reform the nation by application of the idealist principles of Sun Yat-sen. The task was beyond the capacity and in some cases the desires of the Kuomintang. At least in 1927, the Communist competitor seemed eliminated as a result of the repression after their Autumn Harvest Uprising. This hope too proved vain.

Mao Tse-tung's Communists had, it is true, very nearly been destroyed. The peasants, sick of civil war—by then endemic—had refused to rally, often killed stragglers; and the Nationalist Army held on, eroding Communist strength. By October, Mao had six thousand troops but only two thousand under arms. The Autumn Harvest Uprising was a disaster. It was followed by debacle when the Canton Commune, established on December 11, lasted but three days and was crushed in the insurrection. All the news was bad: "The peasants did not help us. . . . The workers of Hongkong did not display the least sympathy for the insurrection."[6] Throughout China the party apparatus was shattered and thousands of members had been killed in battle or executed in relays. Mao was fortunate to escape with one thousand demoralized survivors to the Hunan and Kiangsi mountains in South China. There, temporarily secure, he began to rethink his philosophy of revolution. As was appropriate for a devout Marxist-Leninist, he began an analysis of the nature of Chinese society—the study of war is the study of society—to find valid strategy and tactics. Mao had already read widely not only in the orthodox revolutionary canon but also in the political, economic, and military history of the West. He admired Napoleon and knew Clausewitz. Despite his own revolutionary experience and the conventional knowledge of books, Mao recognized that the revolutionary situation in China could not be understood within his existing Westernized conceptual framework. The Chinese Communists needed to adapt the Marxist tools of analysis and the experience of others to Chinese conditions. Mao felt that the special conditions that operated in China were that it was a semi-colonial, semi-feudal country with an uneven political development; that the Red Army faced a big and powerful enemy in the Kuomintang; that the Red Army was small and weak; and that the leadership of the Communist party was born of the agrarian revolution. These characteristics determined Mao's strategy of revolutionary war.

A new or at least revised strategy of revolution had to be evolved to give the party the appropriate response to "the Chinese situation"—at every level, from the clash of Chinese classes to the behavior of the individual revolutionary soldier. As early as 1928, he evolved his Three Rules and Eight Points for revolutionary-military conflict. His contemplation of the Chinese revolutionary problem

was not, however, a process isolated from events; for amid
his analysis, he, and with him the revolutionary movement, was buffeted by an almost continuous series of
Kuomintang attacks.

Chiang Kai-shek undertook five Annihilation Campaigns between 1930 and 1934 in an attempt to use his
ten-to-one superiority to trap and destroy Mao's forces.
In one of military history's premier campaigns, Mao with
mobility, daring, and incredible execution repeatedly
evaded destruction until he could strike an unexpected,
concentrated counterblow. Despite his mauling by the
communists, Chiang Kai-shek persisted, narrowing Mao's
options, cutting away space to maneuver, and eroding his
strength. Finally, incapable of continuing mobile warfare
from his narrow base, Mao broke contact and in 1934 and
1935, in the Long March, withdrew to distant Yenan to
regroup and reconsider. The subsequent immensely fruit-
ful work of reorganization and political mobilization, constantly challenged but not prevented by Kuomintang
probes, could not be carried on to a higher stage because
of the Japanese invasion of 1937. During the campaign
against Japan from 1937 to 1945, Mao had ample opportunity to test his theory in the field. Applying his principles, honed in battle and tempered in defeat, by 1945
Mao's armies had secured nineteen areas with a population
of one hundred million. The last-minute Russian occupation of Manchuria further strengthened his position in the
next and final stage of the revolutionary war.

The Kuomintang had been sapped by the protracted
conflict with both Mao and the Japanese. The Kuomintang
revolutionary élan of the Twenties had evaporated. Much
of the old, hard elite had become corrupt and soft. The
idealistic program of reform had remained largely a program. China had not been united, the warlords eliminated,
the land redistributed, or order and justice restored. China
was still feeble, still humiliated. On January 18, 1931, the
Japanese had moved into Manchuria. The government in

Nanking was helpless. In July 1937, Japan made further territorial demands, and on Nanking's refusal attacked. The Chinese did hold out three months in Shanghai, but elsewhere the story was grim, one defeat after another, desertion, collapse, treachery, and the deterioration of the capacity to resist. Chiang was driven to withdraw to isolated Chungking, his regime largely discredited on the field of battle. Mao, once the Americans entered the war and thereby apparently assured the eventual defeat of Japan, showed less interest in fighting the Japanese and more for the ultimate struggle with Chiang. By the end of the war, neither external aid nor internal readjustments could cope with Mao's gathering momentum. By 1949, Chiang and the Kuomintang had collapsed and the survivors withdrawn to exile in Taiwan. By then, except for a few final elaborations, Mao's theory of revolutionary war had been perfected. Out of the revolutionary processes and military conflicts of over twenty years, Mao had woven into doctrine his experience and practice. For the first time revolutionaries had a fixed gospel for people's wars, written in blood and crowned with victory.

Mao's thought is based on the Marxist-Leninist world view, but he did not mechanically follow either the Russian example or Western Marxist strategies. There were additions, corrections, and novel approaches discovered during his lifetime of revolutionary activity. For Mao first there are the people, immobile, without vitality, unaware of their potential, exploited and repressed. The permanence and stability of such a society are an illusion. War inevitably evolves from the system of private ownership, from the existence of classes in society. To wage the war successfully the people need only be politically mobilized, and to recognize their destiny and vocation. They will then overwhelm the exploiters:

> The mobilization of the . . . people throughout the country will create a vast sea in which to drown the

enemy, create the conditions that will make up for our inferiority in arms and other things.[7]

Since as a class the people have been submerged and exploited, they begin the struggle from a position of weakness but this "apparent" weakness can itself be exploited to unbalance the repressive class while political mobilization progresses. The first step is to go to the masses, as nothing can be accomplished without them, everything with them.

> Without a political goal, guerrilla warfare must fail, as it must if its political objectives do not coincide with the aspirations of the people and their sympathy, cooperation, and assistance cannot be gained.[8]

Politics is organizing the masses. War is an aspect of this process, politics is bloodless war, war is the politics of bloodshed. The battle is not between armies for land but between classes for the possession of the future. The purpose of battle is to agitate the masses. The Red Army is a furnace which melts down and transforms its members, liberating them spiritually, incorporating them into the class of the future. The new emerging class, involved in a continual conflict, must inevitably emerge triumphant if the doctrine is followed.

First, above all else, the masses must be mobilized—a trying and lengthy process, during which repression must be avoided. This was possible in China because the vast spaces could be used to yield time and the time allowed an opportunity which produced political cohesion and ultimate victory in 1949. After the Autumn Harvest disaster, there was room to retreat, although room alone was insufficient for skill, and stamina made it possible to exploit space. When Chiang's troops finally closed the net around the Communists early in 1934, Mao, after the loss of sixty thousand troops and under the threat of famine, broke through the encirclement and trekked west out of reach of the Nationalists. Ultimately, after all its twists and turns, the Long March led the Communists to haven; more important, the success of the Long March sowed the seeds of revolution in eleven provinces.

> Without the Long March, how could the broad masses have known so quickly that there are such great ideas in the world as upheld by the Red Army?[9]

And for there to have been a Long March, there had to be space, the big country.

For the Chinese revolutionary war, the basics, then, were a big country, the support of the people, and a secure base. The secure base, however, was as much a base of mass support as a geographical area. Mao also insisted that, under the direction of an expert leadership, all military, political, cultural, and economic action on the national and international levels be coordinated. Finally the revolution should keep the initiative. These preconditions and operating procedures were incorporated into a calibrated revolutionary process. According to Mao, the three stages in revolutionary war are strategic defense, equilibrium, and strategic offense. These, of course, correspond to the stages in Mao's own revolutionary war: the implication, as is the case with much of Mao's analyses, is that the laws valid for China have a more universal application—Mao felt that his model could be applied elsewhere, not confined to China alone "but will be world-wide."[10] Mao, of course, opposed the *mechanical* application of the laws of war.

> Thus the different laws for directing different wars are determined by the different circumstances of those wars—differences in their time, place, and nature . . . the laws of war in each historical stage have their special characteristic and cannot be mechanically applied in another stage.[11]

Mao's declaimers aside, his principles or laws were inside China and out accepted by many as universal.

> Comrade Mao Tse-tung's theory of people's war is not only a product of the Chinese Revolution, but has also the characteristics of our epoch. The new experience gained in the people's revolutionary struggles in various countries since World War II has provided continuous evidence that Mao Tse-tung's thought is a common asset of the revolutionary people of the whole world.[12]
>
> —Marshal Lin Piao

> It is obvious—and writers on the theme have said it many times—that war responds to a certain series of scientific laws; whoever ignores them will go down to defeat. Guerrilla warfare as a phase of war must be ruled by all of these; for besides, because of its special aspects, a series of corollary laws must also be recognized in order to carry it forward. Though geographical and social conditions in each country determine the mode and particular forms that guerrilla warfare will take, there are general laws that hold for all fighting of this type.[13]
>
> —Che Guevara

For each of Mao's stages, there is a method of warfare: guerrilla-war, positional war, and mobile war—an evolution from the elusive tactics of the guerrilla to the victory of the Red Army. In his extensive analysis, the nature, problems, strategy, and tactics of each are explored at length. Most important, progress from one stage to another is not inevitable. Retrogression is quite possible, as was the case in China after the Japanese invasion in 1937; but with a patient and wily leadership and constant analysis of the developing contradictions within the process, victory is assured.

In the first stage, once the national consciousness of the inhabitants of a guerrilla zone has been awakened by constant agitation in a program of enlightening and by the example of guerrilla conduct, an ocean is thus created through which the guerrilla fish can swim undetected. To be sure that his fish would not disturb the waters, Mao had produced Three Rules and Eight Remarks for his Eighth Route Army.

> RULES — All actions are subject to command; do not steal from the people, be neither selfish nor unjust.
>
> REMARKS — Replace the door when you leave the house, roll up the bedding in which you have slept; be courteous; be honest in your transaction; return what you borrow; replace what you break; do not bathe in the presence of women; do not without authority search the pocketbooks of those you arrest.[14]

Secure in his friendly sea, the guerrilla can perform his three vital functions: to conduct a war on exterior lines in the rear of the enemy, to establish bases, and to extend the war area. The means to do so are alertness, mobility, and attack. On their own initiative the guerrillas can attack a weak point and, when threatened, move with the fluidity of water and the ease of the blowing wind. Such a strategy of offensive-initiative will lengthen the periods in which the enemy must remain on the defensive. During this time work among the masses can be zealously expanded. The growing pool of mass support will allow the opening of other guerrilla-fronts, which will in turn permit the acceleration of mobilization. Eventually, the enemy, frustrated by the jigsaw war of evasion, will be unable to continue his operations effectively. At this point the revolution will have passed into the next stage—of positional warfare—a stalemate of attrition. Tactics are aimed at

72— 7778

C. L. HARDY LIBRARY
ATLANTIC CHRISTIAN COLLEGE
WILSON, N. C. 27893

"protracting the war, gradually changing the general balance of forces and preparing the conditions for our counter-offensive."[15] During this stage the revolutionary forces maintain both flexibility and mobility, and may continue guerrilla-tactics. Positional warfare is a less desirable but essential preparation for the final stage of mobile warfare, at which time the conventionally organized revolutionary army goes over to the offensive in the final stage. In mobile warfare, where the revolutionary army may still lack field superiority, the key is the concentration at a single point to win a major victory rather than the tactics of protracted attrition. While many such concentrated victories may be needed, such a strategy—cut off one finger rather than wound ten—can have a disproportionate effect on an already bewildered and uncertain opponent. By the final stages of mobile warfare, with the masses mobilized and the oppressors in disarray, the protracted conflict will conclude with the collapse of the exploiters torn apart by their society's contradictions, isolated from the people, frustrated on the battlefield—relics of history.

Long before Mao's doctrine reached its final polished form or his scattered polemic articles could be collected in sets, the more imaginative military theorists had been attracted to his ideas. As early as 1941, Samuel B. Griffith of the United States Marine Corps had begun translating Mao into English. Theoretically the most vitally concerned with Mao's writings should have been the other Asian revolutionary leaders of still inchoate Communist parties. Attempting unsuccessfully to translate the Western demigods Marx and Lenin into meaningful concepts for societies still generations removed from the possession of a proletariat class, they might have grasped, however, at Mao's peasant revolution. Even Lenin in 1920 and 1921 had indicated that the submerged colonies might be able to create socialist societies; but no one except Mao had produced a method.

Most Asian revolutionaries continued to look to Moscow or to their own traditions. In any case, for much of the period that Mao was fighting the Japanese and occasionally the Kuomintang, most revolutionary leaders as well as most military theorists were too deeply involved in the Second World War to follow the ideological developments within the Chinese Communist party.

Mao, whether anyone yet listened or not, had created the basic theory of guerrilla-revolution, a doctrine so intensive, so closely reasoned—and effective in practice in China—that all further additions would be little more than elaborations constructed on the Maoist foundation. The revolutionary-guerrilla envisioned by Mao, unlike the partisan-guerrilla, had been converted to the validity of the new ideology *fight for the future not the past*, to transform the old order, to destroy existing institutions, to create a new system, not to restore an old regime. For Mao the wave of the future was Chinese communism. Other Marxist-Leninist revolutionaries would claim that the guerrilla-revolutionary represents classes heretofore submerged, repressed by history, without traditional institutions. Guerrilla-revolutions could and did eschew the Marxist-Leninist base and claim to represent historically repressed nations or peoples and to aspire to create a new state rather than a new communist society. All would use the same weapons and tactics of the weak against a powerful order imposed by the nature of history or by the power of the oppressor. Superficially, their activities appear identical to those of the guerrillas of restorations; but in reality the two, whatever they are labeled and however alike are their daily activities, are quite different.

For example, while Mao continued his struggle in China, half a world away in Yugoslavia in 1943 an observer would have found Mikhailovich's Chetniks and Tito's partisans using identical military techniques against the Germans, but for diametrically opposed goals. Mikhailovich was fighting for the restoration—the return of the old order—which would arrive on the bayonets of the victors once the Germans had been defeated. Tito was fighting a revolution for a socialist Yugoslavia against both the Germans and advocates of the old regime. In time, Mikhailovich, justifiably perhaps, decided that the greater enemy to restoration was not the Germans but the revolutionary Tito, and switched his focus of attack. It had, of course, been easier for Tito to mobilize his partisans by drawing on historic, patriotic wellsprings; but basically his men had been as much converted to a vision of a new future as inspired by a pure love of country. Most guerrilla movements, resisting the imposition of an alien order, whether they be Russian partisans or American Indians, are forces of defensive conservatism, motivated primarily by traditional aspirations. They are not revolutionary-guerrillas and are consequently irrelevant to revolutionary theory.

The new theory was not in fact overly concerned with guerrilla-tactics *per se*—independent, disciplined forays. In his theory of war Mao has applied many of the particular tactics necessary in guerrilla-war—possession of the initiative or flexibility—on a higher level. Guerrilla-tactics occur not simply at one stage of revolutionary war but can be applied strategically often at a higher stage. Thus a guerrilla-war of national liberation may at some stage make limited use of classical guerrilla-bands and guerrilla-tactics—on the other hand whole regiments or armies may reflect the guerrilla commitment. Thus it is not possible to distinguish guerrilla-revolution by the presence or absence of guerrillas. The key is the revolutionary aspiration expressed through the medium of guerrilla-strategy, based wittingly or not on Mao or devised independently, that the weak can defeat the strong under certain conditions and by the judicious use of certain tactics adapted to local conditions. Such a strategy foresees not an accommodation with the opponent but his ultimate replacement by a new system.

With the defeat of the Axis in 1945, there appeared

to be excellent opportunities, particularly in Asia, for the nationalists and revolutionaries—the previously weak—to seize power in the old colonial areas before the imperialists—the formerly strong—could re-establish their grip. Control might be won quickly by the daring. The victory of the British Labour Party, however, with its known intention of dismantling the Empire, restrained many potential rebels in Asia who anticipated imminent independence. The same was not the case everywhere, for the Dutch and French were apparently intent on re-establishing their former empires. In the East Indies the Dutch found that they would have to fight their way back into control, a process beyond their resources. In Indochina the French found awaiting them a Democratic Republic of Vietnam established on September 2, 1945. Although the French managed a temporary *modus vivendi* with the forces of Ho Chi Minh, Vo Nguyên Giap, Troung Chinh, and the others, Indochina was to be the site of another people's war.

Ho and Giap at first hoped to be able to achieve their republic by diplomacy, then by conventional military tactics; however, the French were reluctant to lose Indochina and even to offer modified autonomy. French pride was at stake; French prestige, French economic interests, the memory of French defeats during the war all played some part in an intransigent policy that only tended to unite all Vietnamese nationalists in opposition. France's inability to move swiftly from an emotional commitment to empire to a recognition of the new strength and determination of Vietnamese nationalism confronted Ho with a choice of fighting or withdrawing for another day. Ho had begun developing a regular army as early as 1945 and, after the collapse of various agreements, he ordered a series of surprise attacks on the French on December 19, 1946. The French proved too strong. Ho's Republic went unrecognized and his army was scattered. Under heavy French pressure, the Vietminh were forced to withdraw into guerrilla-warfare. Simultaneously mobilizing the people and harassing the French, Giap as military commander managed to concentrate his forces in several isolated redoubts—secure base areas. Stretched too thin on the ground, the French were never able to concentrate on these, Giap in turn was too weak to escalate the war. The Vietminh's initially uncertain position was greatly strengthened by the arrival of the Chinese Communist Army on the northern border in December 1949. With China as an even more secure redoubt, Giap built up his forces and cleared the French out of the border area by the end of 1950. The stage of stalemate seemed past, Giap's forces were nearly equal to those of the French in numbers and could maneuver and concentrate in major formations. Fighting a war distant from Paris and for uncertain ends—no decision having been made on Vietnamese independence—the French were tied down in a series of defensive positions. Still they were better trained, better armed, and better commanded and held the loyalty of a substantial portion of the population. Despite his reservations, Giap decided that the stage of stalemate was passing and the time had come to move into phase three, the general counteroffensive. Giap's offensive achieved some immediate success in the autumn of 1950, but the French inflicted limited defeats on him in January, March, and May of 1951. He withdrew to the previous stage, reconstructed his army, and with more care again undertook mobile warfare against an opponent who increasingly was tied into a static defense system. The French Army had morale problems, command problems, and no sense of direction from the Parisian politicians. The Vietminh, too, less sanguine than the previous year, anticipated a long war.

Giap even during the rebuilding kept up his offensive while attempting to reinforce the still uncertain support of the peasants. At the end of 1951 he became—contrary to the appropriate stage of the war according to Mao—involved in a protracted battle of position, suffered serious casualties, but eventually forced the French to withdraw from the area. He then avoided positional battles, striking where the French had placed only token defenses in the mountains, and thus forced the French to extend themselves on the defensive or abandon the area to Giap. The French depleted their forces in the Red River delta to reinforce the mountains and, with limited forces, weakened the Delta without creating an adequate defense in the mountains. With the promise of the Allied Geneva Conference, announced in January 1954, to "deal" with Indochina, Giap decided to risk once more positional warfare, laying siege to the French position at Dien Bien Phu. The Geneva Conference opened on April 26, as did Giap's final assault on Dien Bien Phu. The garrison surrendered on May 8. The Vietminh had lost fifteen thousand men and the capacity to continue the war in the immediate future. Giap had violated Mao's dictum, sacrificed his army in order to win a political victory, which in turn was quite in accord with Mao. The victory over well less than ten per cent of the French Army in Indochina was significant, but the impact in Paris was crucial. Dien Bien Phu was not catastrophic for the French Army but most assuredly was so for French ambitions in Indochina. Giap had gambled and won. Under the Geneva agreements the French withdrew, leaving Indochina divided into four: Laos, Cambodia, the Democratic Republic of Vietnam in the north, and a second Vietnam in the south.

Out of the partial victory came a series of theoretical works—the second-generation ideology of people's war. Much of the work, like Mao's, is polemic, dogmatic, convoluted in style, and limited in detail. More important, much of the work is simply like Mao's "The people to the army . . . what water is to fish."[16] It is possible that the Vietminh had independently discovered Mao's formulae; but, although little is attributed to Mao, much of the Vietminh theory is a paraphrase.

The first step in what Giap calls the Resistance War

was mobilizing the people to launch a people's war, "using the enormous strength of the people to vanquish the aggressors."[17] Once under way, the war not unexpectedly passes through three stages:

> The general law of a long revolutionary war is usually to go through three stages: defensive, equilibrium, and offensive. Fundamentally, in the main directions, our Resistance War also followed this general law.[18]

As Troung Chinh had written earlier, this process of revolution would of necessity be protracted:

> The guiding principle of the strategy of our whole resistance must be to prolong the war. To protract the war is the key to victory. . . . The more we fight, the more united our people at home will be, and the more the democratic movement will support us from outside.[19]

During the protracted conflict, the command must be prepared to return to a previous stage, but ultimate victory is certain provided there be resolute leadership, flexibility, the initiative, and the support of the masses. Guerrilla-warfare can be waged with mediocre material and without modern arms if the pressure becomes really great, but once the people have been mobilized there can no longer be doubt about the ultimate end.

Giap's stress on the spirit of the masses is, if anything, greater than Mao's. Mao, of course, had more to work with: more space, more weapons, and, once the Japanese had gone, less adamant opposition. For Giap, even with his limitations, the opposition, doomed in any case by history according to Marx, could not deny the people victory as long as the rules were followed, the pace of development maintained, and the masses faithful:

> In the Resistance War, guerrilla warfare played an extremely important role. Guerrilla warfare is the

form of fighting of the masses of people, of the people of a weak and badly equipped country who stand up against an aggressive army which possesses better equipment and technique. This is the way of fighting the revolutionary war which relies on the heroic spirit to triumph over modern weapons, avoiding the enemy when he is stronger and attacking him when he is weaker, now scattering, now regrouping one's forces, now wearing out, now exterminating the enemy, determined to fight him everywhere, so that wherever the enemy goes he would be submerged in a sea of armed people who hit back at him, thus undermining his spirit and exhausting his forces. In addition to the units which have to be scattered in order to wear out the enemy, it is necessary to regroup big armed forces in favorable conditions in order to achieve supremacy in attack at a given point and at a given time to annihilate the enemy. Success in many small fights added together gradually wear out the enemy manpower while little by little fostering our forces. The main goal of the fighting must be destruction of enemy manpower, and ours should not be exhausted by trying to keep or occupy land, thus creating final conditions to wipe out the whole enemy force and liberate our country.[20]

Although Giap and Ho not only added a new classical example of validity to Mao but also a variety of elaborations, the essential remained unchanged. The stress on the power of the spirit over the machine was greater than with Mao, but this merely underlined a basic acceptance of the power of the ultimate weapon in revolutionary warfare: the vitalized masses.

The impact of Ho and Giap—and Dien Bien Phu—was immense, both for the world's fresh crop of revolutionaries and, even more so, for the disconcerted forces of order. When the French had brushed aside Ho's Democratic Republic in 1946, much of the world was still intent on tying up the loose ends of the World War. Mao was a cipher to all but the specialists and the old Asian hands, and people's wars were unknown. By 1954 and the Geneva Agreements, a great deal had changed, and not only in the nature of irregular war. Instead of the world being rapidly divided up into monolithic blocs or even tidy, traditional spheres of influence, the great postwar current—a wave of nationalism in the colonial world—produced at last new and sensitive nations, usually violently anti-imperialist and often dedicated to social revolution as well as national independence. The East–West competition, the rampant new anti-imperialism, the constant atmosphere of change, instability, and threat created conditions which seemed ideal for people's wars of various hues. The guerrilla-revolutionary had a central role.

As has been noted, the key which distinguishes a revolutionary-guerrilla from other guerrillas is his ultimate aim. Since most guerrilla-patriots fight under the banner of national liberation, at times the borderline between restoration and revolution is blurred even to the participants. The passage of time while traditional aspirations have been denied or gone unrealized, perhaps after centuries of occupation, may of course transform the nature of the struggle. For eight hundred years, with remarkable lack of success, the Irish had by a variety of means sought separation from British control. The long heritage of rebellion and the consciousness of nationality aside, what the Irish partially won in 1921 was a totally new political entity—a partial revolution at least. The African nationalists in Mozambique or Angola, whatever their rationalizations about their heritage, seek to create a new nation entirely without ancestor. The American Revolution, on the other hand, was fought, at first at least, as much in order to be left alone by the British as to create revolutionary and better institutions. Basically, resistance can last only so long, can only be renewed so often, before sufficient time has passed to allow the imposed order apparent legitimacy while the old ways fade or are mutated. At that point then, only revolution and not resistance is possible. If such a revolution must be engendered without exterior aid by conventional forces, organized, directed, and fought by the people, then there exists an opportunity for the revolutionary-guerrilla.

The new theorists of guerrilla-revolution have stressed above all else that such change can best be engendered by war. The coup, the general strike, conspiracy, teeming mobs on the barricades, or assassination in the palace are, if not adventuristic romanticism, at least secondary weapons in revolution's arsenal. This may be the symptom of revolt: the people's spontaneous and violent resistance to change perceived as intolerable. If these secondary weapons—unreasoning revolts sparked by reason—can be harnassed and escalated, they too may play a revolutionary role. None need necessarily be eschewed, but none can replace the guerrilla, only supplement him; for the essence of political mobilization—the cornerstone of victory—is the guerrilla catalyst. Political power must be won in battle, not picked up in the streets; and revolutionaries without armies must begin at the beginning—and in the beginning is the guerrilla. In time, at a later and higher stage, the guerrilla may act in conjunction with regular forces; but his example still holds the central position. The guerrilla mystique at any stage dominates the revolution. His tactics in the hills, his spirit opposed to mechanistic force, his initiative, mobility, and persistence become the basis of even the conventional revolutionary army. The necessary means of the guerrilla become the strategy of the revolution even if the military tactics are no longer guerrilla.

Not all of the revolutionary theorists, however, would acknowledge that use of guerrilla-strategy or guerilla-technique necessarily indicates the existence of True Revolution. The true believers of the Left would deny that any revolution with or without the guerrilla which does not bring the triumph of the exploited class can be so classified: an independent Ireland or Cyprus are superficial shifts within the bourgeois power structure. Many revolutions abort or are corrupted in process, many through failure of nerve never mature fully or exploit their potential for greater change: contemporary Ireland is still very much within the British Isles and "independent" Cyprus, divided and bitter, retains much of British Cyprus. The changes, however, are hardly superficial, although recognizably less than total.

For many revolutionaries, the difference between true Marxian revolution and superficial revolution may be a matter of semantics or communist arrogance, since ultimate victory is expected to clarify all. The question is academic. After Dien Bien Phu the guerrilla-revolution became the way of the future par excellence. The guerrilla in fantasy is a hero in a camouflage suit, carrying a submachine gun, shifting through the jungle, protected by a sea of people, hunted futilely by the ever blundering forces of authority —quicksilver on the hill. His very presence guarantees the revolution. The guerrilla is for some no longer simply a means to secure power but almost the only means. And the proof for the revolutionaries, no matter how they define their revolution, lies for all to see in the past successes, based on the dictum of the theorists of guerrilla-revolution—Mao, Ho, and Giap devised, tested, and tempered in combat.

The doctrine of guerrilla-revolution had by 1954 become more than laws or principles about war. It was also the soil for a new political myth of considerable power and broad attraction. For the truly dispossessed—the peasants without history or hope, perpetually exploited, wretched, denied all but the opiates concentrated power used to drug the masses—the new myth contained their previous inarticulated desires to act upon history, to create a future. Through guerrilla-revolution they could fight not for warlord or religion or colonialist but for themselves. And those who advocated revolution, peasant or no, who saw the doctrine as means to the desired end, they too were uplifted by the new myth. Some, of course, desperate to achieve change in the face of entrenched power, confused the myth with reality, the image of that quicksilver on the hill with the capacity of the guerrilla. These were led into the realm of actual fantasy; and even those more hard-minded, more realistic, were often more daring because of the power of the new myth.

The second great postwar insurrection began with the opening of the FLN campaign in Algeria in 1954. Here both the French and the Algerians sought to apply not only the tactics but also the theoretical lessons of Indochina. The power of the doctrine of guerrilla-revolution not simply as an explanation of how the masses might achieve victory but as a belief that such a possibility existed was so great that the French theorists felt impelled to find a counterdoctrine—that might in turn be the basis for a new myth in the hands of the West. Thus, for the purposes of theory, Algeria proved more fertile for the French, who finally evolved *la guerre révolutionnaire,* to counter the appeal of the nationalist FLN. In this theory the Algerian conflict was viewed as one battle in a total, global confrontation waged within sovereign states, between communism and the forces of Western civilization, spearheaded by France and more particularly the French Army. The French attempted to use the army as a psychological-military weapon to convert the masses. *La guerre révolutionnaire,* or *la guerre subversive,* was defined as partisan warfare plus psychological warfare equaling revolutionary war. A variety of novel techniques was evolved or adapted to the Algerian countryside, but without political success. The Algerians held on, waiting for the French to lose heart. The FLN redefined the "inevitable victory" as the inability to lose: the guerrilla-revolutionary with the people's backing could not be defeated, even though he could not in turn inflict a defeat on the French. This faced the French with three alternatives: endless and futile war, genocide, thereby removing the sea of people, or withdrawal. The FLN felt confident that in time Paris would recognize the final alternative as the only valid one. The bitter, protracted conflict, which as in Indochina the French seemed unable to win and unwilling to lose, greatly encouraged revolutionaries elsewhere. Special conditions might have applied to the guerrilla-revolutionary failure in Greece, where the new theorist complained that the Greek guerrillas had followed orthodox Stalinist doctrines, and the orthodox communists that they had not even followed these properly. The insurgency in Malaya had not gone as well as was hoped, partly because the revolution was dominated by the Chinese, partly because the lessons of Mao had been imperfectly understood, partly because British public opinion seemed willing to support suppression longer than had the French; but yet the campaign had not ended and British patience might not be eternal. The failure of the Mau Mau in Kenya was not so much a defeat for guerrilla-revolution as a portent for the future of Black Africa. It had taken the British years at great cost to suppress what had been a premature, poorly organized, inadequately led, tribal-based revolt. More care in preparation, more organization, a broader base, full adherence to revolutionary theory as applicable in Africa—all would play a part the next time. More important, most important, the Myth had come to Africa, the imperialists were no longer inviolate nor their empires perpetual: the masses too had a weapon that, used more shrewdly, more consciously than the Mau Mau had done, would prove effective. Thus, despite the apparent "failures" in Malaya, Greece, and Kenya, each had seemed a near-run thing, each had in fact despite obstacles and errors very nearly succeeded, and each had been suppressed only at great cost and over a long period of time. Given a relatively mature revolutionary situation, there was increasing feeling that victory was, if not inevitable, then a real possibility.

During the Algerian war, two more insurrections seemed to underline the lesson's inevitability. In Cyprus, Grivas's EOKA seeking unity with Greece—*Enosis*—opened a terror-guerrilla campaign against the British. Despite the isolation of the island and strong British reinforcements, ultimately London agreed not to *Enosis* but to independence for Cyprus. Thus Grivas, clearly no revolutionary, had, by the application of the tactics of guerrilla-revolution and with the support of the people, demonstrated the power of the doctrine—even in a flawed cause. In Cuba, with one failure on hand, Fidel Castro and a small band of revolutionaries landed and, after near-annihilation, developed a guerrilla campaign in the hills of the Sierra Maestra. Castro's using the guerrilla-bands in the hills to create severe dissonance in the dictator Fulgencio Batista's control system forced the regime to respond to his challenge. Castro's guerrilla example and Batista's ineffectual repression engendered first admiration and then support for what was perceived as a liberal, anti-authoritarian struggle. Urban-based resistance organizations added to the challenge, the middle class and the intellectuals were committed, the United States government showed no enthusiasm for the continuation of Batista's regime. The dictator had proven too inefficient to stamp out the rebellion and his methods too crude and brutal to maintain the support of the Cubans. Castro's psychological victories in the hills whittled away at Batista's credibility and, consequently, his support. Without ever coming to grip with the guerrilla-bands, without suffering any significant military loss, Batista's regime collapsed in January 1959. Castro added another victory banner to the flags of people's wars.

Out of Algeria came a corollary to the general theory. It was in large part from the Algerian war that Frantz Fanon developed his ideas. A psychiatrist, born in Martinique, who wrote widely on the problems of colonialism and revolution, Fanon argued that for a "native" to become a man violence must be the midwife. Freedom, Liberty, Pride could be achieved for the submerged and wretched only through the catharsis of violence. To make the omelette of true independence the eggs *had* to be broken; neither purchase nor gift would fill the psychic hunger of the exploited. Through revolutionary war the rebel was transformed and the base for a truly indigenous society created. Unlike Mao and Giap, who saw revolutionary war as a means of vitalizing a historically submerged class, Fanon felt violence would create a new, free man. Through guerrilla-revolution Fanon offered the black man a new myth to replace those so long and so placidly accepted from the white colonizers—revolt not only against oppression and humiliation but also against the white-imposed myth of inferiority. By so doing, the black might enter the mainstream of history, grasping the future with pride.

A second corollary, developed by Castro, was the central position of the guerrilla rather than of the vitalized mass.

> The guerrilla is bound to be the nucleus of the revolutionary movement. This does not mean that the guerrilla movement can rise without any previous work; it does mean that the guerrilla movement is something that can exist without political direction.
> That in most of our countries the guerrillas are the embryo of liberation armies and constitute the most efficient way of initiating and carrying out revolutionary struggle.[21]

This meant that even when the masses—the exploited peasants of the world—still could not understand the significance of the new doctrine, still could not be attracted by the power of the new myth, still did not realize that they were entering history for the first time as directors rather than directed, then the use of guerrilla-revolutionary doctrine would force a hothouse growth of class consciousness. The few guerrilla-revolutionaries would by their example start the chain reaction to release the latent power of the people. Not only would the visible chains of oppression be broken but also the invisible chains of passive acceptance of innate inferiority welded by centuries of the master's myths.

With the termination of the struggles in Cuba and Algeria, the new general theory of people's wars had come increasingly to dominate revolutionary thinking. In 1960, the most important adjustment advocated by Che Guevara in *Guerra de guerrillas* was that the people's forces need not wait until all or most conditions become favorable to the revolution. And at the point the Myth becomes fantasy, faith, not good works, guarantees solution. Thus, without a mature revolutionary situation—orthodox as an explanation for both failure and hesitation—the guerrilla could by his example vitalize the people. Certainly, the prospects of success for a movement like Grivas's EOKA had, in objective terms, seemed remote and yet it had had remarkable success. Certainly in the Algerian case the lack of a united, committed "Algerian" consciousness, the long exposure to and attraction of French culture, the experience of the French Army, and the presence of a large French population had all argued against success. And yet the FLN had succeeded.

Neither of the two new corollaries, Fanon's Transformation Through Struggle or the Cuban–Che guerrilla-*focos,* added as much to the basic doctrine of guerrilla-revolution as they did to the myth of the guerrilla. In the case of Fanon, failure in the field or at least failure to achieve victory was no longer necessarily real "failure," for the nature of the protracted struggle encouraged the transformation of the "natives" into men. Thus, while victory was certainly desirable, repeated failure paid repeated benefits—those involved in guerrilla-revolution triumphed even as their opponents scored military "victories." The Cuban thesis elaborated by Che, on the other hand, offered justification for instant action, for undertaking a guerrilla-revolution in the face of even the most imposing odds. A revolutionary could thus begin the revolution, reap the dividends promised by Fanon even if the victory proposed by Mao remained elusive. Fanon enhanced the power and attraction of the Myth by emphasizing the spiritual benefits that a protracted armed struggle would guarantee. The Myth needed time to blossom fully. Che on the other hand, impatient with delay, offered immediate benefits. Fanon felt that a revolution without a myth would be impossible, that the creation of a myth in the clash of battle was basic. Che wanted only the clash of battle and so corrupted the Myth, so misunderstood the doctrine, that he created a fantasy out of his desires. Out of hope, desperation, and true belief, the revolutionaries of the world undertook another decade of people's wars in South Vietnam, in Latin America, in Africa. The armed struggle waged by guerrillas vitalizing the masses—the new revolutionary myth, often twisted into fantasy by the desperate and naïve—swept into fashion over the old orthodoxies of political mobilization, parliamentary infiltration, trade union militance, and balanced insurrections. There was abroad not simply a new revolutionary theory but a new revolutionary myth—and the old revolutionary myth-makers had to accommodate it.

Nowhere was the impact of the new myth more apparent than in the communist world. There, by the end of the decade, Peking and Moscow had become competitors. And the proprietorship of world revolutionary strategy a disputed asset. The new doctrine of guerrilla-revolution, that owed so much to Mao, had attracted vast excitement and interest far outside the communist circle and Moscow wanted not only to identify such concern with Russian communism but simultaneously to downgrade Mao's militancy. In November 1960, at the meeting of eighty-one of the world's Communist parties in Moscow, a declaration, the last signed by both China and Russia, was issued supporting valid national-liberation struggles. World communism had accepted its "duty to render the fullest moral and material assistance to the peoples fighting to free themselves from the imperialist and colonial tyranny."[22] On January 6, 1961, Khrushchev endorsed revolutionary wars—a late conversion as far as Peking was concerned. For the remainder of the decade, both Russia and China proclaimed their unswerving support of world-wide wars of liberation, in an increasingly bitter competition seeking control, among other things, of the high theoretical ground of world revolution. Both Moscow and Peking stressed that national wars of liberation were in fact only aspects of a world revolutionary struggle against imperialism in all its guises. Even for less ideologically committed nationalists the contention that the world was gripped in a general struggle made sense. Many of the pure nationalists had already succeeded in winning independence, passing to the seats of power, content with security, not suspecting further internal conflicts. Those still on the outside grasped the world-wide imperialist conspiracy as a visible enemy, an explanation of defeat and a rationale for subversion. The Chinese extended the vision. In December 1965, Marshal Lin Piao, Defense Minister and Vice Chairman of the Politbureau, explained that the people of the countryside, the exploited peasants of the world, the true international masses, would isolate the cities of the world—North America and Western Europe—so that they would drop like rotten fruit. The ultimate contradiction had been revealed between the urban-imperialist and the rural-peasant masses—and the ultimate weapon: the peasant-guerrilla. The cities of the West could not win a protracted conflict with the peasants of the East. In Vietnam, Giap had said, "If we win here, we win everywhere."[23] Che Guevara urged more Vietnams to finish off America. In January 1966, in an effort to give formal order to world revolution, torn between Moscow and Peking a Tri-Continental Solidarity Conference met in Havana; but, not unexpectedly, the delegates could not arrive at a consensus on strategy and tactics.

Thus by the mid-Sixties, a general theory of revolutionary war had been fully elaborated, but it contained deviant strains. Its basis was Marxism-Leninism, its major prophet was Mao, and its great disciple Giap. There was the doctrine as propounded in Vietnam, in Algeria, and in Cuba. After or with that came dissension. The major division was between those who believed that there was no path to national and social liberation but the armed struggle* and those who insisted on having more than one arrow in their quiver. Because the prudent could not well remain revolutionary and still deny the call to revolt, the division was often not so much on the ultimate necessity of armed struggle but on the timing: Peking called for, if it did not itself support, revolutionary adventures anywhere at anytime, while Moscow insisted on the necessity of mature conditions. Many revolutionaries, like Castro, desperate with delays that doomed so many in Latin America to poverty, misery, and humiliation, and frustrated by the institutionalized injustice of the oligarchical regimes, simply could not abide caution.

> The essence of the question is whether the masses will be led to believe that the revolutionary movement, that socialism can come to power without a struggle, that it can come to power peacefully. And that is a lie.[24]

Castro, speaking of Latin America, insisted that the urgency for liberation necessitated action, "since no one

---

* "The fact is that revolutionary warfare is the key to African freedom and is the only way in which the total liberation and unity of the African continent can be achieved"; Kwamé Nkrumah: *Handbook of Revolutionary Warfare* (London, 1968), pp. 20-1.

really has an honest answer or a consequent action that
implies a real hope for almost 300 million human be-
ings . . ."[25] Someone, somewhere, had to strike the first
blow—immediately. The time-honored idea that the revolutionary faced only a single option—Liberty or Death—
now became crucial in distinguishing the true believers
from those sufficiently content to hedge their bets. If
the revolutionary-guerrilla doctrine was valid and if the
weight of humiliation and oppression could not be borne,
then man must act or be less than a man, by acting
must face death to win liberty. On this point, Moscow
usually came out poorly, since, rhetoric aside, it had
to hedge revolutionary commitments in order to protect Russia's international position. Even among the impatient, there was dispute about the minimal objective
factors necessary for success, causing detailed theoretical
arguments over the virtues of Che's ideas or the validity
of urban violence or the value of establishing zones of
self-defense in the countryside. All of the minor deviations,
however, did not detract from the basic validity of the
doctrine, which, when obeyed, would lead to ultimate
victory, or from the power of the new doctrine to go beyond mere explanation of a strategy and to embody the
aspirations of the masses.

For leaders like Grivas, the doctrine was simply an
effective means, a combination of tactics and techniques,
based on mass support, to win national liberation. For
Grivas, "the liberation struggle of the Algerian people has
nothing in common with Mao's Chinese social revolution . . ."[26] The noncommunists agreed that a true national
struggle has certain dynamics, but felt the communists
had simply grasped the nationalist strategy as an instrument of revolution. However dressed up, in three immutable phases or as the vital focus of mobilizing the masses,
guerrilla-tactics remain tactics. Many in the West saw
people's wars and all their conglomerate theory as no more
than old tactics in new red bottles. Their analysis, like Walt

Rostow's speech to the members of the American Special Forces in 1961, was hardly disinterested or objective, for the anti-communist forces chose to see guerrilla-revolution as a tactic that could be met with a countertactic.

> There is no rule or parable in the Communist texts which was not known at an earlier time in history. The operation of Marion's men in relation to the battle of Cowpens in the American Revolution was, for example, by rules which Mao merely echoes; Che Guevara knows nothing of this business that T. E. Lawrence did not know or was not practised, for example, in the Peninsular Campaign during the Napoleonic wars, a century earlier. The orchestration of professional troops, militia, and guerrilla fighters is an old game whose rules can be studied and learned.[27]

The Americans felt in the early Sixties that their guerrillas in green berets could play the old guerrilla game without recourse to any body of revolutionary doctrine. For the French Army fighting in Algeria, the opposite was true; for them there was no old game but a totally new world challenge, necessitating a totally new ideology of defense, *la guerre révolutionnaire*. But *la guerre révolutionnaire* as a theory failed in practice in Algeria and as a counter-myth converted no one, while the American commitment to the techniques of counterinsurgencies could not by replacing black pajamas with green berets steal the magic of the Myth or even counteract the revolutionary-guerrilla in the jungle.

The new wars of national liberation continued to take up vast amounts of time and energy on the part of academic theorists and practicing combatants. A veritable flood of analysis, memoirs, modest proposals, and detailed investigation was poured out concerning the new doctrine. The frustrated American involvement in Vietnam in the Sixties enhanced Giap's stature as a prophet of his time, and the awakened West sought an alternative to defeat. The failures of guerrilla methods in Malaya and Greece and the Philippines were pored over for the key to victory. The campaigns in China and Algeria became texts. Anti-insurgency almost as much as nuclear strategy became the core concern of the academies. A variety of general and special theories was developed but none challenged the prestige of the war of national liberation. Even one victory in 1967 by the Arab nationalists in South Arabia over the already withdrawing British seemed to cancel out the lengthy series of abortive efforts elsewhere in the minds of the militant revolutionaries.

Always there was Giap in Vietnam facing the serried might of America, slipping back and forth from one stage to the other, flexible, daring, indomitable, confounding the technological might of the United States with the spirit of the masses, a continuing triumph of black pajamas over B-52s. None of the detailed scholarly analyses, none of the disclaimers from the practitioners of the Right, none of the memoirs of successful anti-insurgents had any serious impact on the converted and the faithful. The more illusions stripped away in print, the more misinterpretations corrected, the more logic introduced, the more firmly committed became the revolutionaries to the armed struggle —and to the myth of the guerrilla. What had been done in China and Algeria, what was being done in Vietnam, could be repeated in Latin America, in Africa, and in the Middle East. The theory of guerrilla-revolution, now myth embodying as well the aspirations of the wretched, held world-wide attraction for the suppressed masses.

For a decade Castro had, with varying degrees of enthusiasm, supported a series of armed struggles in Latin America. Admirers of ideological rivals followed Havana's lead, often in futility but always with conviction. Most of the rebellions, ill-prepared and poorly led, collapsed early on. Increasingly the weight of evidence indicated that mature revolutionary conditions might indeed be necessary or that at least a *few* conditions favorable to revolution should exist. Guevara, however, failed to lose the faith. In the final form, his theory, propounded by Régis Debray in *Revolution in the Revolution* in 1967, proclaimed the immediate necessity of establishing guerrilla-*focos* in Latin America. From these injected germs of revolution, the peasant masses would be infected and, rising up, would sweep away the imperialist governments. The prime responsibility of the revolutionary was to make revolution, to become a guerrilla forthwith. The most fertile field was the exploited peasant, who would be mobilized by the guerrilla example. None of the *focos* worked, including of course Che's own fatal attempt in Bolivia. Ten years of unrelieved failure did have a slightly sobering effect on some Latin American revolutionaries. Even to relatively disinterested observers both the need and inevitability of revolution remained patent.

> Latin America's social and economic structure is decadent, corrupt, and generally unsalvageable.
> That a change is coming is obvious. That it will come through revolution is certain. That revolution entails the possibility of violence is unavoidable.[28]

For some reason, however, the inevitable revolutions sponsored by Castro and Che failed to materialize.

Sometimes the reasons were easy to discover. Tiny groups of dedicated men landing from boats in an unfamiliar country, without proper organizational support, without the commitment of any segment of the population, without adequate supply lines, facing the determined opposition of a regime possessing the resources of repression had, at best, faint hopes of success. Attempts by young university students, highly politicized, highly enthusiastic, to take to the hills, when even within the university there was divided support for such an adventure, had equally small hopes of creating peasant support in the hills before the armies caught up with them. Everywhere the revolutionaries were split by party, by personality, by suspicion; everyone wanted revolution, many accepted the way of the guerrilla, but no one seemed to trust the other or the Castro–Che center in Havana. Each ill-prepared, romantic rush into the hills only honed the regimes' tools of oppression, further discouraged potential rebels and disinterested peasants, and broadened the rifts in the Latin American revolutionary movement. The revolutionaries persisted. The limited theory of Che was broadened a bit to allow "guerrilla" activity—assassination, theft, kidnapping, arson—within the cities. Che, as a myth personified, remained even as his theories were accepted only as stepping stones to the future. Some in the jungle hills of Venezuela or Guatemala still clung to the concept of the *foco,* but increasingly the struggle moved to cities, where a revised doctrine might still work even without the peasant masses or the catalyst of the guerrilla-band.

In Africa, the armed struggles were largely anti-colonialist, based on the new black nationalism facing the armies of imperialism, rather than the once-removed, nominally independent oligarchies of Latin America. After the abrupt removal from the scene of Kwamé Nkrumah, who had tended to broaden the list of "imperialists" to include newly independent states without sufficiently congenial governments, this was particularly true. Since most of Black Africa had been granted, rather than had seized, independence, the armed struggle was against the unrepentant white bastion in the south, where political agitation and nonviolence had failed. In the course of their protracted struggle, the southern Africans came increasingly to accept Fanon's thesis that much of the victory was in the struggle. They were fighting not simply for national liberation nor for an economic and social revolution but to transform themselves and their people.

The national liberation of people is the reconquest of
the historic personality of that people, it is its return
to history as a means of destroying the imperialist
domination to which it has been subjected.[29]

With some notable exceptions, the Africans were less
dedicated to the details of Marxism-Leninism and to defining the ultimate institutions of their nation, focused as
they were on the overwhelming need to achieve the nation
first. Thus some movements managed to accept both Chinese and Soviet support without alienating the liberal
West. All the liberation movements shared, however, the
conviction that the armed struggle was the only means to
victory and that through the struggle the Africans would
undergo metamorphosis, emerging as the pure crystal of
proud new nations—born in battle.

The most recent convert to the theory is the Arab
Palestine movement. Although, before June 1967, several
marginal movements and, for other purposes, the radical
Ba'athist regime in Syria had urged guerrilla-war à l'Al-
gérie, not until the devastating defeat of the conventional
Arab armies did the guerrilla come into his own as the new
hero of the frustrated and desperate Palestinians. Then
the Palestinians, demonstrably one with the wretched of
the earth, found that the myth of the guerrilla-revolution
fulfilled their craving for hope and offered a means to
rise above the despair of the June disaster. The theorists
of the major movement, al Fatah, had long urged that
guerrilla-tactics could be turned into guerrilla-strategy,
that the might of Israel could be defeated by the guerrilla.
Ultimately the Israelis would tire of a protracted war of
attrition and be swept away by the mobilized Arab masses
led by a vanguard of Palestinian guerrillas. Unlike Latin
American variants, most of the Palestinians, following the
Algerian example, were grouped in an apolitical front
keyed to national liberation and not to defining future
institutions. The revolutionary aspect of the armed struggle

in the Middle East, as in Africa, was the transformation of the Arabs.

> The struggle for freedom is the only means of liberating the oppressed from the illusions, imposed by colonialist suppression and bias, and that is the only way to eliminate despair and indifference.[30]

Hopefully, this liberation would not be limited to the Palestinians but would extend throughout the Arab Nation. For the Palestinians, if Israel were an outpost of imperialism then the conventional Arab governments were little better since they repressed the vitality of the Arab masses as the overt colonialists had done before them. The inevitable victory would sweep away not only the Zionists but advocates of the old order. The al Fatah guerrilla in the Golan Heights or the Gaza Strip would by example create a new breed, the truly liberated Arab, by releasing and transforming the incredible energies of the masses.

Yet Palestine is not yet liberated. The promise of the doctrine of guerrilla-revolution often seems delayed or thwarted. The liberation of Bolivia or Mozambique seems no closer despite the careful application of the tenets of guerrilla-revolution. Some movements seem hopelessly quixotic, brief flashes of daring; others apparently have mobilized the masses and generated momentum and yet are still denied victory. In Africa and the Middle East, revolutionary officers seize power through coups and the guerrillas in Kurdistan or the southern Sudan fight on. No matter how elegant the new doctrine, no matter how glowing the specific successes in Cuba or China, the difficulty of successful application appears to be severe. Part of the reason is that the necessary conditions for revolutionary success are apparently somewhat different from those detailed in the doctrine; in fact, the actual nature of guerrilla-revolution is somewhat different.

First, to have any chance to attract the people, the guerrilla-revolution needs a sufficiently valid cause which can mobilize a basic core of militants without alienating the masses. This can occur within any geopolitical context. Such a valid cause must also appear sufficiently viable, capable of success even if not particularly desirable, to the people if the revolutionary is going to be tolerated. The people by no means need to be converted to the cause in order to create conditions which the hard core need for operations. Toleration is sufficient, and toleration in part is dependent on the realism of the revolutionary vision and the capacity to achieve a level of success. If the vision is faulty, provoking the opposition of substantial portions of the people, then the population will no longer remain disinterested and can only be coerced, assuming the revolutionaries have achieved a sufficient level of performance to be capable of coercion. If the revolutionary capacity is minimal, however attractive its vision to the people, then no one is going to bother to back a sure loser at great personal sacrifices. A war, however just, must have a chance of success, for converts to blood sacrifices no matter how glorious are a rare breed.* With a just cause and a

---

* There are almost always alternatives to Liberty or Death—the Warsaw Ghetto Rising being a notable exception—and if Death is absolutely certain, no matter how humiliating may be existing circumstances, tolerating the intolerable somehow becomes possible. There is little doubt that a handful of men determined to secure a Black Republic in America could cause untold damage and despair in New York City or Chicago—but to what purpose. Certainly guerrillas could at least begin again to operate in the Soviet Ukraine, but for how long and for what purpose. Violence as protest or violence as an aspect of larger political processes has a certain validity, but violence that can lead only to the grave for both participants and cause requires provocation apparently almost universally lacking. Even the leaders of the Irish Easter Rising of 1916 assumed that all the rebels would not be executed but that the death of the commanders would vitalize the Irish people to seek what they deeply felt was a feasible goal. Neither a Black Republic in America nor a Free Ukraine appears at the moment a feasible goal.

reasonable chance of success, the original hard core of converts can undertake the mobilization of the people.

Since the mobilization depends in large measure on the effectiveness of the armed struggle, the prospects for ultimate success of a guerrilla-revolution also depend on the reaction of the opponent. Some regimes can be swept aside like Farouk's in Egypt, eliminating the need for a protracted struggle, but a remarkable number of outwardly feeble governments have had the power to resist. Others, obviously potent and determined, clearly have the capacity to resist a swift revolutionary victory.

To some degree, for ultimate success a revolt must also possess legitimacy in the eyes of the opposition. If a protracted conflict, like the Algerian but unlike the Chinese, cannot or does not expect to terminate with a military victory, then the will of the opponent must be broken. To do so the rebels must offer a viable alternative to the existing order. No one could, or should, deny that Mao or Ho represented not only legitimate aspirations but an alternative to the existing order. The dedicated in the Kuomintang or the unrepentant foreign legionnaire might be willing to fight to the last, but there were fewer and fewer volunteers for the final battle and more defectors to the new order or émigrés to a more comfortable haven. In some cases, the alternative to revolutionary victory is simply the destruction of the entire existing society or state which engenders, as in South Africa and Israel, the most uncompromising, total resistance. The paper tiger proves to have saber teeth. Even the imperialists occasionally draw the line. In Malaya the communists were visibly interchangeable with the Chinese population. A nationalist-communist Malaya was hardly palatable but a Chinese-communist Malaya was unthinkable, both to the British and to the Malays. And the British fought for twelve years to prevent it. The same was true in Kenya, where, whatever legitimacy the Mau Mau could acquire at a later date, in 1952 it was inconceivable to the British that the forces of darkness and death, representing much less than a united Kikuyu tribe, could rule Kenya. The British government and, most particularly, the white settlers saw the alternatives as order and chaos, civilization and barbarity. Less than a decade later the potential of the African nationalists was accepted as a matter of course—but not in 1952.

Simply to announce the existence of a national revolutionary movement does not automatically achieve viability: the hodgepodge of tribal groups intent on murder and plunder in the Congo threatened even their advocates; the little bands of bearded students in the hills of Latin America are often pawns in the power game, not players. The revolutionary cause must represent an alternative legitimacy, however distasteful, or anticipate an adamant refusal of the opponent to lose heart. If the revolutionary has the power to force victory, then his legitimacy in alien eyes is immaterial, but most guerrilla-revolutionaries begin from a self-confessed position of weakness.

Consequently, revolutionary wars have had a remarkable chance of success within an imperialist context. In much of the world, colonialism is an accepted evil. Equally important, empires in the formal sense no longer pay, certainly not in prestige. The security and prosperity of advanced countries can be maintained as readily without tinting the map various colors. With the heyday of imperialism long over, a colony should be an ideal target. Most insurrections within empires have really been over a matter of timing, since most empires have been in the processes of self-destruction. If an anticolonial revolution seems to threaten national security, however, prognosis for success is poor at least until the times change or the perceived nature of security is re-evaluated. If the revolutionary enters the armed struggle too soon or at too delicate a point, the imperialist may be willing to pay a very high price indeed, and often over a very long time. Even a colonial power opposed by the overwhelming majority of the people and under attack by revolutionary-guerrillas can continue to derive very real strategic benefits from its position.

Despite the widespread and often effective partisan resistance movements during the Second World War, the Germans did not evacuate France or Greece because the price they paid to stay was well worth it. In the Fifties, the British military establishment insisted on the possession of Cyprus—the entire island: Cypriot bases were felt to be too vulnerable without British control of the island —and paid Grivas's price. Despite the EOKA campaign, the Anglo-French attack on Egypt in 1956 was mounted from the Cypriot bases, validating the strategic assumptions made in London for maintaining control of the island. In time, for a variety of largely non-Cypriot reasons, London accepted a "solution" which guaranteed the permanent possession of the bases—and an independent Cypriot government determined to maintain the British presence. London had its cake and let EOKA munch on the crumbs of independence. On the other hand, once the East of Suez strategy had collapsed, the British had no need of Aden and withdrew, under pressure but under a level of pressure they could have withstood indefinitely.

For the revolutionary opposing overt or covert imperialism, it is vital to persuade the opponent that his perceived vision of security is ephemeral, a temporary misjudgment. The guerrilla-revolution is basically asking a question: Do you feel it necessary to pay the price to keep your present position? The price the revolution can inflict may be high or low, but is seldom intolerable if vital security interests are at stake. The price may be sufficiently high so that the opponent returns to examine the word *vital* at some length. Is a French Algeria really vital to the continuation of France? Is a British presence in the Palestine Mandate truly vital to British strategic interests? Is a Portuguese presence in Africa vital to the nation's future? The question usually must be asked again and again, communication by violence being a faulty method of discussion, which is why the conflict is protracted. Once answered in one area, whatever the special conditions, the next proposition usually receives a swifter reply. The British in Central Africa did not really wait for the nationalists of Zambia or Malawi to pose the question and thereby begin paying the price. Among the other factors, the Mau Mau in Kenya had given adequate warning for London to dump the whole Central Africa involvement even more rapidly than the potential questioners had foreseen. The point is that it is the perception of the word *vital* that matters. The all-but-Pavlovian response of Washington to a perceived threat in the Dominican Republic may indicate how vital at the time the Caribbean question appeared to be to Washington. In the same way as long as the Pentagon and the President accept some form of the domino theory and the vital nature of American interests in all of Southeast Asia, then full evacuation of South Vietnam is very unlikely unless the American population makes clear their disagreement with the government's analysis.

The question is addressed not only to the regime in power but over the heads of the politicians to the people behind them. If the regime under question is in fact dependent on those people—on their votes or their support —and the question cannot be kept from them, then they play a significant role in defining *vital*. If the regime's population is mute, denied a part in the political dialogue, then the price is largely the cost of anti-insurgency. Thus, to date, Portugal can measure the price of the African wars in terms of military losses, low, and budgetary costs, high. In the case of Indochina, Washington has discovered that the price of anti-insurgency—both military losses and budgetary costs—has been far higher than anticipated, but the most expensive price has been the serious division of the American people over the administration's definition of *vital*.

For a revolutionary opposing a nominally independent state the question to the regime is whether the state and society will continue to exist as organized. The answer given at first is that it will, for the only alternative is abdication, most unpalatable for most governments at any time. The revolutionary must depend on forcing the appropriate answer through the appropriate use of force. The government, assuming it does not collapse swiftly, thereby eliminating the prospect of a protracted war, may in fact reorganize both the state and society under pressure to reform, but the maintenance of control remains through the process a vital interest to be defended to the end.

Consequently the guerrilla-revolution must possess ultimately the capacity to raise the price to an opponent; in other words, the armed struggle on whatever level must be efficient, must be able to produce sufficient pressure to raise the price beyond paying. Clearly the price level during guerrilla-revolutions varies both in time and from one armed struggle to another. The price at a later stage might be more the regime would have paid at an earlier one and the price that an independent and popular government would pay might be far more than would an uncertain and unpopular colonial power. Clearly the reason that guerrilla-revolution is so often protracted is that the means to raise the price can only be accumulated slowly through the mobilization of the people—a process that an efficient antirevolutionary regime does everything to hamper, keeping down the price and maintaining control in the process.

As long as the regime's defense is relatively effective and largely tolerated by the population, the guerrilla-revolutionary must depend on counterforce, the conversion of the population, and the growing inefficiency of the government to create conditions where the revolution cannot be prevented. This process, following the Chinese pattern, has really only been repeated in Cuba. Elsewhere there has been insufficient force, popular indifference, or effective counteraction, or all three. Magsaysay in the Philippines could keep the Huks isolated in central Luzon, convert the population to mild enthusiasm for his regime, and wage an effective counterinsurgency campaign. To put together all these facets of an internal guerrilla-revolution, it is vital to start, if at all possible, with at least one or two assets in the bag: a strong force in being, or monopoly of a deeply felt issue, or the existence of a repressive, inefficient, and unpopular government. Evidently these conditions have seldom existed simultaneously. Too often the guerrilla-organization has started from scratch in a society where the people do not feel unduly exploited and the government manages a reasonably effective response. Then the guerrilla must persist, bide his time, work for mass mobilization, and keep up the pressure.

The difficulty for a potential revolutionary in assessing his prospects is that it is remarkably difficult to judge, in advance, the response of the people to what must seem to the hard-core believers an undeniably just cause or the real difficulties of mobilization or the future efficiency of the counterinsurgency response of the regime. For a cold-minded pragmatist, devoid of ideology, the prospects of guerrilla-revolution against certain regimes would remain most doubtful indeed. To organize a secret army in Wales or bomb squads in an American university would clearly seem to be acts of fantasy; but there were many to call Lenin a dreamer, if not mad. The contention that someone, someplace, must strike the first blow is based not simply on pure faith but on the assumption that until the blow is in fact struck there is no sure and certain way to predict the result. Thus the "certain conditions" for success evolve at least partly out of the armed struggle. And in very many cases the resources necessary to begin the armed struggle can be slight: a small core of the committed, perhaps without room to maneuver, without arms or exterior assistance, without visible signs of mass support, but with a determination to begin, to strike the first blow.

When that core of the committed strike in the name of the exploited, they are emboldened not by a doctrine alone but a new political myth, that of the revolutionary-guerrilla. The myth of the guerrilla has been extrapolated from a technique of attrition to revolutionary tactics and then to a psychomilitary strategy possessing the capacity not only to win wars of national liberation but also to transform men. The Myth has allowed the masses onto history's stage as the major actor. The exploited of the ages, heretofore recipients of their masters' myths of submission and humiliation, now, promised future salvation in exchange for present submission, have their own myth of action. The attractions of the revolutionary-guerrilla proved so appealing that even those without recourse to jungles and rice paddies have grasped the strategy as the ideal means to achieve change in communities resistant to change. Incapable of patience, despising prudence, the young want immediate transformations in societies structured, at best, for slow, erratic evolution. Despairing of conventional democratic means and the fashionable stratagems of nonviolence—both painstakingly slow to produce results—the impatient have gone beyond confrontation to guerrilla-politics. The lastest elaboration has been to bring the strategy and tactics of Mao or Che into the streets of Chicago or Tokyo. The new guerrilla-politics of rhetorical violence, paramilitary costumes, symbolic bombs, and wild riots may in some cases lead to the urban-guerrilla campaigns of Latin America, but in most instances the means remain the end. Often the strategy of the guerrilla-revolution has been carried past the baroque myth to the rococo fantasy, surface decoration hiding a vacuity. The idealists dress themselves in the costume of the guerrilla and their aspirations in the language of revolution. They have, like many of the guerrilla-revolutionaries, mistaken movement for momentum, the word for the deed, the myth for the doctrine. The way of the guerrilla offers for them, much as it does for the African or the Palestinian, an opportunity to act, to evade the chronic dissatisfaction with the evils of the present, to link their lives and their cause with the new heroes on the distant hills.

The myth of guerrilla-revolution offers many things to many people. The affluent, middle-class, American radical has a guidebook guaranteeing a route to change without the frustrating tolls ordinarily required by the system. For the orthodox communists it is the appropriate road signposted by natural laws to achieve the victory of the masses over the inevitably doomed power of imperialistic capitalism. For the poor, the exploited, the despised, the wretched, it has become the means for liberation not simply from the chains of exploitation and oppression but from societies which have twisted their minds, stolen their treasures, emasculated them, corrupted them, and debased them. The guerrilla has become not simply a soldier but a savior. In the jungles of Venezuela and Angola, on the bleak hills of Samaria, in the cane fields of Luzon, and the rice paddies of Laos, the guerrilla fights on assured of the gifts of victory granted by the changeless laws of war. The theory is simple, elegant, sure—and without a revolutionary theory there is no revolutionary practice—but those who mistake the Myth for objective reality may find the practice of revolution leads not to victory but to fantasy, and often an early grave.

PART II

The Battle Seen Through a Glass Darkly: The Practice of Guerrilla-Revolution

The seizure of power by armed force,
the settlement of the issue by war,
is the central task and
the highest form of revolution.
            —MAO TSE-TUNG

REVOLUTIONARY PRACTICE has been complex, confused, and uncertain. Revolutionary-guerrilla warfare has often drifted far from theory, has in fact often been devoid of theory, being developed pragmatically, entirely by necessity. The basic theories with most of their variations and elaborations have been firmly screwed into specific experience, an experience adjusted by hindsight and dogma. As the theoretical canon developed, new evidence had to be fitted into increasingly rigid molds. Rationalizations had to be found for successes gained in the field without recourse to "right" thinking, and explanations devised for failures based on proper principles. Thus, what was actually happening during the course of a campaign was often twisted, knowingly or not, into what should be happening. Consequently, schismatic alternatives, particularly when successful, have been incorporated by new definitions. Ignominious failure has been publicly explained within existing rules and regulations, even if private analysis has revealed the actual misconceptions. The result has been that the various guerrilla-theories often bear only marginally on guerrilla-practice, and guerrilla-practice wedded firmly to theory has at times led directly to disaster. The great basic truths, like most prophetic words of wisdom, are still held to be valid; but the application of the word to the deed has proved so disheartening that even the most naïve have some doubts about the absolute applicability of the formulas of revolution.

Since both the theorists of revolution and of orthodox military strategy have showed little interest in the guerrilla before Mao, almost no one has noticed the potential implications of the first great success of the revolutionary-guerrilla techniques in the twentieth century—in Ireland during the Troubles. After an insurrection, largely limited to Dublin, in April 1916, which was admired even by Lenin as a necessary foundation for future revolution, the Irish people, as the rebels had planned, were vitalized by the Rising and angered by the British repression. The leaders of the 1916 Rising—Pearse, Connolly, Clarke, and the rest, martyred at the moment of their execution by the British—joined the pantheon of almost forgotten Irish Hero Patriots and the neglected tradition of revolution was renewed. The ancient Irish myth was again watered with patriot blood. The Irish, or at least the Catholic Irish, within a year found their latent nationalism more demanding than their previous loyalty to Britain. Although the Easter Republic of 1916 had been apparently buried in the smoking ruins of central Dublin, by 1918 the ideal had been resurrected as 75 of the 103 newly elected members of the Westminster parliament pronounced themselves in Dublin the new Dáil of an independent Irish Republic. With only the very distant American Revolution as an example, the new republic had to scramble about pragmatically for means to impose recognition on the awesome power of the British Empire. The myth of rebel Ireland was alive in the island, but the means to transform it into reality remained undisclosed.

The greatest immediate advantage was that, Protestants aside, most of the Irish had by personal conviction opted for independence from Britain. The people were mobilized without further necessity of example (the Easter Rising had done that) nor of proselytizing; the scope of the election victory had demonstrated the conversion of the people. The problem was to discover the means to establish what had been proclaimed. Between 1918 and 1921, the Irish discovered a means to go with the myth. Two simultaneous processes were launched, if somewhat uncertainly: an irregular military campaign to make the island ungovernable by traditional British methods and a parallel program to establish shadow Irish institutions to replace the "legal" institutions. The military campaign of the IRA, carefully balancing small, evasive guerrilla-bands in the hills with assassination and terror in the cities forced an ever increasing British commitment to severe, although self-defeating, repression. The guerrilla-terror campaign, however, did not achieve sufficient momentum to permit the successful creation of functioning Irish institutions, although the British were in their turn unable to impose order. The Irish had not won by 1921 but neither had they lost. Britain could not win, at least not without increasingly brutal methods, anathema to much of the population of the United Kingdom. In many ways Britain was a strained and divided nation exhausted by the "victory" of 1918 and unwilling to unite behind a policy of coercion that would entail further sacrifices. Haunted by the specter of massive unemployment, class violence, and social chaos, the Cabinet could not depend on general popular support to force a military solution on Ireland and yet could not recognize Irish aspirations without endangering British security. A political compromise appeared, for the British Cabinet, the only way out of the dead end of coercion. The Irish, isolated without significant international support, exhausted by the strain of the long campaign, and fearful of British negotiating skill, were torn between compromise and loyalty to the ideal of the Easter Republic. Mistrustingly they opted to treat with London. The result was a dubious formula embodied in a formal treaty. The Anglo-Irish Treaty of 1921 gave Ireland not the republic but a Free State all but independent, although separated from six counties in the North where the loyalist, largely

Protestant population remained within the United Kingdom.*

Here, apparently, was a glowing revolutionary example. A tiny nation, isolated on an island within a great and arrogant empire, could without conventional arms or exterior intervention force extensive concessions from a major and reluctant power. Once determined, the Irish people could not be cowed by military force. The British were forced to choose between genocide and compromise. Yet few noticed. The leadership of the proletariat did not approve of a nonproletariat revolution without barricades and red flags.

The submerged nationalists in Asia and Africa were more attracted to the theories of nonviolence or to the polemics out of Moscow. Much the same fate awaited the Arab Revolt of 1936–9 in the Palestine Mandate, where forty thousand British troops could not cope successfully with a combined general strike and terror campaign. In Palestine, too, the solution was political when Britain, tidying up in expectation of general war, produced with a flurry of excitement a White Paper, which partly satisfied immediate Arab aspirations by limiting Jewish immigration.† If peoples as hampered in resources as the Irish and as disorganized as the Palestinian Arabs could "revolt" to advantage, then logically the process could be exported, interpreted, and repeated. No one bothered. A real op-

---

* The formula of solution, the oath as much as partition, could not be accepted by a substantial section of the IRA. The result was a short and bitter civil war won by the new Free State. A concomitant feature of many revolutions is civil war to determine the exact nature of the victory; i.e., who will determine the specifics of the future. Such a struggle is as often fought before victory is secured as, in the Irish case, after "liberation" has come. In the Irish case, the hard core of the IRA never gave up their loyalty to the 1916 Republic, and still exist as a clandestine faction.

† One of the most curious aspects of the largely successful Arab Revolt of the Thirties is that the contemporary Palestinian fedayeen theorists have paid so little attention to their fathers' experience and have gone far afield to find their mentors in China and Cuba.

portunity to use guerrilla-tactics as a revolutionary weapon in Europe came with the outbreak of civil war in Spain in July 1936. Unlike Ireland or Palestine, the Spanish Civil War involved at least the emotions and often the active intervention of practically every variety of European political, social, and religious creed. Soviet Russia and socialist Mexico aided the Republic. Nazi Germany, fascist Italy, and authoritarian Portugal intervened in favor of the rebel Nationalists. Volunteers from dozens of countries, organized into the International Brigades, fought to defend Spanish democracy and/or socialism against the conventional expeditionary forces from Italy and Germany. Using Spain as a sand table, the military mandarins of Europe had an opportunity to test their concepts and their hardware in practice. During a period of considerable military innovation, ranging from the first extensive use of massed tanks to the anarchists' novel military formations, the guerrilla still found no significant place. Inevitably there were partisans, urban conspirators, and mild commando raids but on an often spontaneous, seldom closely organized level. Agents of the Russian NKVD did sponsor some partisan bands, but they remained a sideshow.[1] While a great many lessons were read out of the Spanish Civil War, pored over at length in military academies or radical seminars, none related to partisan activity, military or revolutionary. Although Alberto Bayo Giroud published *La Guerra Será de los Guerrilleros* in Barcelona in 1937, not until 1960 did his *150 Questions for a Guerrilla** attract general interest.

In retrospect, of course, it is somewhat difficult to find explanations for a nonevent—the failure by either side to consider seriously the guerrilla option. To some degree,

* Bayo, a Cuban who was a devout Mason but a noncommunist, took part in various revolutionary ventures in Latin America, including training Fidel Castro's men in Mexico in 1956. After Castro's victory he was promoted by the Spanish government-in-exile to brigadier general and returned to Cuba as a *commandante* in Castro's army.

neither side had sufficient military resources to be interested in a sideshow that would cost, if little, still too much. Perhaps more important in this most ideological of wars, neither the Republicans nor the Nationalists found attractive the independence from central control that even a sponsored and directed guerrilla movement would require. To the Nationalists, armed guerrilla-bands might have appeared revolutionary, while to the Republicans, increasingly under the influence of the communist policy of instilling discipline and orthodox organization on the army, the same bands would appear romantic, unrevolutionary formations. The lack of spontaneous guerrilla-bands after the chaos of the first months of the war attests to the lack of popular support of the Nationalists in areas still widely controlled by the Republic and the efficiency of the Nationalists in intimidating potential rebels in the areas they controlled. Apparently both sides—for example, Franco's vaunted Fifth Column in Madrid or the peasants of Andalusia—felt that armed resistance, difficult to organize in any case, would be unnecessary since rescue would come through the use of conventional armies, Nationalist or Republican. There was an *alternative* to guerrilla resistance; Franco's Nationalist Army and the new Republican Army neither materially nor ideologically felt the capacity or need for a guerrilla force. Not until Franco's victory was there no longer an alternative for the unreconstructed revolutionaries. Thus, in Spain, the only serious guerrilla campaign began after the end of the war, in March 1939, when the communists turned to the guerrilla option.[2] By the eve of the Second World War, Spain had engendered at best only marginal interest in the guerrilla. There was no theory and no interest in practice.*

During World War II, the rapid advances and dis-

---

* Some indications of the almost total lack of interest within the military establishments of most countries can be seen in Britain, where as late as 1938 only a single, self-appointed specialist was examining the possibility of guerrilla operations.

organized retreats often created optimum opportunities for partisan-guerrillas, and some of the indigenous resistance groups had revolutionary or nationalist programs and were fighting not simply to restore the old society; but this tended to be overlooked by the Allied leadership, which concentrated solely on the defeat of the Axis. The campaigns of the European partisans added to the knowledge of guerrilla-tactics and indicated that the countertactics of the Axis could mobilize the people, awakening the apathetic, and broaden the base for further resistance. But, with the exception of Tito, these revolutionary potentials were not incorporated into revolutionary doctrine. In any case, it was far better to have revolutionary partisans tying down German divisions in Yugoslavia than facing those divisions in Italy. Many of the advisers and observers attached to the Greek or Yugoslavian resistance organizations became increasingly aware of the postwar aims of their temporary allies, but the problems of the moment continued to drown out the political settlements of the future.

While there remained considerable interest in the resistance movements and their contributions and potential, in the West theoretical analysis concentrated on their roles as adjuncts to conventional military practice. In future wars there would be a tactical place for the partisan in orthodox strategy. Other ventures into irregular war proved more exciting but less useful. Within the various Allied military establishments a variety of special forces emerged. Most were commando-partisans trained to make deep penetrations, like Merrill's Marauders, Wingate's Chindits, or the Long Range Desert Group. Many of these groups attracted a great deal of romantic publicity but played relatively little part in Allied strategy. They were irregular, difficult to integrate, useful for nasty jobs but were no key to the future, although in time various special forces would be incorporated into the regular establishments. While the military establishment might not like the little "irregular" operations, there was no doubt that the mass partisan operations could be most useful. The communists in particular agreed; for where socialism could not be delivered on the bayonets of the Red Army, the partisans might be able to seize power alone.

There was, however, for the revolutionary no significant commitment to a general theory of guerrilla-warfare as a result of experiences in the field. The European communists, anticipating chaotic postwar conditions, hoped for insurrections based on the partisan core coupled with political agitation. The nationalists, particularly in Asia as noted, had much the same aspirations—to present the returning colonial power with a *fait accompli,* a *de facto* government supported by a partisan army turned conventional. When a swift seizure of power was denied or resisted, the forces of revolution might be forced to return to partisan activity, but except in rare cases no one anticipated depending solely on the guerrillas as the key to change. Whatever the subsequent rationalizations of the successes and failures, most of the postwar wars were fought at first pragmatically, without any new theory of a people's war, although in communist cases there were ample orthodox, Moscow-oriented ideological explanations until the power of Mao's doctrine became increasingly relevant to field conditions.

In Europe, devastated by six years of war and occupied by huge armies, the prospects for revolution, guerrilla or no, were not great. Russia had a firm grip on Eastern Europe and in the West the communists, even, if so inclined, did not have the capacity to rebel openly against the Allied armies. Tito in Yugoslavia, with 350,000 men under arms and the Red Army on the border, managed to prohibit the return of the old order. In only two areas did extensive campaigns develop. In Palestine, two Zionist underground organizations, the Irgun Zvai Leumi and the Stern Group, had begun extensive terrorist operations in the Mandate as early as 1944. In Greece the

Popular Liberation Army (ELAS) of the communists, without the presence of the Russian Army and with British troops to oppose, failed to seize power and in 1946 went over to guerrilla-warfare. Thus, in Palestine, the Irgun and Stern Group opted for the tactics of irregular warfare divorced from any revolutionary theory, while in Greece the ELAS attempted to incorporate guerrilla-tactics into orthodox communist doctrines concerning insurrection.

When Menachem Begin and the Irgun began their revolt in the Palestine Mandate in January 1944, they had no general doctrine of national revolution to go along with the isolated Irish and Arab examples.* With an intuitive grasp of both British mentality and morality and the fears and aspirations of his fellow-Zionists, Begin put together out of very little a highly effective terrorist campaign. From time to time cooperating with the tiny Stern Group, advocates of individual terror, the Irgun rapidly made life untenable for the British and order impossible in the Mandate. The Jewish Agency at first opposed the campaign but later sporadically, and quite secretly, coordinated resistance activities with the Irgun. The more troops the British sent in, the more targets there were available for the Irgun. Ambush by ambush, Palestine slipped into anarchy.

The key to Begin's strategy was not to be found simply in the tactics of terror but in his analysis of the British response to those tactics and the nature of the Zionist community in Palestine. The British, harried by what had been called in Ireland a campaign of murder from the ditch, overreacted, condemning the Zionist community at large, who in turn gave the Irgun growing toleration if not admiration. British morality did not permit a decline to open brutality and massive repression. The British could

* Several members of the Irgun had been most interested in Katherine Chorley's *Armies and the Art of Revolution* (London, 1943), but this provided hints and guesses rather than a theoretical base.

wound but not kill, insult but not eliminate. At the same time, the presence of Ben Gurion and the Jewish Agency—the moderates—who negotiated with clean hands and vast international support, drove the British to distraction. The most minimal Zionist demands negated the most limited Arab aspirations. There was no solution satisfactory to both; worse, no solution that would guarantee the minimal British security requirements. Britain could impose a solution on the Zionists but only by recourse to a strategy far too reminiscent of the most recent final solution. Begin, actively supported by only a small minority of the Zionists, in turn themselves a minority in Palestine, could not determine the nature of the political solution but by 1947 had made certain that the ultimate solution would have to respect the Zionist presence. Deeply embittered, the British dumped the problem on the United Nations and withdrew. Ultimately the state of Israel was established with United Nations' sanction and defended by conventional forces, but in 1947 Begin as much as anyone had established the central fact—only force could prevent a Zionist state. He knew the British lacked the will and the Arabs the means. His revolt had succeeded.

In Greece, on the other hand, the ELAS, overburdened with inappropriate communist theory, never grasped what Begin had intuitively perceived: to authority, the alternatives to a determined mobilized people are either compromise or murder. At one stage, the ELAS controlled, or operated in, nearly four fifths of Greece; nevertheless, it failed not only to convert the people but also, worse, by brutality and terror, it alienated them. The ELAS's use of fear to control the people, a process hardly alien to European communism, proved effective only so long as the Greek government was too feeble to protect the countryside. Once the tide began to switch, vast amounts of popular "support" evaporated. After that, one strategic blunder followed another, culminating in a grossly ill-advised attempt to hold ground by conventional warfare in order to secure international recognition as a "revolutionary government." Increasingly isolated from the people, trapped in the bleak, wild mountains of the north, deserted by Tito, the ELAS insurrection collapsed.

Even so, the Greek government had needed three years, 150,000 men, and substantial Anglo-American support to defeat thirty thousand men representing ideas hardly grounded in Greek traditions. Although subsequent communist analysis dwelt largely on the lack of proper and mature revolutionary conditions, the premature decision for the armed struggle, and contradictory and vacillating leadership,[3] there is no doubt that less terror and longer persistence in guerrilla-tactics would have gone far toward compensating for party errors—in fact, might have won the day. Mao instead of Stalin might have won the day. For the world of Moscow, the key to successful revolution remained in mobilizing the masses by traditional political means, a process which when completed would lead to an armed struggle. That the Greek masses might be immune to mobilization in the communist cause by orthodox communist means could not be considered by Moscow. With proper prior planning, the supreme moment of maturity would inevitably occur. In 1948, Moscow would support the instigation of the armed struggle in Asia under conditions considerably less mature than in Greece; but there would be other closely reasoned, theoretical reasons for that series of blunders.

The first two irregular wars in Palestine and Greece had been fought by the insurgents without recourse to guerrilla-revolutionary theory. As noted, the orthodox critics of ELAS attacked the Greek communists for failing to follow the orthodox rules while the radical critics felt that ELAS had been too rigid to take advantage of shifting Greek conditions. To a degree both criticisms were accurate. ELAS had, of course, been stiffened with traditional Marxian theory but had managed major strategic errors without any novel ideological explanation. Out of the

Greek war came only a variety of tactical lessons, of varying merit, for both sides. In Palestine the Irgun had managed to secure a half-a-loaf with the establishment of
Israel in part of the Mandate. Menachem Begin of the
Irgun had fought *his* war largely without previous examples other than the Irish Troubles and, of course, completely without a general revolutionary theory of war—for
he was attempting to create a nation, not a social revolution, in either Marxist-Leninist or Maoist terms. Both of
the limited wars, revealing the West to the opportunities
available for rebels, attracted more tactical than theoretical
concern. Although Begin wrote *The Revolt* and some of
the ELAS activists produced articles in self-criticism,
there was no very serious impact on traditional Western
thinking about the nature and practice of guerrilla-warfare.
Neither did the Irgun or ELAS consciously contribute to
the theory of guerrilla-revolution then arriving simultaneously at maturity in distant China; but both provided most
useful examples of what could go right and wrong: Begin,
a sophisticated use of tactics; and the ELAS, the dangers
of theoretical obsolescence when involved in a potentially
mature revolutionary situation. Essentially unhampered by
a rigid ideology that determined the nature of his tactics,
Begin could, when the situation altered, afford to be op-
portunistic, shift with the flow of events, discard previous
assumptions, and adopt new means. The ELAS perception
of conditions in Greece, and therefore the means to exploit them, had been largely determined by what orthodox
communist theory indicated *should* exist. Perhaps if the
ELAS had been more flexible tactically, less interested in
working by the revolutionary rules, the Greek experience
would have gone the other way, a triumph instead of a
near-run failure.

The possibilities of limited wars in an uncertain world
as a major means of policy had, however, attracted considerable Soviet analysis. Eager to fill the gap left by the
withdrawing imperialist powers, the Soviets revived the

Comintern as the Cominform in 1947 and Zhdanov urged the overthrow of colonial oppressors. In February 1948, at Calcutta during a communist-front students' conference, Soviet delegates urged the various already eager Asian parties to begin the armed struggle. In Burma, India, and Indonesia, already independent, the communist-led revolts floundered mainly because the target nations were already liberated.

In Malaya, still under British rule, the insurgents, with their wartime experience and a valid call for independence, apparently made immediate progress. The leadership of the Malayan Communist party, however, having made a variety of tactical errors largely based on misperceptions of the nature of the British response, could not move to the stage of liberated zones and was forced to depend on guerrilla operations from out of the jungle. These operations were less than sophisticated, apparently even—or particularly—in the eyes of various Chinese communist envoys, although the British appeared sorely pressed for several years. But with the British moving Malaya toward independence, the communists lost their monopoly on nationalism. Their tactics in the field did not improve as rapidly as did British counterinsurgency, and their increasingly coercive means to secure popular support began to alienate the Chinese population. The British finally managed to contain but not end the revolt. Not until 1960 would Malaya be secure, following a bitter twelve-year effort.

In the Philippines the Huk guerrillas, also with wartime experience, faced a corrupt government obviously under American domination and for some time managed to expand their operations on the island of Luzon. Between 1946 and 1950, approximately twenty-five thousand troops of the Philippine government failed to destroy half that number of Huks in Central Luzon and in the process alienated much of the population. Under this pressure, the Huks maintained their position even if their numbers did not increase remarkably. For many of the peasants, the government and the system lacked credibility. After the advent of Ramón Magsaysay as Secretary of National Defense, the entire thrust of the government campaign shifted. Magsaysay offered the Huks All-Out Friendship or All-Out Force. The Friendship that Magsaysay offered was not limited to the Huks, for he sought not simply reforms administered from distant Manila but through intensive personal contact with the peasants to create a presence and thereby a belief that there was an advocate for the countryside in Manila. Simultaneously, the option of Force was applied by far more sophisticated methods tied closely to the reform program and Magsaysay's perpetual appearances. The 1951 election, scrupulously fair, underlined the responsiveness of the system—the government could and would accommodate legitimate demands, the welfare of the countryside would be a national goal. With visible reforms, with the new counter-insurgency tactics, with the charisma of Magsaysay, the capacity of the Huks to resist declined. Desertions began. Rewards to informers brought much of the leadership into the net. Centers in Manila and Panay Island were cleaned up. In 1954, Luis Taruc, military leader of the Huks, surrendered. The Huks or what was left of the organization went underground to wait for a better day.

The struggle of the Mau Mau in Kenya, little understood and often analyzed from afar with inappropriate tools, seemed to fit the new pattern of guerrilla-revolution. Undeniably the Mau Mau were members of the Kikuyu tribe, oath-bound to the movement that had evolved out of or parallel to the Kenya African Union, hiding in the mountains of the Kenya highlands, pursued by the British using the increasingly refined techniques of counter-insurgency. The Kenya emergency was proclaimed by the Governor on October 20, 1952, two weeks after the assassination of Senior Chief Waruhiu, the leading government spokesman in Kikuyu country. The British then swept up almost all the articulate, dedicated leadership of the Kenya African Union. Potential Kikuyu spokesmen were jailed or interned and the leadership of the Mau Mau bands that had fled to the hills fell to lesser, although sometimes talented, men. If there had been a conspiracy, the core had been removed. The British condemned the Mau Mau as an atavistic, tribal movement of barbarism and evil. Those who fought in the hills, if captured, had to be rehabilitated, for the British saw Kikuyu and African aspirations in the terms of abnormal psychology rather than reform or revolution. No accommodation with the forces of darkness and death could be contemplated, and for years the British Army, backed by the white Kenyans and at times the other tribes, hunted down and eliminated the bands in the hills. The defeat in the forest did not end the struggle for self-determination but after 1956 only accelerated it, although by more conventional tactics. At the time of Dien Bien Phu, however, the only really certain information was that guerrilla-resistance to the British continued.

Thus, by 1954, only Mao and Giap, leaving the special example of Begin aside, had won two clear victories for guerrilla-revolution in the first wave of postwar insurrections. On the other hand, the fate of the Malayan, Philippine, and Kenyan insurrections was still uncertain. The first rounds were indecisive but promising, and the more so since the doctrines of Mao, Ho, and Giap, particularly after Dien Bien Phu, had world-wide circulation.

Increasingly, it was to Mao and his disciples Ho and Giap that the theorists of both the East and West turned for an explanation of the successes and failures of guerrilla-revolution. The advocates of the new theory increasingly felt that the way of Mao would be universal, particularly in the emerging Third World, and tended, awestruck by his success, to ignore all the blunders of the first great victory in China as well as the Chinese Communists' hidden assets, unmentioned in Mao's theory. They believed that, whereas the Irish and the Irgun had fought without theory and the ELAS with the wrong one, Mao had followed his own dictates to the letter. To "explain" Malaya or the Philippines one need only restudy the history of modern China. There the masses had been converted and mobilized, the guerrillas had held the initiative and worn down Chiang Kai-shek, the war had progressed through the three inviolate stages. There were, however, certain special circumstances in China unmentioned by the theorists—revolutionary or counterrevolutionary.

To begin with, the point should be made that except for a very brief period after the break with the Kuomintang, Mao was not really fighting a guerrilla-war in the conventional, military textbook tactical definition. Most certainly he was developing on the ground guerrilla-revolution; but there was ample space outside the limited control of the Kuomintang for him to fight an irregular, somewhat unconventional war with relatively large units. These units used guerrilla-strategy and, of course, cooperated with small, irregular units elsewhere that more closely resembled the traditional conception of guerrillas. Mao stressed the great importance of the guerrilla as a means to mobilize the masses—particularly in view of Chinese conditions—and as the embodiment of the masses' aspirations and virtues. He also generalized his doctrine of war from the essential nature of guerrilla-operation. To analyze Mao's "guerrilla-tactics" as military means misses the point of a guerrilla-strategy as a part of the revolutionary process. Consequently his tactics owed much to the guerrilla but his actual formations were far more conventional and his revolutionary strategy highly unconventional. First, Mao did not defeat the Japanese by guerrilla-tactics; in fact, he did not defeat the Japanese at all, even while conducting what was clearly a nationalist campaign. In 1945 the Japanese, admittedly at some cost, were still in control of all of China that Tokyo needed. Second, Mao did defeat Chiang Kai-shek but only after over twenty years of war and after the invasion of first the Japanese and then the Russians. Furthermore, Mao's army was motivated not solely by communist doctrine but by a clear recognition of the frailties and failings of the Kuomintang, increasingly a selfish and brutal elite incapable of restoring order or creating a decent society. Mao not only had converted to his cause those committed to revolutionary change but also had wide support among those many who wanted a strong, united China, which Chiang Kai-shek could not deliver. Mao, of course, made provisions for various tactical means to incorporate opposition to the Kuomintang into a revolutionary front using those who had been driven to his cause for negative reasons as well as those converted to a specifically communist view of the future. Emphasis, however, remained on the essential attraction that the cause offered. When, in time, the new volunteers realized the essential nature of the struggle, they were expected to become converts. The intensity of the distaste for the Kuomintang may have motivated the volunteer who might desire a future very different from the one envisioned by the communists, but in time the attraction of the communist cause would transform him.

The promise of land, of protection, of a better day for China attracted peasants exhausted by years of chaos, intrusions of warlords, and institutionalized corruption. Mao had followed the traditional formula for successful Chinese revolution and gained the support of the peasants and the scholars, but as much because of the arrogance and gross inefficiency of the Kuomintang as because of historical laws. The corruption of the last dynasty, the failure of the Nationalists to reform China, the brutality and corruption of the wrangling warlords had long alienated the peasants, who if nothing more sought the order that Mao promised, and the intellectuals, who if nothing more sought honesty in power. And power had surely corrupted the Nationalists beyond redemption, beyond salvation even if the vast resources of America were added to the scales. China deserved more than the Nationalists could offer and the only organized force of redemption, a force that had maintained a purity of purpose and avoided corruption, was the communists. While all wars which are viewed as "just" have an evil enemy, Mao was blessed by 1945 with a visible rascal in the Kuomintang. The rascals—and there were, indeed, many rascals—were thrown out. The nature of the Kuomintang paper tiger had as much to do with Mao's success and the mobilization of the masses as did the laws of revolution. There was, it is true, a law defining all revolutionary opponents as paper tigers; even if at first they refused to act as they should, they would in time, for careful analysis would reveal the basic exploitable contradiction. Mao's analysis, founded on Marxist-Leninist principles, indicated that the class structure of China, although different from European models, still permitted the revolution of the peasant masses since the Kuomintang tiger could be isolated from the people, whose interests and aspirations were opposed to those of the ruling class—just as the capitalists of the West ultimately faced defeat at the hands of the proletariat. Unlike most theorists, Mao accepted the fact that special conditions had existed in China; but like most, he insisted that his basic formula for revolution had universality. All paper tigers might not be as corrupt as the Kuomintang but all capitalist tigers were, nevertheless, made of paper.

While Mao had insisted that there were natural laws of revolution, he stressed that constant analysis of local variables would determine guerrilla-revolutionary strategy. Obviously Giap in Vietnam was from time to time and from place to place less perceptive than Mao, for he jumped his fences too soon—having misinterpreted the pace of revolution. Still the Vietnam guerrilla-revolution against the French apparently ran to the Mao dictum. There were, however, some slight adjustments. First, without sufficient space Ho and Giap had to make do with China as a redoubt, which was fortunate, for without space

Mao's doctrine should not work. Second, Ho received rather substantial external aid, which was an asset not delineated by Mao. Finally, the mobilization of the masses proved more difficult than anticipated. In the early stages, with the colonialist French clearly visible as the oppressor, nationalist sentiment was easier to acquire. As the direction of the war drifted more visibly to the Left and the French fumbled about putting together a local government of sorts, the mobilization of the masses did not go as well. Those more dedicated to Christianity than communism or those intent on their ethnic separatism or simply those who saw no future in Ho's state had to be intimidated into conversion. In theory, neither Mao nor Giap opposed judicious terror, but the emphasis had always been on mobilization by the purity of the guerrilla conduct and through the demonstration of the validity of the Maoist doctrine. More important than the theoretical problems of terror was the partial success of 1954, achieved, as predicted, by the move to the third stage with the victory at Dien Bien Phu. With adjustments and after some initial errors, Mao's ideas had worked rather well for Ho and Giap.

Elsewhere revolution, as noted, had not fared as well, and not solely because the Mao doctrine had been incorrectly applied. In Malaya, one of the most successful counterinsurgency operations in a protracted conflict had been undertaken by the British. The basic step had been the promise of independence, around which the Malays could rally. The key strategy was to isolate and protect the vulnerable villages, create walled ponds instead of permitting a sea for the guerrilla fish. The British then settled down to the long, long processes of winkling the communists out of the jungle, ambush by ambush over the years.* What no one in the revolutionary camp liked to

* The British subsequently felt that the basic organizational step had been to centralize all activity, civilian and military, in one man and his agencies—a step which would have been impossible if the British had been cooperating with a fully independent Malaya.

discuss was the simple fact that the insurrection had been largely dominated by the Chinese of Malaya. Communist revolutions are supposed to be color blind. In Malaya the racial aspect of the revolt was a vital asset for the British in their efforts to deny support to the guerrillas. A majority of the Malay people, addicted to none-too-latent anti-Chinese sentiment, had their doubts from the first. The same was not true in the Philippines; but there the Huks could not claim a monopoly on nationalism.

In Malaya the communists were at first fighting at least for independence as well as communism. In the Philippines the Huks did corner the market for purity in a corrupt society; however, once the basic reforms of Magsaysay became visible or, more important, once an atmosphere of reform could be discerned in Manila, the Huks were reduced to urging an alternate and highly violent route to change, not the one road. Both Mao and Ho had managed to represent nationalist sentiment as well as radical reform, thereby easing the task of vitalizing the masses. After the arrival of Magsaysay, the Huks could claim a monopoly of neither. Despite their handicaps and their tactical errors in the field, the revolutionaries in Malaya and the Philippines had, nevertheless, nearly managed to duplicate Giap's success.

And if the Mau Mau emergency were, indeed, a struggle for national liberation, and even today there is no consensus in Kenya, the preparations for insurrection were minimal, the theoretical basis for armed rebellion slight, and the tactical successes few. Yet even with the loss of the entire central leadership, the lack of arms, ammunition, training, and central direction, the forest bands lasted for years and caused the British untold anguish. The cost in Kikuyu lives had been great, but the Mau Mau had written the future of Kenya in blood. The British would have to recognize the appalling cost of future repression in Africa and the relative ease with which determined men could turn balked aspirations into the tinder of revolution.

And unlike the Chinese in Malaya and the Huks in the Philippines, the Black Africans did have a monopoly on nationalism and after the Mau Mau emergency a means to accelerate the process if the imperialism needed prodding.

The other revolutions, in Burma, Indonesia, and India, did not even come close. The communists had failed to capture the high ground of nationalism. The people of new nations, no matter by what means or in what forms independence has come, appear to identify nationalism with the regime that has secured it. The communists had not; moreover, they were poorly organized, their political structure often unrelated to the masses, and their program less than universally attractive. Despite the obstacles, some guerrilla-bands continued sporadic and disjointed campaigns for as long as even a few of the faithful remained. Absolute pacification in isolated areas proved very, very difficult. Victory had escaped the revolutionaries; but here and there in the mountains resistance did not quite flicker out. The theorists were not disheartened. The huge effort necessary to defend against revolutionary war, if not as encouraging as a victory, was a hopeful indication that with deeper analysis the special contradictions could be found and the flickering guerrilla-bands in the hills could flare up into the wild fires of revolution burning so fiercely in Vietnam.

The next great success in Algeria came despite the presence of far more obstacles than had faced Giap in Indochina. The French had been bloodied in Indochina but had become versed in revolutionary-guerrilla doctrine. The French Army, not the FLN, had practiced the tactics of irregular war. In Algeria, the French had the certain loyalty of the *colons*, not the doubtful backing of distant and alien Asiatics. French control of Algeria was firm. Still, the FLN appeared far better off than the Irish had in 1918. The Mediterranean is wider than the Irish Sea and Algeria is not an isolated island but abuts Tunisia and Morocco, potential havens. Although the Algerians across the sea would not have as great an impact on French domestic opinion as had the Irish, closer to the center of power and the conscience of the public, the Algerian population within metropolitan France could carry the struggle into the cafés of Paris and the streets of Marseilles. Television and radio, too, would make it more difficult to isolate events in Algeria from the French public. Unlike the Irish, who had to depend on their exile population and their own agents in the international arena, the FLN had the firm support of the Arab states and the sympathy of the world's anticolonialists. Then, too, the Algerians, *colons* aside, were religiously and racially far more different from the French than the Irish from the English, making polarization and mobilization easier. In 1918, the Irish felt they faced an Empire victorious in the great war, proud, united, confident, secure in its destiny—although in time the divisions in Britain, exhausted by "victory" and weary of war, became more apparent. France, however, did not even appear to have the capacity to resist. France had been demoralized by the defeat in Indochina. One faction felt that France's Indochina debacle had dishonored the nation, violated the historical mission of the French, and required atonement so that the defeat could be expunged by a victory in the field. These ultras seeking glory were balanced by others who felt that the imperial mission had been dishonorable, that there was no glory in military adventures, that the Indochina campaign had been a misguided adventure. Neither pole seemed to speak of the same France nor envision the same future. France seemed without a mission acceptable to the nation. The government was a shifting collection of wrangling politicians. France seemed a declining nation, bitter, divided, uncertain, surely a paper tiger. The FLN was riding the crest of the wave of nationalism, battering the rocks of old empires. If they had fewer assets than Ho and Giap they apparently had far more than the Irish in 1918. The FLN, of course, gave little thought to Ireland and much to Asian events; but if Ireland could win, then with Mao and Giap in hand, many observers would assume that so could Algeria. The armed struggle was launched in November 1954.

For some time everything went according to plan for the FLN. The French had been caught by surprise, the people showed every evidence of supporting the liberation of the nation rather than maintenance of the French connections. The concepts of *la guerre révolutionnaire* held no charms for the Moslems, who did not see the struggle as a battle between Western civilization and communist atheism. The countermyth remained a fantasy of the theorists. The French persisted, evolving ever more effective military counterinsurgency tactics. The number of FLN blunders mounted, culminating in the battle for Algiers in 1957, when they lost seven thousand men and the last of their military momentum. By 1957 the FLN had reached the edge of military defeat. The French Army had not quite reached the point of reducing the level of insurrection to banditry, but the few guerrilla-bands were small and scattered and the urban cadres depleted and desperate. The French, despite their original difficulties, had proved highly effective but the FLN refused to accept defeat or accommodation. Ferhat Abbas had already adjusted the revolutionary theory:

> The guerrilla fighters have never looked for a military victory over the French army. We know that a great nation can exterminate a little people. But the guerrillas remain invincible and in existence so long as their political objectives are not reached.[4]

There was not going to be a next stage in Algeria. Instead, the FLN would persist until France lost heart. So the French Army had not quite won but the FLN had not quite lost—and the simple existence of resistance, the outward symbol of the Algerian people's option for Liberty or Death, did the trick. The French did not even manage to secure as much from the final negotiations as had the British in 1921, who had carved out an enclave in Ulster for their *colons* and hatched the not-quite-independent Irish Free State. French Algeria disappeared without a trace, except for the brief raucous klaxons in Paris hooting the fading slogan of the diehards.

Algeria had not followed the steps of Mao's doctrine. There had been no three-stage procession. The laws of the battlefield had at first seemed to work as planned, but then initiative and mobility were lost. The determination and skill of the French Army harried the guerrillas into hiding. Instead of moving on to a higher plane, the FLN had been forced to lower the stakes and reverse the process—although not in time for the French, and time was the real key to the FLN victory, not force. In China, Chiang Kai-shek lacked the force to smother the rebellion militarily. So had the French generals in Indochina. In Algeria, just as in Ireland, the rebels could be overpowered militarily but at a very great moral cost. The basic law had worked in that, once the Algerians had been mobilized and had opted for liberty at whatever cost, the French could not win without exterminating a little people. In these conditions military victories were barren and costly. France grew tired of the cost. An unjust colonial war that divided the country and ate up blood and gold without paying visible interest could not be a "military" success. Even then the generals might have been able to persist, if the realization had not finally dawned in Paris that a French Algeria was not basic to French security. Prestige, pride, even honor might be at stake but not the existence of France. The FLN had not so much won as the French had lost, and they *had* lost and there was an independent Algeria. And next to China and Vietnam could be emblazoned Algeria—the spirit of revolution again made flesh.

Both the Vietnam and Algeria wars were fought within the context of anticolonialism. The next success, in

Cuba, was, like China, an example of internal revolution, thereby re-emphasizing the universality of the theory. According to later appraisals, Castro had set up the *foco*, vitalized the peasants, orchestrated the violence in the cities, while escalating guerrilla activity. Then at the appropriate moment the revolutionaries had confronted Batista, whose regime, rent by internal contradictions, collapsed. There were no special Cuban conditions that significantly should alter the general doctrine's validity. There always are, of course, special conditions; but, for many revolutionary theorists, the Cuban ones did not seem relevant. The re-emphasis was on the vital military role of the guerrilla-*foco* and the importance of peasant support. In reality the real value of the *foco* for the Cuban revolution was not in the guerrillas' military effectiveness but in the continued existence of a highly visible dissidence that produced severe strains within the Batista regime. Provoked to brutal repression, particularly in the cities, Batista squandered if not the support of the people, then certainly their toleration. The longer the guerrillas remained in the hills the more desperate and self-defeating became the regime's policies of repression. All classes, except individuals personally involved in the regime, became disenchanted. All the guerrillas needed to do in order to produce sufficient dissonance to fragment the regime was to exist. The "war" in Cuba was almost entirely psychological. Militarily the guerrillas had almost no effect. Psychologically they were profoundly important. Second, few peasants were at first recruited and those were from among groups with special grievances. The revolutionary catch-all phrase "peasant" covers a multitude of individuals and groups with widely varying aspirations and commitments. In Cuba, the peasants did, indeed, become alienated from the regime, but so did the bourgeoisie. In Cuba peasants did, indeed, eventually fight in the guerrilla-bands, but so did the workers become involved in urban insurrection.

Because the ultimate custodians of victory had spent the years in the hills and had, many for the first time, come to recognize what they felt were the innate virtues of the peasant, they not unremarkably stressed those aspects of the revolution most visible to the peasant. Since the guerrilla and the peasant had elsewhere played a major role in the making of revolutions and the Ho–Giap doctrine assigned them major roles, the Cubans tended to assume that surely they had done so in their own revolution, which of course they had, but these were only two among several major roles. Finally the errors of Batista, which were legion, were not stressed. Nothing could have been more advantageous for revolutionaries, with or without theory, than the combination of brutality and inefficiency in the Havana regime. Batista, like Chiang Kai-shek, proved a paper tiger. The Cuban assumption was that all the tigers of imperialistic capitalism would, like Batista, be vulnerable to the peasant-guerrilla.

For the next decade, while Cuba became the breeding ground for Latin American revolutions, which failed one after another, the Cuban "lessons" revealed more about the Cuban revolution. Either the lessons were valid only in Cuba as it was from 1956 to 1959 or something desperately important had been overlooked. There were ample specific excuses for the failure in Latin America: the *focos* had bad luck, the conventional communists or the radical Trotskyites had betrayed the true way, or the revolutionary leadership had fallen heir to pride and schism. For one, Guevara never lost faith that revolution could be engendered by the presence of a *foco*, just as it seemingly had been in Cuba, but the doubtful had second thoughts. Moscow, never admitting to second thoughts, stressed that the mature conditions must be available, as they obviously had been in Cuba. Just exactly *what* they were has managed to escape investigators. The theory of the armed struggle, Russian orthodox version, was still valid. The theory had not failed the Cubans; it was just that the

Cubans had failed the theory when they attempted to export revolution.

By the early Sixties, guerrilla-revolution had finally attracted high-level opinion in all quarters. President Kennedy called on America to face the new challenge. Premier Khrushchev pledged Soviet backing to wars of liberation. De Gaulle appeared, a *deus ex machina,* to pull France out of the Algerian morass. While the French troubles had attracted the main attention, elsewhere the tactics of the guerrilla seemed to be spreading. Grivas had already, more or less, won in Cyprus. Nasser had used fedayeen-guerrillas against Israel. Guerrilla-*focos* were appearing and disappearing in Latin America. There were mini-insurrections throughout Asia and even a low-level campaign in Northern Ireland by the unreconstructed IRA. Where the theory seemed most vital as the Sixties progressed was South Vietnam, where Giap seemed once more at the breakthrough stage. There the threat was most readily perceived in Washington; and there the United States intervened in strength to buttress what some conceived of as the Southeast Asia dominoes and to fulfill uncertain commitments to the tottering government. When aid and comfort proved insufficient to deter the Vietcong, Washington raised the stakes. Hanoi replied in kind, and the war settled down deep in the stage of attrition.

Giap, the Hanoi high command, and the Vietcong found that the practices which had worked so well in China and the north were insufficient in the south. The masses of the south had many other first loyalties than to their heritage as a suppressed class. Even with the massive American presence, the north did not have a monopoly on nationalism. The ties of Catholicism, Buddhism, ethnic purity, French culture, self-interest, and, particularly, suspicion of the northerners often proved quite strong. There was certainly mass support for the Vietcong, partly national, partly ideological, partly self-interested, but not sufficient to move to the next stage of the war

without widespread conversions. Such conversions, however, were made desperately difficult by the rising
American commitment that funneled in troops, weapons,
advisers. The Americans applied not only the more sophisticated techniques of counterinsurgency but undertook
massive search-and-kill operations coupled with a constant
air attack. Even if the often clumsy American intervention
could not drive the Vietcong back to an earlier stage, the
work of mobilization was severely hampered. The Vietnamese backlash at the huge, often brutal American intervention did not compensate for the new difficulties that
limited further mobilization. Clumsy or not, the American
intervention was *impressive,* even if distasteful to many
Vietnamese previously neutral. Impatient with delay, and
provoked by the large-scale violence of the American
campaign, the Vietcong pursued as one tactic a terror
campaign to intimidate the reluctant masses and destroy
the fragile institutions of the state. The tactics of terror
were almost always directed at discrete rather than
random targets. At times, however, in order to reveal the
weakness of Saigon, grenade or rocket attacks had no
specific individual as the target.* The government was
the target not the victim. Although some assassinations
were ordered for reasons of vengeance, the northerners'
major purpose was to eliminate holders of specific positions, headmen of villages or agents of pacification, so that
they could either be replaced by the Vietcong or if that
were not possible by no one. Thus, after the occupation of

* Douglas Pike, hardly sympathetic to the Vietcong, makes the
point (*Viet Cong, The Organization and Techniques of the National
Liberation Front of South Vietnam* [Cambridge, Mass., 1966], p.
250) that the "NLF cadres regarded the proper use of terror as
terror applied judiciously, selectively, and sparingly." He even sug-
gests (ibid., p. 252) that perhaps Hanoi disapproved of an intensified terror campaign in February and March 1964. After the
American build-up, however, not only were there more targets and
a higher level of fighting in general but also there was a greater
pressure to react to American provocation and presence.

Hué during the Tet offensive in February 1968, the Vietcong methodically eliminated their opponents, a more effective tactic than the American counterattack that killed an estimated four thousand civilians—friends, foes, and the disinterested alike.

Terror, according to Mao, Ho, and Giap, was quite within the bounds of the theory, but the extent of the terror campaign in the south went far beyond the examples in China and the north. Elimination of self-defined class enemies after the revolution had been an accepted practice; however, in the south the process during the war became standard operating procedure. Once the Americans had intervened in force, it appeared even more necessary to maintain a hold on the masses, who might otherwise opt for the other side, so replete with wealth, equipment, and men, and so willing to use the brute power of military technology to effect their ends. To a considerable degree the Americans eased the Vietcong task by the ill-directed use of excessive fire power, indiscriminate bombing, and instituting free-fire zones that endangered all civilian inhabitants. The Americans in effect alienated and thereby "organized" many of the Vietnamese for the Vietcong.

Regardless of the American "terror" disguised as military operations, the Vietcong's use of terror, the level of violence, the carefully contrived use of murder, indiscriminate assassination, and public executions seemed to play an almost strategic role in the Vietcong and, later, North Vietnamese policy. American figures, hardly infallible but indicative, for 1970 up to September 30 put the number of civilians abducted at 6,000, the wounded at almost 10,500, and the killed at 4,956. In 1969 the figures were 6,907, 15,063, and 6,090.* Even if inflated, there has been

* The differences in approach can be seen in Jonathan Schell's *The Village of Ben Suc* (New York, 1967) which tells of the Vietcong, who organized the village in 1964 after kidnapping and executing the government-appointed village chief, and the Americans,

ample collaborating evidence from non-American journalists as to the extent of Vietcong terror—and to the effectiveness of that terror.[5] In theory, terror should not have
come to dominate either the good example of the guerrilla or the attractions of the faith. In theory, it should not
have been necessary to intimidate the masses rather than
vitalize them. In theory, there just should not have been
so many class enemies. In practice, however, terror proved
remarkably successful and, once addicted, the leaders of
the people's war showed no intention of drawing back for
theoretical reasons but, rather, of evolving theoretical
justification:

> We should not take advantage of the situation to
> terrorize, assassinate, and torture indiscriminately.
> We should fully understand the policy of using
> violence and implement it correctly and democrati-
> cally.[6]

If the masses refused mobilization, then terror would
be used to bring them to their senses, to their class destiny,
for it was the reactionary terror of the American forces
that prevented further mobilization. Naturally the rationale was that all the victims were class enemies, which meant
in practice that whoever was killed was by definition a
class enemy. The masses were not being terrorized, only
their enemies. "Each comrade must kill one reactionary."[7]
The important divergence by the Vietcong from the theory
is *not* the level of violence, which for the revolutionary is
immaterial, not the fact of murder, which is what war is
about, but the reason for its use. The theory cannot really
reconcile mass slaughter with mass mobilization. Supposedly South Vietnam is a mature revolutionary climate,
otherwise why has the war been continued for a decade.
The masses *must* be vitalized in theory and in practice

---

who in January 1967 organized the village by moving all the 3,500
inhabitants to a distant "safe" area. There was no longer a Vietcong
Ben Suc, but there was also no longer a Ben Suc.

even if terror is the only way. The needs of the battlefield have become paramount over the niceties of theory.

This refusal of the masses to mobilize on schedule creates the most basic divergence of revolutionary-guerrilla theory and practice. What had worked in China and in North Vietnam, had seemed such an inevitable process, did not do so as properly in South Vietnam or even in Algeria, despite the remarkable degree of revolutionary success in both. The alternative course has been to force the doctrine laws to work properly by recourse to terror often defined as counterterror. The people are alienated from their oppressors by intimidation, driven to enthusiasm by fear—both quite effective revolutionary tactics at certain times but, not only undesirable and often high risk tactics, also among the unmentionables. In Algeria the steady toll of executions and assassinations of the dissident, disloyal, and disinterested Arabs far surpassed the number of French soldiers killed.* The masses had to be vitalized by the sword—and largely they were. In Kenya only ninety-five whites, soldiers and civilians, were killed by the Mau Mau, but 13,972 blacks lost their lives, many killed by the Mau Mau.† In South Arabia probably more Arabs lost their lives in the last days of the emergency as

* It has been estimated that over ten thousand of the Moslem members who had served in the French Army were killed (*Le Monde*, hebdo. 734, November 1962, pp. 8–14) soon after the FLN came to power, and this was only the last installment. Early in metropolitan France the toll of Arab deaths, 779 killed and 2,725 wounded in 1957, 900 and 1,500 in 1958, and 237 and 421 up to June 1959 (George Armstrong Kelly: *Lost Soldiers, The French Army and Empire in Crisis, 1947–1962* [Cambridge, Mass., 1965], p. 239) indicates the scope of the terror operations.

† Julian Paget: *Counter-Insurgency Operations, Techniques of Guerrilla Warfare* (New York, 1967), p. 104. The total number of black deaths may be considerably higher than the official figure of 13,972, since body counts in the mountains were often impossible and the losses due to malnutrition, disease, and unreported operations must have been high indeed. The British claimed to have killed 11,507 Mau Mau and listed 1,817 African civilians killed by the Mau Mau.

the competing revolutionaries sought to seize the fruits of victory than the British had lost during the entire course of the insurrection.* Even in the relatively pure nationalist wars like the one in Algeria, the masses tended to prove remarkably intractable. Often the more sophisticated Front tactics of the doctrine have been neglected and the National Liberation Front is little more than a slogan raised over narrow party interests that—in theory—have had the support of the masses. Certainly the basic premise that once the people are mobilized then victory is ultimately certain seems valid; but the inevitable, immutable mobilization has proven evasive.

The simplistic converts to theory tend to see masses as masses and not as collections of individuals who define their status in other, less general terms. The theory insists on mass mobilization and, when successful, the revolutionary claims that the people made everything possible. Obviously, if all the people *are* mobilized behind a slogan of Liberty or Death, then the only alternatives are Victory or Death. The exploiters are left with genocide as the only alternative to defeat, and, moral qualms aside, the technological difficulties of genocide are beyond most capacities. All the people, however, are never mobilized. Most people at most times do not want to be bothered. In the euphoria of the struggle or at the moment of victory, the revolutionary commanders may say so, but often with a few unspoken caveats. In Cyprus all were mobilized behind EOKA except the communists and Turks; in Ireland the IRA had the support of all Irishmen except the Protestants; in Algeria there were reluctant Arabs in Paris

* During the emergency between 1964 and 1967, fifty-seven British security forces and eighteen civilians were killed as well as seventeen local security forces and 290 local nationals (Julian Paget: *Last Post: Aden 1964–1967* [London, 1969], p. 264), according to British statistics; but the final fighting between the NLF and FLOSY could not be included, since no statistics could be kept and the bodies were often buried on the spot. The estimates by local journalists were, however, usually in the hundreds.

as well as in Algiers. In point of fact, most of the masses need only to be disinterested to provide a neutral ocean for the guerrilla fish. T. E. Lawrence almost alone accepted this premise, suggesting that ninety-eight per cent of the Arabs could have remained passively sympathetic without affecting his campaign. Obviously the more support the better, and some support is essential. Revolutionaries of whatever denomination suspect the neutral and seek full commitment. There is obviously no more effective technique than to leave the oppressor isolated, alone in his castle dependent on mercenaries; but successful rebels have not always had to depend on total backing, even if according to theory they should have done so, must have done so.

Much more significant has been the remarkable failure of practice to accord with theoretical predictions. What works can readily be incorporated into theory, but what does not work requires more extensive explanation. And the theories simply do not seem to work very often or very well. All rationalizations about mature revolutionary conditions and the analysis of the special contradictions in every society aside, the theory proposes a model in which revolution is not only inevitable but imminent. The model has become not simply a doctrinal projection but the basis for a world vision that no longer needs transfusions of victories in the field to exist but only the acceptance of the myth of the guerrilla by the faithful. The actual limitations of the theory of guerrilla-revolution, however defined or denied, no longer have for many men particular relevance.

The world is ripe for revolution, seething in discontent, groaning under exploitation, rent with contradictions. Wars may, as the theory indicates, be protracted. Many attempts, well intended and pregnant with hope, may abort. Yet few of the promised victories occur. In Africa, for example, during the Sixties there were over eighty coups—romantic adventures—attempted with a remarkable record of success, and yet in the same period revolution according to the theory succeeded only in Algeria, and perhaps Zanzibar. Many of the coups could be categorized as revolts, not part of a revolutionary process that transforms more than the personnel of the Cabinet; however, it had to be accepted that in some instances—Egypt in particular—the coup led to revolutionary changes. Coups seem to work, and wars of national liberation do not— and that is heresy. The litany of failure in Latin America is long. Everywhere there is hope, in Laos and Thailand, in Venezuela and Guatemala, in Angola and Mozambique; but nowhere is there clear-cut, undeniable success. Outside of Southeast Asia even the prospect of minor victory appears remote. The general and special theory has often proven too general or too special on the battlefield but victorious as a myth. The reasons are as complicated as the Myth is simple.

A basic difficulty of any theory of all human conduct is that it is apt not to be sufficiently inclusive. Despite explanations about special analysis for special cases, the theory of guerrilla-revolution transformed into myth persists in labeling complicated phenomena with simplistic labels—the masses, the imperialists—which have had a remarkable attraction for many desperate men. Mao, Giap, even Che have presented revolutionaries with a rule book which analyzes history largely in class terms, leaving little room for the peculiarities of the human spirit or the diversity of human institutions. The special contradiction must be discovered in the form of class contradiction, for the existence of classes determines the existence of such contradictions. This model does not always work, although, of course, with a wise or shrewder manipulator it might. During the Sixties no such wizard appeared. Instead a collection of acolytes, true believers in the Myth, persisted in their faith in the theory, and believed that the exacting practice of the gospel would be sufficient. Some in desperation may have had no choice, but others stubbornly acted out their special disaster according to the rule book. They provided again and again the exceptions to the rules.

For the contemporary revolutionary, the most unfortunate aspect of the new myth has been the stress on vast generalizations outlining the total confrontation between two great mutually exclusive armies of the future and the past: the masses and the imperialists. It has long been a tempting and alluring vision, Them and Us, the Saved and the Damned, but as a fulcrum for specific policy, it is difficult to use effectively at every point at which the Myth fades into fantasy. For many contemporary revolutionaries, all opponents are lumped into one tidy camp: those who are doomed by history, evil exploiters of the people, rich in machines, poor in spirit, the counterpart of the teeming, loyal masses. Simply labeling the enemy a doomed imperialist does not necessarily doom him or change the balance of power. The Palestinian Arabs insist that the Israeli is an imperialist, befuddled by fragile Zionist theories, a certain victim to a war of national liberation. The Israeli, possessed of his own myths, clearly thinks otherwise and has and will react otherwise. The Afrikaner, equally endowed with his people's myths, does not perceive himself as a "colonialist," an alien intruder in a Black Africa. To call the Israeli or the Afrikaner an imperialist, to prove it to your own satisfaction, does not mean that he will return to Rotterdam or Warsaw. Both are chosen people, destiny's children, whose myth's reality can be proven to their own satisfaction on the field of battle, validating their existence. The Bolivian or Venezuelan governments assume that their regimes are legitimate whether or not the men in the hills call them imperialist fronts. The "pawns" in La Paz and Caracas have refused to rush into exile, confident that they represent the nation.

When applicable, the label can be most useful, as the Vietcong have found, since despite all the reasoned explanations of the American commitment, there remains a basic "imperialist" content to American intervention. For example, Washington might feel truly responsible for the various dominoes, deeply, perhaps morally, committed to their defense; but basic American strategic interests are at stake above and beyond pure idealism. By the mid-twentieth century, such recognizable imperialism has become an excellent target and obviously open colonialism even more so. A great many such "ideal" targets for revolution, however, have refused to act like fading colonies just as many peasants have proven obtuse about their class loyalties. Still, to label an opponent as imperialist is most useful, if not the ultimate weapon. Even more difficult of application has been the tidy label of national liberation. Many nations not only feel unimperialistic but quite satisfactorily liberated. Some of the nations to be liberated exist only in the imaginations of the liberators or within lines on a map. When used, however, as something more than a handy cachet, nationalism is by far the most effective basis for revolutionary war. The world-wide vision remains: the vanguard of the vitalized masses fighting wars of national liberation against bestial imperialists; no matter if the masses won't mobilize, the nation is invisible, and the imperialists are local liberals.

No matter what the guerrilla-revolutionaries think they are doing or how they define their war, if their armed struggle is not to slip into this fantasy world, certain conditions seem to be necessary for even an outside chance of success. The new generations of experts on counterinsurgency have regularly stressed certain, almost essential, factors that permit the waging of guerrilla-war. Some of the more salient features postulated have almost always included the existence of extensive, isolated, and inhospitable terrain; the guerrilla possession of secure base areas preferably beyond the national boundary and the reach of the counterrevolutionaries; and an unprepared and disorganized government. While space and ineffectual opposition are prized assets, they are no means essential.

A guerrilla-revolution need not be waged solely or even primarily by classic guerrilla-tactics but by a mix of techniques, although those converted to the theory and attracted to the Myth seem to prefer the guerrilla option. A guerrilla-revolution can occur in narrowly limited space against a highly effective opponent even if these are admittedly not optimum conditions. Even in a tight little island like Cyprus, almost swamped with British troops and police, a guerrilla-*cum*-terror campaign was possible. Clearly, the smaller the country, the more likely a guerrilla overload becomes and the more likely it is that other tactics should be sought. Similarly, the question of a protracted guerrilla-revolution is unlikely to occur if the opponent is going to fold at the first trumpet blast. Then the revolution can be made from the seat of power rather than during the armed struggle. Thus, guerrilla-revolution can most easily exist in countries sufficiently disorganized to allow a growth of insurgency but sufficiently structured to prevent its swift success.

It is not, however, really the size of the country or the degree of control that determines the prospects of success for a guerrilla-revolution but the relation of the revolutionaries to the population and to their opponents. Effective guerrilla-revolution is as much a political-psychological struggle to convert and intimidate as it is an armed struggle to grasp victory on the battlefield. Guerrilla-revolution is about people, the struggle to mobilize them during and by means of an armed struggle that isolates their opponents from them. Increasingly isolated, increasingly dependent on naked coercion achieved at higher and higher cost, both moral and spiritual, the opponent may well collapse without substantial guerrilla-revolutionary military victories.

In vast areas of the world, it is obviously quite possible to begin a guerrilla-revolution, though not necessarily to finish one. With rare exceptions, the easy targets of overt imperialism have gone, leaving only the more difficult

independent if "reactionary" states. Within these, however, there are usually sufficient pools of resentment,
ethnic dissidence, economic exploitation, religious bigotry,
linguistic separatism, or historic humiliation for the guerrilla fish to swim in for some time. With a relatively tiny
core of the devout, capable of being replenished, and a
measure of popular toleration even if geographically
limited, the revolutionary can cause a disproportionate
amount of chaos for an indefinite time. If the popular
support is reasonably broad, complete, and permanent,
pacification is apparently nearly impossible. For eight
hundred years, the British could never quite keep the lid
on the rebellious Irish. When dissidence is founded on
racial differences and in many cases on religious or linguistic dissent, the regime's hope for order lies in revolutionary exhaustion or institutionalized repression. Pure,
naked oppression—no one's favorite option—has worked
out usually only if the oppressed have accepted an
unstated premise that continued support of rebellion, however limited, has far worse consequences than the existing
supposedly intolerable conditions. The obstacles, then,
that face a guerrilla-revolution's success are formidable
but the prospects of launching the struggle are excellent.°

° Since the basic investment to begin and continue guerrilla-
revolutions is minimal and yet can produce disproportionate benefits, several powers have been willing to underwrite revolt. In
many cases, successful revolt is unnecessary, even undesirable—only
the continuation of disorder, which indebts the patronized guerrillas,
garners the enthusiasm of friends of their cause, and forces a
substantial investment on behalf of reactionary order. The Russians
get a maximum return on a minimal investment in southern Africa,
where Moscow favors guerrilla-revolution, but would acquire little
in Latin America, where revolt would disrupt both Soviet foreign-
policy initiatives and local communist organizations. China, with
few foreign policy initiatives at hand and a minimal overseas organization, has been universally attracted to the concept. Western theorists, echoing Moscow's concern about mature situations, can see little
chance of guerrilla-revolutionaries' succeeding within communist
states (Hungary or Czechoslovakia or Tibet); but other patrons
of revolution have not been overly concerned with success, only

Throughout the Sixties, there were many men in many places who cared not how great the obstacles to success might be, were inclined in any case to believe their oppressor inherently frail if overtly potent, and, clinging to the grail of a just cause, persisted in the armed struggle. Nothing gave them as much comfort as the presence of the doctrine of guerrilla-revolution nor as much trouble as its application. The techniques of the guerrilla are well known and easily learned, the tactics require some level of natural talent, but the strategy of guerrilla-revolution proved not only ineffectual but often self-defeating. Those who knew that the new myth of action embodied the exploited people's belief that they *could* make a revolution did not despair. The faithful kept the faith. Many had no other choice. Others had invested too many lives, too much hope. Some were led beyond the power of the Myth to the realm of fantasy, acting out revolutions in a deadly drama. So the guerrilla-revolutions continued out of the Sixties and into the Seventies, in the jungles of southern Africa, in the narrow alleys of Gaza and Nablus, and on the wild highlands of the Andes. The guerrilla persisted or died, pursuing the revolutionary trade, seeking the inevitable victory, validated by theory but so far denied in practice.

---

the spin-off benefits of the struggle. On a somewhat parallel case, Moscow has much to gain by the continuation of the Israeli–Arab confrontation but is threatened by the element of disorder within the Arab world created by the Palestinian fedayeen, whose activities could bring premature Israeli retaliation. In any case, the great attraction of intervention is that so little spent on so few can return so much prestige and position—even Cuba or the People's Democratic Republic of Yemen can play the revolutionary game.

PART III

Three Case Studies
in Guerrilla-Revolution

*War, at this Time, rages over
a great Part of the known
World; our News-Papers are
Weekly filled with fresh
Accounts of the Destruction
it every where occasions.*
    —BENJAMIN FRANKLIN

CASE STUDY ONE

The Winds of Change Blow North: The Wars of Liberation in Southern Africa

Today's mission
comrade

is, dig the basic soil of Revolution
and make a strong people grow
　　　—MARCELINO DOS SANTOS

THE BLACK–WHITE CONFRONTATION in southern Africa is now nearly five hundred years old. Since the arrival of the Portuguese off the mouth of the Congo River in 1482, there has been a cycle of exploitation and pacification, temporary accommodation and open war, coercion and toleration; for, essentially, the Black African has not been able for long to absorb or to expel the white settler. In the Portuguese areas until recently, the course of penetration has been in the grand tradition: the string of forts, the network of traders seeking gold, ivory, and slaves, and the endless wars of pacification. Even in the twentieth century the huge Portuguese colonies remained largely backwaters with some of the interior still not pacified. There was a minimum of economic or social development and limited European colonization. The impact of the European on South Africa, on the other hand, had been quite different and often quite violent; for the Boer and Briton had come not only to exploit the wealth of the continent but also to stay.

On April 6, 1652, Jan van Riebeeck had started the first Dutch settlement at the Cape. Joined by the first of the

Huguenots in 1688, the old Europeans gradually evolved into a new breed, the Afrikaners, pushing north into the often empty areas for new land, competing with the Bantu moving south. In 1795, Britain occupied the Cape for strategic reasons, accepted its cession from Holland in 1814, and in 1820 encouraged the arrival at the Cape of five thousand settlers. All through the nineteenth century, the competition between the Boer and the Briton continued simultaneously with constant wars on the expanding frontiers: the Kaffir Wars, the Basuto Wars, the Matabele War. With the end of the Anglo–Boer War in 1902, the future domination of South Africa had apparently been won by the British. The Boer Republics were absorbed. African resistance had been broken and even far to the north Matabeleland and Mashonaland were controlled by a British company. The future seemed to lie open to Britain: the Boer faced assimilation and the Bantu tutelage.

Within the decade, all the forces were present in South Africa which would transform the course of events in the next fifty years. In 1907, Mohandas Gandhi, who had arrived from India in 1893, began the first of his Satyagraha campaigns to gain political acceptance for the Indians, who with the Coloureds had until then been, and would continue to be, unassimilated. In 1910, the Union of South Africa, with Louis Botha as Prime Minister, appeared and the mechanism for direct British intervention was removed. In 1912 the African National Congress (ANC) was organized to seek a satisfactory *modus vivendi* with white South Africans. In 1913 Hertzog founded the Nationalist party to seek Afrikaner aspirations within the existing system. To many, if the prospects for a homogeneous South African nation seemed faint, the possibilities of a tolerant and democratic pluralistic society did not.

What hopes there were showed little sign of fulfillment in the years after World War I. The militant Afrikaners had no desire to be absorbed into the mainstream of British politics represented by the United party. In turn, the United party showed no overwhelming interest in absorbing the Indians or the Cape Coloureds, much less the Africans, into white society. There were sporadic violence, race riots, a massive strike of Rand miners, even a brief African rebellion; but more often there was surface calm. However, no slow fusion of races, no gradual agreement on values, no lessening of tension could be detected.

After World War II, there was a growing militancy on the two flanks. The Nationalist party, under D. F. Malan, expanded its appeal and its effectiveness so that in the election of May 26, 1948, the United party was rejected at the polls. The new government under Malan, advocates of apartheid, deeply suspicious of the Briton, dedicated to creating a society abhorrent to most Western ideals, gave every indication of permanence. The astute, among them many within the United party, did not see how the election results could be reversed in the future, a future which consequently would be very different from that conceived by liberal opinion. Almost at the same time that Malan came to power, the African National Congress, after long years in the polite doldrums, issued a militant Program of Action. Most important, the Youth League, led by articulate and impatient young men like Oliver Tambo and Nelson Mandela, dominated the thinking of the Congress rather than the more patient nostrums of the movement's elders. If nonviolence remained the basic strategy, the insistence that the pace of progress be accelerated was increasingly loud and clear.

Essentially, the weapon within the arsenal of nonviolence selected by the ANC was the boycott. To be effective, the leadership would have to persuade a large and untrained mass to seek, at some expense, goals which at best were distant and more often quite mysterious. Shaping and politicizing the African mass was a formid-

able undertaking, since the elite leadership was often
isolated from the tangle of tribal and class antagonisms
that hampered unity of action. Insufficient preparatory
work had been done and there were too few existing
African institutions. The trade unions were weak. Social
and welfare organizations were often tribally based. The
antagonisms between city and country were often more
real than Fronts or Congresses. Outside the black organizations, the Coloureds remained highly passive and the
Indians—the target of black attacks during the Zulu riots
of 1949—suspicious. Given the awesome handicaps, ANC
managed relatively impressive results through much
of the early Fifties. Boycotts, protests, marches, monster
meetings, and appeals to conscience, all part of a general
defiance campaign, encouraged the leadership. The Congress Alliance was formed to draw into the struggle the
other radical groups, including white radicals and many
communists. In 1956 a bus boycott in Johannesburg
organized by ANC attracted international attention, but
like all the other tactics resulted in no visible change,
rather generating increasingly repressive measures by the
government.

The nationalist grip on the country under the new
Prime Minister, J. G. Strijdom, had in fact been strengthened as the repressive machinery was elaborated and refined under ANC pressure, a tendency which would
continue for a decade. Whatever Gandhi may have
thought of the universal validity of Satyagraha, the
Nationalists felt that even superficial compromise was
unnecessary, certainly unwise, and a violation of the
Afrikaner's historical mission. All the sound and fury of
the escalating ANC campaign could not really threaten the
state. As the ANC campaigns against the system grew
more intensive so did security measures. The effort to
break the notorious pass system failed in 1958 and the
treason trials began. Strijdom was replaced by H. F.
Verwoerd and progress toward apartheid, toward the

elimination of radical dissent, toward a polarization of white–black opinion continued.*

In 1958, ANC was split by the "Africanists," who suspected the infiltration of Europeans and communists into the movement and also expressed a willingness to accept violence if need be. In 1959, the "Africanists" established the Pan-African Congress (PAC) under Robert M. Sobukwe and Potlako K. Leballo and opened a militant campaign against the pass system. Essentially the PAC was still using the politics of nonviolence, the tactic of confrontation and not that of rebellion based on conspiracy. It still hoped the government would give way, rather than be forced to give way. There was, however, no good will on the part of the nationalist government. On February 3, 1960, Prime Minister Harold Macmillan spoke of the winds of change before the South African Parliament. The nationalists felt no necessity to bend before the breeze. The Africans stepped up the pace of defiance. On March 21, 1960, at Sharpeville the police opened fire on a crowd of demonstrators, killing 67 and wounding 186.

International opinion was horrified. The Africans of ANC and PAC were appalled at the callous brutality. Many of the whites, particularly those clustered around the United standard, were deeply concerned, particularly about the future security of the state. There were tremors in the world of South African finance: the market fell by over ninety million pounds in three days. PAC-ANC pro-

* Of all the nationalist leaders, Verwoerd was by far the most able. With his firm grip on the mind of the Afrikaners, he was able to extend Pretoria's narrow vision to the necessity of coming to terms with Black Africa by some other means than keeping the wagons in a circle. His policy of maintaining a low profile and expanding South African penetration, even at the cost of welcoming Black African diplomats, transformed the situation in southern Africa. That his vision of an alliance of black and white states developing separately is anathema to African Nationalist opinion does not mean that it does not have an overpowering logic, given the present situation, nor a remarkable record at present of success.

tests developed throughout the country. There was a revolt against the Bantu authorities in Pondoland. There was more talk of capital taking flight, of a massive black uprising, of catastrophe around the corner. The government, however, had no intention of losing its nerve. A state of emergency was declared, army reserve units mobilized, and PAC and ANC banned. The impressive array of repressive legislation allowed the government to ban meetings, jail thousands of ANC and PAC members, exile others to remote locations, and detain the suspected. By 1961, the overt African organizations had been disbanded and great numbers of the activists imprisoned so that the always fragile communication and control network collapsed. Any legal successors to ANC and PAC would be narrowly confined by the continually growing corpus of legislation and the constant vigilance of the security forces.

As well as inflating their own impact, the African leadership elite had obviously, from the first, grossly underestimated the determination and capacity of the Afrikaners. The Boer was dedicated to a mission, he was a man ruthless in his pursuit of *his* dream, and he was in possession of all the repressive machinery of a vast, wealthy industrial state. Difficult as it is in retrospect to accept, the allure of nonviolence, even after Sharpeville, had not lost all its charm. For some time militant leaders of PAC and ANC insisted that they would use violence only if the government did not recant. As a policy statement in 1948, this might have had some slight relation to reality; but by 1961 it was postponement of the obvious. In June 1961, Mandela and several of the militants of ANC still on the run founded Umkonto We Sizwe to direct sabotage operations—but sabotage which would endanger no lives. PAC sponsored Pogo, a similar organization; and an interracial group, largely white, founded the National Liberation Committee (NLC) and began sabotage operations in October. Umkonto We Sizwe followed in December and the stage of illegal resistance was under way. During the period of nonviolent politics, the leadership at least held to the strategy that they could force the South African government to bargain under domestic pressure and international influence. What was expected from a sabotage campaign was far more cloudy. If the campaign of bombs and arson could generate sufficient momentum, a highly unlikely premise, the same dead end would loom ahead; for even if the British panicked, the adamant, uncompromising resistance of the Afrikaner was certain. A Briton, perhaps, might compromise or else prefer an exile in England to a race war; but the Afrikaner had for centuries shown his faith in the African mission, and low-grade sabotage was not going to move him.

More restrictive legislation was brought in. More arrests were made. More men and women were detained. One by one the key leaders of the underground were picked up. Mandela was captured in August 1962. The drastic penalties for "treason" and the continuing arrests could not immediately stamp out the violence; but the vestiges of centralized control deteriorated. More and more the "campaign" depended on local initiative and regional frustrations. The often-rumored PAC master plan for a general rising in 1963 apparently aborted under police pressure. With or without central direction, the number of incidents of sabotage and terror remained high as local groups carried out sporadic attacks. Consequently the level of repression continued and the level of arrests was high: from February 1962 to December 1964, 2,436 persons were charged with sabotage, although about 1,000 were found not guilty; there were usually about 8,000 political prisoners; and 1,095 people came under ninety-day detention. On June 12, 1964, Mandela and his colleagues received heavy sentences at the Rivonia treason trials, the most spectacular of a long series of judicial extravaganzas. By the end of the year, from the point of view of the government, the worst seemed to be over. While there had been a considerable number of sabotage incidents, almost all had been quite minor. A substantial portion of the African leadership was in prison, in detention, or in exile. Their white allies, particularly the communists, had been infiltrated and apprehended. The old PAC and ANC political organizations were fragmented and the sabotage organizations crushed. Internal opposition and subversion continued to exist but on a low level. All the potential white sympathizers had been frightened off or intimidated. The Coloureds and Indian population watched from the sidelines. By 1964 African resistance became exile-based, desperately searching for some means to strike back at the white *laager*.

In 1961, the year when South Africa had seemed to totter on the brink, the acquiescent nationalists in Angola suddenly shattered Portuguese complacency. The transformation was so sudden that many somber, if distant, experts caught napping accepted the inevitable: that Black Africa was on the move and that if the Afrikaners could not cope, then certainly the Portuguese were lost. In 1958, there had been only one thousand Portuguese troops in Angola and by 1960 still only three thousand. Little seemed to change with the passing of the years. The price for coffee was down; the international press was complaining about the forced-labor system; the turgid pace of life went on day after day. A visitor would find little difference in the Angola of 1940 or of 1930. Portugal was too poor even to exploit the colony properly. There was no domestic opposition in Salazar's Portugal to develop an anti-imperialist issue, nothing more than vague talk in Luanda about an independent Angolan destiny; and what there was of African politics seemed limited to constantly shifting alphabetical letterheads and a handful of frustrated Westernized and often exiled bourgeoisie. With only a few exceptions this was essentially the case; however, the exceptions proved vital, for all was not well in Angola. There were longstanding grievances on the part of most tribal Africans: forced labor, widespread unemployment, brutal tax collectors, discrimination, lack of education or welfare services, and Portuguese arrogance and repression. Efforts to exploit these by the various inchoate African political groups and the ethnic associations based in Northern Rhodesia had not been particularly successful. The few local leaders were urban, Westernized, largely isolated from the rural peasant and often, for that matter, from the stimulation of the outside world.

In December 1956, the Movimento Popular de Libertação Angola (MPLA) was founded, with one of its major components being the Angolan Communist party. The MPLA, under the leadership of Mário de Andrade, Dr. Agostinho Neto, and other Westernized Mbundu urban-intelligentsia, had attracted largely the Kimbundu from north-central Angola. The development of a clandestine organization proved difficult, for the Portuguese security police, Polícia Internacional e de Defesa do Estado (PIDE), arrived the following year and clamped on tight security measures. The culmination of repression came on March 29, 1959, when extensive raids resulted in the arrest of many members and the exposure of hundreds of others who were forced to flee to exile in the Congo. MPLA opened a headquarters in February 1960 in Conakry, sufficiently distant to reassure PIDE. There was still obvious unrest in Angola. Riots followed the arrest, flogging, and jailing of Agostinho Neto on June 8, 1960. On another front, Barros Necaca had organized a party among the Bakongo but to avoid repression had to keep activity to a minimum. Instead, he asked Holden Roberto, long resident in Europe and the Congo, to go on the road to acquire international support. In 1958, Roberto then created the União das Populações de Angola (UPA) and began an odyssey to garner aid and comfort. Although PIDE was aware of much of the political maneuvering and Lisbon felt sufficiently concerned to reinforce the army, the situation did not seem especially ominous. Some of the sporadic outbreaks of violence could be traced to religious sects or traditional tribal discontent. Tribal barriers seem to prevent any real all-Angolan front organization, and there was always the heritage of inertia.

In 1960, the independence of the Congo to the north, led by men who publicly favored the liberation of Portuguese territories, brought an exile-base menace a great deal closer. Roberto, who had held long conversations with Frantz Fanon*—then representing the Algerian FLN in Ghana—Nkrumah, Lumumba, and the powers of the emergent Third World arrived in the Congo in mid-July. How effective he would be remained problematical. The MPLA–UPA division, despite protests that unity was the goal, continued and a variety of other movements appeared, joined, and hived off one or the other. Both MPLA and UPA, moreover, publicly continued to favor nonviolence. It would appear that the Portuguese were prepared for a campaign of subversion or even infiltration, but not open rebellion. This, apparently, for the time being was the intention of MPLA and UPA, still hopeful of intimidating Lisbon into concessions as had the nationalist movements in the British and French empires. Early in 1961, there was serious trouble in the Kasanje country but no firm evidence of "outside agitators." On Feburary 4, 1961, the MPLA or at least several hundred Africans armed with clubs attacked Luanda's main political prison. The cycle of retaliation and response tapered off within a week.

Then on March 15, a widespread, ill-coordinated series of bloody attacks on white settlers occurred almost simultaneously throughout the areas on the Congo border and down as far as the Dembos region. The degree of control or even of immediate responsibility of UPA was

---

* Fanon's insistence on the necessity of the armed struggle apparently greatly influenced Roberto, although the decision to give up nonviolent means was made for him by Angolan events.

probably minimal. Whatever nationalist "military" organization might have existed, the rebellion collapsed almost immediately in an orgy of atrocities, arson, and wanton murder. Luanda was stunned. The settlers in panic withdrew or were withdrawn into the major cities. In the first wave of assaults, over one thousand Europeans were killed and tens of thousands of blacks. The Portuguese reprisals were immediate, indiscriminate, and ruthless. Badly shaken by the extent of the carnage and justifiably horrified by the rebel brutality, the response in hot blood was to slaughter any African in the disaffected areas. The final total was in the thousands. The Portuguese Army rushed into the vacuum, re-established a semblance of order. The rebels receded into the countryside. There was no wild second wave of screaming Africans driving the Europeans into the sea, which had momentarily seemed a possibility; but there was no return to the past. The revolution had come to Angola to stay.

In the first six months, the Portuguese Army, rapidly reinforced, moved through the countryside with a minimum of restraint. By the end of six months, the estimated number of Africans killed ran well over twenty thousand. Perhaps over five hundred thousand Angolans fled to safety in the Congo. Large, formerly fertile areas were left deserted and desolate; the villages burned in air strikes; the fields fallow; the population dead or gone. UPA was largely unready and unable to take advantage of the extensive Portuguese repression or of the opportunities that the withdrawal of the European population opened up. Inside Angola, much of the leadership and armament remained indigenous and third-rate; but the "rebellion" did not burn itself out—giving UPA headquarters an opportunity to try and sort out the chaos. A military structure was developed, arrangements were made to give exiles military training, arms were collected, agents dispatched, and bit by bit during 1961 an element of control and coordination created in the guer-

rilla areas. A far more centralized campaign was opened
by UPA against the Portuguese enclave of Cabinda. By the
end of the year, the UPA guerrillas there numbered three
hundred under the command of Alexandre Taty. Again
the Portuguese response had been ruthless: thousands
had been killed or deported and over half the population had fled into the Congo. At the end of the year, both
sides were strained. Roberto was scrambling to create
a military-revolutionary organization, to maintain the
momentum of March, and to fight off nationalist competitors. The Portuguese with limited resources in place
were hard pushed to wipe out the elusive and deadly
guerrilla-bands before the infection became endemic.

The UPA monopoly on the liberation struggle was
challenged in October 1961, when MPLA moved its
headquarters to Léopoldville with substantial international support assured. Soon MPLA claimed that its
guerrillas were operating within Angola and, almost as
soon, that one of its patrols had been wiped out by
UPA. The UPA–MPLA rivalry would continue despite
various efforts to create a front organization if not a
unified party. Angolan nationalist politics remained a
seemingly endless spiral of internecine disputes, ethnic-
based schisms, enthusiastic front groups, and often
bloody competition in the jungle. All the kaleidoscope of
the various alphabetical groups, merging and splitting,
was repeatedly complicated by the rapid switches in
the Congo government. For example, Lumumba supported Roberto but his successor Kasavubu did not,
while his successor Adoula did—each change seemingly
leading to the hiving off or the rushing in of the opportunists. Under Tshombé, the number of organizations
mushroomed still further so that at times it appeared that
whenever two nationalists gathered there were two parties
and a front. More than anything else—religion, ideology,
strategy, or values—the difficulties were ethnic, which
no covey of fronts or commitment to Western ideologies

could completely dilute. Coupled with the rampant op-
portunism and the ebb and flow of local and international
support, the strains so fragmented nationalist politics
that few but specialists could follow the intricacies of
the sterile mitosis. In April 1962, Roberto created the
Govêrno Revolucionário de Angola no Exílio (GRAE),
drawing in various splinter groups, but MPLA persisted.
For five years the essential competition remained between
GRAE–Bakongo and MPLA–Luanda–Mbundu, each drawing its strength from the ethnic base and each pursuing
its campaign in an ethnic area.

By the spring of 1962, it was clear to GRAE as well
as to MPLA that a variety of basic assumptions about
the Portuguese response to the rebellion had to be discarded. Lisbon would not be intimidated and the Portuguese Army was proving ruthless in the field. A swift
victory for "rebellion" seemed unlikely, but a more extended guerrilla-war would prove effective. There was
still hope that international condemnation, high losses
in the field, and a recognition of the inevitable would
persuade Lisbon to think again. Both GRAE and MPLA
seemed to possess ample assets to bleed Portugal dry.
The Third World was enthusiastic. The socialist bloc was
helpful. The West, despite ties to Portugal through NATO,
was warm. Portugal was a small, weak, impoverished
country. Certainly, soon, the penny would drop.

It did not. All through 1962, the struggle in northern
Angola continued, shifting into a traditional guerrilla-
insurgency operation with a friendly base in the Congo.
The Portuguese brought in more troops, continued air
strikes on rebel areas, tightened security elsewhere. By
the end of the year, the rebellion was by no means contained but was certainly limited to the north. Both GRAE
and MPLA realized that the guerrilla campaign would be
even longer than anticipated. They agreed on little else
as the squabbling continued. The Organization of African
Unity (OAU) recommended that member states deal only

with GRAE. For a time GRAE seemed triumphant. In July 1963, the Congo government closed MPLA head-quarters. Then an accumulation of disappointed hopes, dissident elements, and organization errors eroded GRAE's pre-eminent position. The Cabinda front was not going well. Tshombé was less than enthusiastic. The Ovimbundu tribe hived off when Jonas Savimbi broke with Roberto in 1964. Dr. Neto reorganized MPLA and launched raids into Cabinda. MPLA did not disappear. By mid-1965, GRAE had been infected with a series of internal eruptions, even a quasi-coup at headquarters by Alexandre Taty. The OAU began to show doubts about the wisdom of recognizing Roberto as the sole leader of the Angolan nationalist movement. While the shifting fortunes of GRAE and MPLA were reflected on the battle-field, as much from a decline of centrally directed supplies as anything else, the insurgency continued at a reasonably high level.

The Portuguese continued to send in reinforcements so that by 1965 there were approximately forty-five thou-sand troops along with a first and second line militia and the ubiquitous PIDE. The army was given a psycho-sociological, hearts-and-minds task, as well as a military one, with mixed results.* Resettlement was introduced with some effect. Many refugees returned home, partic-ularly during the recurring troubled times in the Congo, but many did not, giving the nationalists a solid base for support and recruitment in the Congo.† The Portuguese

---

* Exactly what Portuguese policy is in the countryside of Angola and Mozambique is difficult to determine; however, there is some indication that in Angola a greater effort is being made to convert the peasants. Whether this is a result of lack of liaison with the army in Mozambique or an Angolan–Portuguese Army policy or a conscious Lisbon directive is unclear. Whether it is successful is even more unclear.

† A highly novel nationalist tactic was to take their sea of people with them by moving the local population into the Congo or even moving them along with the columns.

built a network of fortified villages, created early-warning nets, introduced a variety of welfare reforms, constantly patrolled the roads if not the bush* and by 1965 had contained but not eliminated the guerrillas. MPLA was again in the ascent, but GRAE showed no sign of quitting. The standard of training, often abroad, had improved: the level of weaponry was high, in some cases higher than that of the Portuguese; the techniques of international propaganda had been well learned; and despite the lack of unity, there was no sign of a weakening of will. Neither side gave any indication that it was about to blink.

On the other side of Africa, another front had been opened against Portugal in Mozambique, but this time with the errors and mistakes of GRAE and MPLA well in mind. The major premise, accepted almost from the first, was that the Portuguese were going to concede nothing and that the only option was an armed struggle. In 1961, the three Mozambique exile nationalist movements opened separate headquarters in Dar es Salaam soon after Tanganyika became independent. Delegates from one attended the Conferência das Organizações Nacionalistas das Colónias Portuguêsas (CONCP) in December and heard strong pleas for unity—the general desire, in any case. Negotiations in Tanganyika led to the formation of the Frente de Libertação de Moçambique (FRELIMO) on June 1962. The new organization had a most impressive leader in Dr. Eduardo Mondlane, who was then teaching anthropology at Syracuse University. Even before the articulate and sophisticated Mondlane arrived, FRELIMO fell prey to the very schisms and splinters, so damaging

* Portuguese troops have shown little inclination to undertake regular patrols off the roads, although obviously this is not a hard-and-fast rule. There would appear to be more patrols in Angola than Mozambique but in both cases there is a far greater dependence on convoys, forts, and air strikes than is ordinarily the case in anti-insurgency campaigns.

to the Angolan nationalists, which they had hoped to
avoid. A young man, Leo Clinton Aldridge, placed in
charge of military training, created such tensions that
a series of defections occurred, including that of the
secretary-general, David Mabunda, and his deputy Paulo
Gumane, who withdrew to Cairo in May 1963 and their
own party. Once Mondlane was firmly in charge in Dar
es Salaam, there were fewer dissenters. All the competitive
organizations, including the soon-expelled Aldridge's Mozambique African National Union, remained letterhead
organizations except Comité Revolucionário de Moçambique (COREMO), founded in Lusaka, Zambia, and
successor to the Cairo organization, in June 1965. In the
meantime, FRELIMO had gone ahead in the 1962–4
period to lay the groundwork for a cohesive, centralized
rebellion.

The basic assets for an insurgency campaign existed
in Mozambique. There was, if little local understanding
of sophisticated national ideology, yet a very specific
grievance list. The Makonde tribe, spread out over the
Mozambique–Tanganyika border, was open to persuasion. The new Tanganyika government of Julius Nyerere
was quite willing to provide a secure base. There was and
would be more outside aid. The Algerians were enthusiastic and willing to provide military training. The Portuguese, while not as complacent as they had been in
Angola, were still ill-prepared. The essential task was to
organize. From scratch, Mondlane and FRELIMO began
to construct not only a military force but the entire
infrastructure of a state-in-being. To attract converts and
educate political exiles, the Mozambique Institute was
opened in Dar es Salaam under the guidance of Mondlane's American wife, Janet. All the questions of new
legal codes, of medical care, of agricultural cooperatives
were considered. Extensive international contacts were
developed as FRELIMO representatives toured the world
collecting aid and comfort. In January 1963, the first

fifty men left for military training in Algeria. The publicity office in Dar es Salaam prepared to issue an extensive variety of publications, including *Mozambique Revolution* in English, a program beyond the typical smudged mimeographed handouts. Some of the concentration on social and welfare tasks, on building a state in exile may have been window dressing for external consumption; but the level of organization, the internal structure of FRELIMO, and the preparations inside Mozambique were far in excess of those by the nationalists in Angola.

By September 1964, FRELIMO had 250 trained men and a network of support and sympathy through much of the two northern provinces of Niassa and Cabo Delgado. Elsewhere there were support cells including a net far to the south in the capital, Lourenço Marques, but the main center of military operations for logistic reasons would be the north. On September 25, 1964, the campaign opened with a synchronized series of attacks on Portuguese positions. The Portuguese responded as they had in Angola, rushing in troops, striking from the air, burning out villages, and arresting suspected nationalists in the cities. By the end of the year, the Portuguese had perhaps thirty-five thousand troops in the country and had confined FRELIMO activity to north-west Niassa and the Makonde plateau in north-east Cabo-Delgado. Elsewhere PIDE destroyed the FRELIMO apparatus in Lorenço Marques and arrested or drove deep underground any sympathizers in the rest of Mozambique. In the north, the Portuguese Army, despite heavy patrolling, resettlement plans, the traditional string of armed-enclave forts, and repeated air strikes, could not regain full control of the rural areas. In January 1963, a major if distant ally appeared when the Partido Africano da Independência da Guiné e Cabo Verde (PAIGC) under Amilcar Cabral, after over six years of careful preparation, opened another armed struggle against the Portuguese in their West African colony of Guiné. Lisbon seemed quite willing to accept one more drain on the limited Portuguese resources and rushed in reinforcements. *

Despite the three-front war, there was no sudden turn for the better in Mozambique. FRELIMO was still limited to hit-and-run attacks by small groups until the number of recruits coming down the pipeline from Tanganyika increased. After the first elation, FRELIMO headquarters settled down to the long, slow task of raising the stakes in northern Mozambique beyond the capacity of the Portuguese to play. The number of FRELIMO guerrillas in 1964-5 climbed from a few hundred to a thousand and then more. Simultaneously with the hit-and-run war, strenuous efforts were made to set up schools, move agricultural produce north to Tanganyika markets, and recruit young men for military training by the promise of an education. FRELIMO delegates could be found at all the appropriate conferences: the Tricontinental Congress, the Afro-Asian Peoples' Solidarity Organization, the World Council of Peace. The OAU recognized the movement, the Socialist camp was a firm supporter, and through Mondlane's balancing act so were a great many Western liberals. By 1965 the Portuguese in the field, however, showed no more sign of quitting than they had in Angola and the FRELIMO guerrillas no more capacity to escalate the war than MPLA or GRAE.

Between the two inflamed flanks of Mozambique and Angola, the vast British hold on the two Rhodesias and Nyasaland had seemed far more open to challenge as the winds of change blew through Africa. In 1953, the Central African Federation, created out of Northern Rhodesia—

---

* Of all the campaigns against the Portuguese, PAIGC has been the most carefully prepared and the most successful. Logically, the Portuguese determination to stay in Guiné, a grim swampland without visible resources, is an unwillingness to give the nationalists a victory which would encourage a continuation of the wars in Angola and Mozambique. In time, they may have to content themselves with showing the flag in the capital Bissau and one or two urban-forts to cut the disproportionate investment in the enclave.

rich in copper, the Nyasaland Protectorate—poor in everything but people, and Southern Rhodesia—center of the largest white-settler enclave in British Africa, seemed to offer hope for a real multiracial solution to the black–white confrontation. The British government, apparently deeply dedicated to the federalist concept of solving troublesome colonial problems, stressed the economic logic of the union. Economically there was much to be said for the Federation, but the Africans insisted that there was no necessity in cementing three potentially independent Black African states into a white-dominated federation. In 1953, the three African Congress movements, along with a variety of ineffectual labor and welfare organizations, had attempted to exert pressure on the British government, with a notable lack of success. The riots were put down and demonstrations dispersed. The African leadership was uncoordinated, excessively moderate, and had little grasp on the possibility of disrupting British plans for their own ends. They gave their advice when asked, and saw it discounted.

On the surface, the Federation looked most permanent; but for the Africans the theory of multiracialism in practice proved to be a combination of tokenism and the same old discrimination. Dominated by the white-settler community in Salisbury, the Federation seemed no more than a device to hold back the potential black nations of Zambia (Northern Rhodesia) and Malawi (Nyasaland) and Zimbabwe (Southern Rhodesia). In the mid-Fifties, a new and more militant generation of nationalists began to infiltrate the old Congress movements. The nonviolent struggle in the Gold Coast indicated that African freedom need not be indefinitely postponed. The immediate goal in all three areas was to create mass movements capable for the present of eradicating some of the more pressing discriminatory social and economic policies of the Federation. In time, the organized militant masses would be capable of pressuring the British into dissolution of the Federation.

Although there were intensive organizational efforts and occasional campaigns of protest, not until Harold Macmillan replaced Anthony Eden in 1957 was there a feeling that Britain might be willing to reconsider the eventual fate of Central Africa. By then the tension between the moderates and militants, particularly in Northern Rhodesia and Nyasaland, had grown severe. In 1958, the Northern Rhodesian African National Congress broke apart as the young radicals, under Kenneth Kaunda, left to form the United National Independence party. In Nyasaland, the activists were in contact with Dr. Hasting Banda, increasingly suggested as a prestigious savior in exile. In Southern Rhodesia, the African National Congress was reorganized under the leadership of Joshua Nkomo, but much of the spadework already accomplished to the north remained to be done. The Southern Rhodesian authorities were not the British, and African political activity had usually been muted by one means or another.

According to the orders-in-council establishing the Federation, there was to be a review at the end of ten years. As the date, 1963, drew closer, the Africans began to sense a weakening of British enthusiasm for the Federation. The campaign of agitation—boycott, defiance, and demonstration—accumulated more support and produced more uneasiness in Salisbury. In Northern Rhodesia even the sanguine realized that Kaunda and his lieutenants had put together a mass, disciplined organization capable of using nonviolent tactics to exert the maximum pressure on Federation authorities and the British conscience. In July 1958 in Nyasaland, H. M. Chipembere and the radicals finally persuaded Dr. Hastings Banda to come home to lead the next stage. Month after month Banda and the militants toured Nyasaland whipping up enthusiasm. In January 1959, Banda returned from meetings with Nkrumah, Tom Mboya, Patrice Lumumba, and Holden Roberto in Accra and put on the heat. On February 15 there was a riot; not until February 28 could the police clear the Congress people from Fort Hill. On March 3, 1959, a state of emergency was declared and during the night a series of arrests skimmed off the African leadership. In the meantime, the Southern Rhodesian government had already used the troubles as justification for rounding up its own nationalists. The Congress was banned and some five hundred members arrested, but not Nkomo, who was out of the country. Both the Federal government and the Southern Rhodesian government felt that they could keep things well in hand. The British, with memories of the Mau Mau in Kenya, began having serious second thoughts about the Federation's viability.

In London the hard-line Conservatives had left the government, and the new Colonial Secretary, Iain Macleod, was not tied to the old ways or to the Federation. On July 6, 1959, Sir Roy Welensky agreed to the formation of the Monckton Commission to examine the course of the Federation. In 1960 there were mobs and riots. The British grew increasingly sympathetic to African aspirations. In Nyasaland the emergency regulations were lifted and Banda and the remaining detainees released. On October 11, 1960, the Monckton Commission recommended majority rule for the Africans in the north and the right of secession for all three territories. Welensky with some justification felt betrayed. Banda in Nyasaland and Kaunda in Northern Rhodesia had won the day. It was only a matter of waiting for independence that would come more than a decade sooner than most had hoped. The old tried and true formula of defiance and intimidation, of threats, of real violence created a momentum which the British were unwilling to resist and worked to perfection for Kaunda and Banda; but to the south it was a different story.

Essentially, the basic strategical error of the nationalists was to proceed as if the regime in Salisbury were British. The Southern Rhodesian government was determined to maintain the position of the white settler with a façade of multiracialism and indeterminable delay on the principle of majority rule. The will to endure, which did not exist in London, did in Salisbury.* Consequently, the techniques which had proven so successful to the north did not work as well in the south. The National Democratic party under Nkomo, successor to the banned African National Congress, set out to organize the country: huge, enthusiastic meetings were held and great numbers of members signed up; protest and sit-down strikes were initiated. The visible result was the new 1961 constitution, which in the eyes of the more conservative white settlers was quite a compromise. Nkomo accepted it but his militants would not go along. He drew back and the Africans continued to protest outside the parliamentary system. In December 1961, their party was banned, and its resources seized.

As planned, from the ashes came the Zimbabwe African Peoples Union (ZAPU) with Nkomo again as president. The same round of protest, expansion, and consolidation followed. A sporadic campaign of sabotage and petrol-bomb attacks was opened. In September 1963, ZAPU was banned and the leaders restricted for three months. Abroad the organization continued as ZAPU; in Rhodesia its successor was the Peoples' Caretaker Council (PCC). At the same time the Africans were slipping toward sabotage and conspiracy, the Salisbury government lunged to the Right. Sir Edgar Whitehead and "partnership" went out in December 1962 and in came Winston Field and the Rhodesian Front, avowedly hostile to the nationalists' most modest aspirations. Field released the detainees, and with the other hand introduced the death penalty for petrol-bomb attacks and refined the already harsh Law and Order (Maintenance) Act. Some Africans still hoped that

* A continuing and vital question was just how great the Rhodesian will would be, under pressure. With a large first-generation white population, there was and is a feeling that unlike the Afrikaners, the Rhodesians would opt for emigration under threat of sufficient force. Sufficient force, however, has not so far been produced.

Great Britain would force Salisbury to compromise. Others feared Field might declare Rhodesian independence unilaterally. Some, including Nkomo, gave serious thought to a government-in-exile. In the expanding interparty disputes, a rebel group formed around Ndabaningi Sithole. The dissidents were, by and large, more articulate, more impatient, and most disappointed with Nkomo. That tribal and personal antagonisms existed and had festered is equally clear. In any case, the new party, the Zimbabwe African National Union (ZANU), attempted to displace the "discredited" ZAPU, which in turn desperately fought off the challenge.

The ZANU assumption that ZAPU was finished proved disastrous. Not only was ZAPU not finished, but the majority of African nationalists still supported Nkomo. The entire Zimbabwe movement was split. In the townships and out in the country, a vicious, bloody, little ZANU–ZAPU war was fought. Criminals took advantage of the opportunities to settle old scores. Decent people were humiliated or frightened into submission. Beatings and blackmail became the order of the day. Because Field seemed reluctant to take the necessary security measures to smash the nationalists and restore order, the troubles went on and on, dissipating the pool of good will and support that had accumulated over the years from the African population. In the long run, Field's hesitation was brilliant strategy, as it allowed ZANU and ZAPU to destroy each other and to throw away not only the sympathy but the toleration of the African mass. In the short run, however, it lost Field his office; Ian Smith took over in April 1964. Hundreds of Africans were arrested, including Nkomo and Sithole, and were isolated in vast camps. The police stopped turning the other cheek. The highly effective intelligence operations inside ZANU and ZAPU permitted the police to arrest most of those responsible for the continuing sabotage incidents, often men trained abroad and slipped into the country. By the end of the year, there were two thousand Africans in detention or restriction and hundreds more in prison. ZANU and ZAPU had been banned; and the *Daily News,* which reflected African opinion, was closed. Ian Smith sat firmly in power in Salisbury.

In November 1965, Rhodesia declared independence unilaterally. London and Salisbury had found insufficient common ground in their long and complicated negotiations. The British government did not intervene. The independent Black African states were horrified but impotent. World opinion was shocked. All the world was against Smith and the Rhodesian Front, but this mattered little to the black Rhodesians. It had taken the Africans a long time to realize that no one was going to pull the chestnut of black independence out of the fire for them, not even—particularly not—Great Britain. After UDI, the smoldering resentment against the Smith regime could not be organized. Nationalist leadership, increasingly discredited, was either in exile or in detention. The local ZANU and ZAPU organizations were in disarray or defunct. Members of ZANU and ZAPU in Lusaka vowed to carry on the struggle, to move to a new, more violent stage; but at the end of 1965, the once affluent, confident nationalist movement had deteriorated into two squabbling sects isolated in exile.

The early Sixties had seemed to offer nothing but pleasing prospects for black nationalism throughout southern Africa. In South Africa, Sharpeville had shocked the world's conscience and the defiance-*cum*-sabotage campaign had shaken the white establishment. Portugal was under armed attack in Angola and Mozambique. The Central African Federation had been destroyed, and rising out of the ashes would come Zambia, Malawi, and under British auspices, Zimbabwe. The winds of change had turned to hurricane force. The number of free black states multiplied. The Organization of African Unity (OAU) was established in Addis Ababa with a major aim being to finish the job in the South. There was a rising clamor of international support as the United Nations condemned the white bastions. A flood of sympathetic statements, declarations, and manifestoes churned out of New York and Moscow, Paris and Peking. History, justice, and time —not to mention most of the world—were aligned with the African cause.

By 1965 a great many things had gone wrong. In South Africa, PAC and ANC had been banned, their militants jailed or exiled, their successors forbidden, and any lingering white sympathy for the black cause dispersed. A fifty-year tradition, a huge organization, an accumulation of hopes had disappeared under Pretoria's hammering repression. If Zambia and Malawi had escaped white domination, in Rhodesia the internecine struggle between ZAPU and ZANU had frittered away the last chance to challenge the Rhodesian Front. In Angola, the Portuguese had not broken before the first wave and instead undertook an extensive anti-insurgency campaign. In Mozambique, the guerrillas had not been able to expand beyond the two northern provinces or increase the size of their attacks. The OAU–Liberation Committee,* established with such hopes, had proven a weak reed. Most Black African countries soon revealed their conviction that Black Africa's responsibility ended with oratory.† International

---

* Under George Magombe, with headquarters in Dar es Salaam, the Liberation Committee was to coordinate African contributions to the various movements, supply technical and military advice, and act as a clearing house and counseling service. It has very little real control over the movements, no capacity to enforce unity or determine strategy, and, since few of the African states contribute funds, almost no influence.

† In Black Africa only Zambia and Tanzania have given serious aid from the beginning. Ghana lost interest after Nkrumah's departure and Nigeria after Nyerere recognized Biafra. Algeria and Egypt have helped out. Generally, however, there has been a continual decline in support. In the period from June 1 to December 31, 1967, £350,000 was allocated to the seven major movements but only £51,150/7/0 given (ranging from £1,640/15/0

opinion, Third World conferences, United Nations resolutions, warm words in Washington, and huge demonstrations in London had not weakened the white grip on southern Africa. Ian Smith and the Rhodesian Front defied Britain and the boycott with impunity. Lisbon, playing NATO blackmail, evaded sanctions. South Africa had always listened to a different drummer and, while not immune to "opinion," had its priorities straight as far as black "subversion" was concerned. Even the money, weapons, training, and advice from the sympathetic African- and Eastern-bloc states had not tipped the scales. In 1965, the African nationalist movements were wiped out in South Africa and Rhodesia, stalemated in Angola and Mozambique, stripped of their illusions of African brotherhood and the power of righteousness, still splintered and quarreling, still uncertain as to what was going wrong. In Pretoria, Salisbury, and Lisbon, there was a quiet feeling that the worst might be over, that one did not have to be a weatherman to know which way Macmillan's wind of change was blowing.

The choice facing the exiles in Lusaka, ZAPU, ZANU, ANC, and PAC, was more difficult than that presented to those already fighting in the Portuguese territories. In Mozambique and Angola, the fight needed only continue until Portugal bled to death; but in Rhodesia and South Africa, there was no armed struggle to continue. Despite the awesome technical and organizational difficulties, all the exile organizations had chosen guerrilla-war rather than admit defeat. In South Africa, there had been neither ideological preparation nor a base, nor arms, nor trained men. Increasingly, as the activists had to flee, the new exile headquarters channeled them into military training in sympathetic countries. The endless friends won in countless antiapartheid and solidarity conferences proved most accomodating. The major difficulty was geographical,

to ANC to £19,000 for PAIGC; *Sunday Telegraph* [London], May 4, 1969).

for by the time that sufficient cadres were trained and ready to strike, the easy opportunity to infiltrate South Africa had gone.* There was no longer an effective underground inside the country to absorb them, and no way through the wall of white-dominated states.

Along with PAC and ANC, there was a new organization, the South-West African Peoples' Organization (SWAPO), created in 1960. The delay in forming a militant nationalist organization to liberate the old League of Nations Mandate was the hope that an international judicial decision would sever the mandate from South Africa and allow the African population to escape apartheid. When the World Court decided adversely on the Liberian–Ethiopian maneuver to secure a ruling against South Africa's control of the former mandate on July 18, 1966, SWAPO too was left with unpalatable alternatives: should it continue pounding futilely on the doors of international justice or turn to armed struggle? As with the other African liberation movements, once nonviolence had foundered there was nothing left but to fight or disband. Efforts to infiltrate guerrillas through the Caprivi strip produced only very limited success and a series of treason trials in Windhoek.

The most promising target was neither South-West Africa nor the Republic, but Rhodesia across the Zambezi. ZAPU and ZANU had in one form or another been involved in a violent struggle since July 1963 and had even earlier smuggled in trained saboteurs. By the end of 1965, the two organizations had control of a pool of some two hundred trained men. Until 1966, infiltrations had been in dribs and drabs and not particularly effective. The first step in the next stage of the struggle came in April 1966 when a heavily armed, fully equipped guerrilla-column

---

* "The crux of the matter is that we have been stopped AT GUN POINT, from political communication with our people . . ."; PAC: *Principles of the United Front in People's War* (Dar es Salaam, n.d.).

crossed the Zambezi, evaded border security, and moved into the interior. At Karoi, halfway to Sinoia, the column finally ran into Rhodesian security and most of the guerrillas were killed or captured in a series of clashes on April 28 and 29. By the end of the year, the Rhodesian authorities claimed to have killed or captured a total of one hundred guerrillas. Both the ZAPU and ZANU communiqués, which usually revealed more enthusiasm than precision, insisted that the level of struggle was much higher.* In any case, by the end of the year, the prospects for expanded activity had brightened. An increasing number of men trained abroad had become available and others were attending camps in Tanzania. Military equipment made available from the Eastern bloc or China had been accumulated. The intention was to follow up the 1966 campaign with a series of substantial infiltrations. In this stage, the guerrillas would cross the Zambezi heavily armed, move to the various locations of operations, create arms stockpiles, and begin the military training of the population.

The number of the guerrilla intrusions, mainly ZAPU, increased during 1967; but there were serious difficulties. Rhodesian security rapidly tightened control of the uninhabited border areas, reducing the opportunity for penetration by relatively large, uniformed, heavily loaded columns. ZANU–ZAPU security was lax and Rhodesian intelligence often excellent. In May 1967, nine guerrillas penetrated Rhodesia but were hit and scattered.

---

* ZANU and ZAPU claims—after various actions—of twenty or thirty (in one case seventy-two) killed could not even have been verified on the battleground and certainly not in Lusaka. The tales of secret burials and Rhodesian cover-ups are unimpressive. Rhodesian figures released over a long period of time can be correlated to give what appears a reasonable picture, although the one point not stressed is the number of guerrillas still at large. ZAPU–ZANU claims that everything which goes wrong in Rhodesia, including hotel fires and criminal acts, is a result of "operations." This further discounts their accuracy.

A few managed to return to Zambia. Twenty-one crossed the Zambezi in July with no more success. The liberation headquarters claimed that they had inflicted heavy casualties on Rhodesian security, had fought more often in the interior than Salisbury communiqués revealed, and had put far more men into their assigned areas than reports indicated. The Rhodesians insisted that they were fighting largely a border campaign with very light losses and were with few exceptions eliminating all the guerrillas soon after their arrival. Despite vast contradictions in the numbers game, the rate of intrusions was relatively high and the loss rate intimidating. As far as evidence existed, efforts to set up cores of resistance had not succeeded, although obviously some guerrillas were still inside Rhodesia. There was also as yet no indigenous armed struggle; almost all the fighting took place during the attempt to penetrate the security cordon along the border. In Lusaka no decision was made to discard the tactic of sending in heavily armed, readily visible columns of considerable strength. The problems which easily recognizable guerrillas might face once they arrived at a zone of operations often little known to them were evaded. In fact, ZAPU was prepared to up the stakes.

In July 1967, ZAPU and ANC signed a pact to cooperate in the armed struggle. ZAPU would help the ANC guerrillas through Southern Rhodesia so that they could slip across the South African border and open a new front against white Africa. This would give the guerrillas more men in the field against the Rhodesians and would directly involve South Africa in the confrontation. For ANC, it was vital to act if the movement were not to decay into an exile-letterhead propaganda organization. PAC had given every indication that this road was difficult to avoid because the leaders wrangled and defected, the members drifted off, and the sympathy of their recently committed Chinese friends had evaporated. There remained obvious technical obstacles in ANC's new approach. Even if ZAPU had possessed some control of the transit areas, the prospects of a supply line through inhospitable, enemy-dominated country was hardly promising; nor was the state of the skeleton organization inside South Africa likely to provide the essential supplies, intelligence, and recruits. Neither of these problems had to be faced for long—the one serious effort to penetrate the Rhodesian cordon under ZAPU guidance collapsed almost before it had begun. In August 1967, a very large ANC–ZAPU column crossed the Zambezi near Victoria Falls, evaded detection, and moved into the Wankie game park area to the south. There Rhodesian security discovered them and repeatedly hit the column in a series of heavy clashes. Twenty-nine guerrillas were killed, seventeen captured, and most of the rest fled back to Zambia, although not all managed to get across the crocodile-filled river. By the time the ZAPU–ANC joint declaration of alliance was released on September 19, 1967, the fighting in Wankie was long over. All that had been acomplished was to alarm the South Africans, who stepped up their cooperation with Salisbury and sent in South African paramilitary police for field experience. Although ANC–ZAPU alliance continued, there was a noticeable cooling of enthusiasm on the part of ANC. For several years efforts were, nevertheless, continued to infiltrate people through the Caprivi strip from Zambia and on to the Republic or the Mandate, but the terrain and the border patrols made this an incredibly high-risk operation with negligible military results. By 1970, ANC and SWAPO had not gone as far toward futility as PAC, but there was still no answer to the dilemma of carrying on an armed struggle while isolated in Lusaka.

Within another year ZAPU, and particularly ZANU, had failed to solve the same problem. In December 1967, a group of one hundred guerrillas crossed the Zambezi and managed to go undetected for two months; but the Rhodesians were able to track down most of them and completed the hunt in July. During 1968, other columns were sent over the Zambezi in March, again in July, and a smaller foray in August. From the information trickling back to Lusaka, even the most dedicated optimist would have paused in the face of accelerating disasters. None of the columns could get through to their areas, though some managed to wander a considerable distance with Rhodesian security on their trail. Most of the columns were soon badly mauled, leaving only a few scattered escapees who discarded their equipment and uniforms and tried to make their way to a friendly sanctuary. For example, in the July ZAPU intrusions, eighty-one guerrillas were involved and only eight evaded death or capture— seven of those were in a small group in the Chewosre– Zambezi area which never made contact with Rhodesian security. In August, none of the fourteen guerrillas involved escaped.

By the end of 1968, Rhodesian anti-insurgency techniques had been honed to perfection: excellent advance intelligence, constant small patrols, regular night ambushes, tracker dog and air support, and absolute confidence in the outcome of any clash. When there was indication that ZAPU might try once again in December, small planes flew over the Zambezi to broadcast an invitation over loudspeakers. Whether it had any effect or not, no guerrillas came over the river. ZANU and ZAPU had to the end persisted in sending men, however well trained and well motivated—and some proved certainly not to be the latter—who looked like the popular image: in guerrilla-camouflage suits; even with helmets, in one case, festooned with heavy automatic arms and explosives.*
They were forced to act like regular commandos in enemy

* One ZAPU column of twenty-eight men, which crossed the Zambezi in July 1968, carried: 3 light-machine guns and 9 magazines, 3 bazookas and 24 projectiles, 19 AK-47 assault rifles, 6 SKS rifles, 6 automatic pistols, 112 grenades, 150 slabs of explosives, and 40,000 rounds of ammunition. At times, weapons were brought into Rhodesia still greased and in crates.

territory. They found not a sea of friendship to swim through but only the bare border lands crammed with Rhodesian security. Hit regularly and hard, they could only evade detection by discarding all their romantic equipment.*

By 1969, ZANU, never large, had badly decayed. Probably only regular transfusions of Chinese aid kept armed strength near one hundred men. The leadership remained highly articulate and far cleverer than that of ZAPU, but there was literally no rank-and-file. ZAPU was only relatively better off: there were still a couple of hundred trained men in the pipeline but a lamentable lack of recruits. As early as 1967, the two movements had been driven to press-gang methods, greatly disturbing the Zambian government, which repeatedly showed signs of losing patience. Efforts to recoup their declining prestige by moving to another stage of individual agents infiltrating, had limited results. Rhodesian intelligence had vast files, border checks were thorough, and many of the "agents" of dubious quality. By the end of 1969, both ZAPU and ZANU still had the capacity to launch one more wave of "guerrillas" but with faint hope of novel results. Like ANC and SWAPO, they had been reduced to the final expedient of persisting without a viable program of action.

In Portuguese Africa at least, the future, if hard, looked far from hopeless. In 1966, MPLA claimed that the Cabinda had cost the Portuguese fifteen hundred lives and control of a quarter of the enclave. By the next year two new MPLA fronts had been opened in northern and eastern Angola although the Portuguese had gained control of the Cabinda situation, had moved in five thousand

---

* "You cannot hope to gobble up a regular army all at once in a conventional war style, as our brothers tried to do, and still claim to be waging guerrilla warfare. It is wholly unacceptable both in theory and practice . . ."; PAC: *The Wankie Fiasco in Retrospect* (Dar es Salaam, January 1969).

troops and reduced MPLA activity there to a minimum. The eastern front, opened in a small way in May 1966, did put an additional drain on Portuguese resources; but the new front in the Nambuangongo–Dembos area resulted in armed clashes with GRAE. Roberto had managed to make a comeback after Joseph Mobutu's Congo coup in November 1965 and to continue a low-intensity campaign in the north as well as to open a small second front in the Kasanje area. By 1967, in preparation for broadening the struggle, GRAE was building up another rear base in Kantanga under southern leadership. The major new factor in Angola was the appearance of União Nacional para a Independência Total de Angola (UNITA), set up by Jonas Savimbi after his break with Roberto in December 1964. In March 1966, beginning with very little support, Savimbi opened still another front and nursed his movement along until by 1969 there were well over a thousand guerrillas fighting in the wild grasslands of eastern Angola.

Thus by 1970, the over-all picture had changed very little. The slow war of attrition continued, broadened to eastern Angola but excluding Cabinda. Instead of two major competing liberation movements, there were three, which upped the cost somewhat for the Portuguese. In the welter of conflicting figures in the numbers-casualty game, it is clear that the campaign was costing the Portuguese dearly.* Although the dissident areas of Angola are economically marginal, the policy of containment is expensive in men, material, and funds. Several hundred soldiers are killed each year, over fifty per cent of the Portuguese budget is spent on the military, and the investment in Angola and Mozambique of the long-delayed roads, schools, and welfare programs stretch it still further. Some, perhaps much, of the slack has been taken up by

* For the period from February 2 to May 3, 1968, the Portuguese war communiqués and press reported sixty-one of the armed forces and forty-two militia killed in Angola.

the development of oil in Cabinda, the rise in coffee prices, and the growth of the colonial tax base; but the three liberation movements remain confident that Lisbon will not want to pay the price indefinitely.

The situation and the basic assumptions remain much the same in Mozambique. By the end of 1966, Mondlane had finally committed sufficient guerrillas in the north to launch far heavier attacks on the Portuguese strong points. The war in the north intensified, the size of the Portuguese commitment grew, and the casualty list began to resemble that of the fighting in Angola. On October 22, 1965, COREMO had begun a few operations in the Tete area, further stretching Portuguese resources although the level of fighting remained very low. FRELIMO continued to insist not simply on primacy but on exclusive leadership of the Mozambique movement. Mondlane claimed eight thousand guerrillas in the field and extensive control over Niassa and Cabo Delgado provinces. FRELIMO had established all the proposed institutions of the protostate: the bush schools, agricultural cooperatives, and local judicial systems. Military operations tied down forty thousand Portuguese troops and, month after month, inflicted heavy casualties. In response to the Portuguese intention of building a giant dam and hydroelectric complex at Cabora Bassa in Tete Province, FRELIMO opened a second front in March 1968. Infiltration was difficult since Malawi was closed to armed transients and a guerrilla-column takes three months to make the trek from the Tanzanian border on foot, but the threat to the dam was one more drain on Portuguese resources. Despite FRELIMO claims, the Portuguese still maintained a grip on all the urban areas and most of the communications, though movement in the guerrilla areas was dangerous.

During 1968, FRELIMO ran into a leadership crisis as a result of the intertwining of tribal jealousies, racial sentiment, and ideological differences. The Tanzanian government became involved, and conferences were held repeatedly. Even the success of the FRELIMO Congress in July in Niassa inside Mozambique and attended by foreign journalists did not resolve the differences. Then on February 3, 1969, in Dar es Salaam, President Eduardo Mondlane was assassinated with a book-bomb.* There were many who felt the internal stresses of FRELIMO rather than the machinations of PIDE were to blame. Concurrently, Lazaro Kavandame, the Makonde military commander, fled to the Portuguese and denounced FRELIMO.† Kavandame's defection could be absorbed, but the loss of Mondlane was a serious blow, particularly on the international scene, where his presence and prestige had been of inestimable value. Even if within FRELIMO there had been less than universal admiration for Mondlane, he had always dominated the movement. FRELIMO did not immediately fragment into warring sectional and ideological segments. Instead, a new three-man triumvirate was established and the war pursued for some while, if anything, on an accelerated level. Then in December 1969, the strains within the triumvirate became too severe and Uria Simango was expelled. The following year on November 6, FRELIMO suffered a further defection and loss of prestige when Miguel Artur Marupa, former head of the External Affairs Department in Tanzania and a Central and Executive Committee member, defected to the Portuguese. The war of attrition, however, continued.

By 1970 all of the liberation movements had settled

---

* Although the immediate favorite for responsibility was PIDE, an ample list of potential assassins soon developed. Both the other major FRELIMO leaders, Dos Santos and Simango, received bombs so that specific revenge could, perhaps, be eliminated. High on the list was the defector Lazaro Kavandame, as well as other dissidents, not to mention the Chinese, the CIA, even the Cubans. So far neither the Tanzanian police nor anyone else has produced definite proof—or any proof—of guilt.

† Here again rumors are rife as to Lazaro Kavandame's previous contacts with the Portuguese. It is unlikely that his switch or his pleas on behalf of the Portuguese will have any long-term effect on the Makonde.

into the tunnel of attrition without any longer predicting when they might see light at the end. All believed that time, the weight of numbers, and the thrust of world opinion and support would erode the seemingly intractable white bastion. Increasingly, efforts had been made to co-ordinate the struggle, beginning with the union of groups fighting Portuguese colonialism in 1961 and extending through a series of pacts and alliances. Despite efforts to secure unity by freezing out competitors,* there was no prospect of a monolithic movement or even of extensive tactical cooperation.† The efforts of the OAU in the form of the Liberation Committee were futile. Since the promised funds were not subscribed, the penalties of nonrecognition by the OAU deterred no one. All the groups competed for aid from sympathetic powers.‡ Each movement continued to follow an independent course, limited only by the occasional displeasure of the host government.

The governments of white Africa had probably as many outstanding differences as the liberation movements:

* The "solution" of ZAPU for unity with ZANU, or of FRELIMO for unity with COREMO is that the smaller group dissolve and come within the larger.

† Bitterness between the various movements is often very deep and, in Angola, violent. As examples:
"The so-called Mozambique Liberation Front or FRELIMO had long since evolved a method of deliberately sabotaging and hindering the cause of the Mozambican revolution"; COREMO: *O Combatente* (Lusaka), September 30, 1967.
"But these groups did not manage to keep themselves stable for very long . . . later on, in 1965, they created COREMO. . . . At the same time that these maneuvers of the enemies of the liberation struggle were proceeding . . ."; FRELIMO: *Documents of the 2nd Congress* (Niassa, Mozambique), July 1968.

‡ Although all of the major groups are recognized by the OAU, more important is the support of Russia, in increasing competition with Communist China, for the hearts and minds of the liberation movements. Six groups were present at the International Conference in Support of the Portuguese Colonies and Southern Africa held in Khartoum, January 18–20, 1969, and attended by delegations largely of Soviet persuasion.

South Africa had its apartheid, Rhodesia had its token multinationalism, and the Portuguese were proud of their heritage and their African destiny. The Portuguese took a dim view of the prospects of South African economic penetration and Salisbury preferred not to see Rhodesia become a South African province. In South Africa, the reactionary men of the *laager* saw no need and much danger in becoming involved to the north. Under attack, however, all made common cause on an increasingly intimate level. Cooperation of security and military forces has long passed passive consultation. In some areas, particularly the Zambezi valley in Mozambique, Portuguese–Rhodesian operations became closely meshed. If there were still no true centralized control, there was a growing linking on the military security level and a quiet expansion of South African economic influence. A typical example was the Cabora Bassa dam, target of FRELIMO and COREMO, which would supply power to South Africa and which is of deep concern to both Portuguese and Rhodesian security forces.

Not only is white Africa far more unified for protracted war but it has been far more successful in consolidating an expanding grip on the continent. In 1960 the future seemed assured for Black African independence; but what no one could have foreseen was that four of the new states would be allied to white Africa by economic necessity, but allied nevertheless: the three former British High Commission Territories Swaziland, Basutoland (Lesotho), and Bechuanaland (Botswana). Hostages within the South African Republic, they remain nominally independent but economically totally dependent on Pretoria; and Dr. Banda in Malawi felt that, without resources or prospects of developmental funds, he had no choice but to align his country with South Africa and Portugal.*

---

* There is evidence that Dr. Banda made this decision even before arriving in Malawi. While most nationalists recognize the problem of Malawi, the aggressive defense of Banda irritates them more

Verwoerd and his successor J. Vorster quietly came out of the *laager* and extended South Africa's commitment far beyond the Limpopo. Thus, a bloc of white-dominated states stretches across southern Africa from the mouth of the Congo to the Indian Ocean, pierced only by Zambia, which is compromised by its desperate need to export its copper through white Africa.* The confrontation had been pushed beyond, to the center of Africa—the battleground became the edges of the Congo and Tanzania rather than the streets of Sharpeville or of Salisbury. Increasingly unified, bolstered by the South African economic miracle, determined to hold what they have until international opinion recognizes the pragmatic logic of their policies and the emotional chaos to the north, white Africa too feels in 1970 that time is on its side.

If, in the small hours of the morning, some of the leaders of the liberation movements recognize the direction of events over the past ten years and the present stalemate along the border of the *laager*—and some do†— there remains a conviction that justice will not be denied, that there will sooner or later be a shift, a change for the better.

The two most feasible major changes possible, if not probable, would be, first, the collapse of Portuguese resistance as a result of the wounds of attrition or of a transformation in Lisbon, and, second, the collapse into chaos of the African frontier states of Congo–Kinshasa,

---

than the reality of his cooperation. Banda does permit ZANU to have an office but this may be a result of his long feud with ZAPU's Nkomo rather than the thin edge of the wedge.

* Savimbi and UNITA were expelled from Lusaka after an attack on the Benguela Railway. Even on completion of the railway link to Dar es Salaam, Zambia will not be free to give full support to the liberation movements without risking retaliation of one form or another.

† "Yet we must face the hard fact that after many years of such solidarity work the vicious regimes which we confront have survived, even flourished; that our people are more oppressed and exploited than ever . . ."; ANC speech at the Khartoum Conference.

Zambia, or Tanzania. In the first case, South Africa seems willing to a degree to contribute to maintain Portuguese Africa while a revolutionary change in Lisbon, still highly unlikely, might not be exportable to Angola or Mozambique.* Even a more liberal government in Lisbon assured of South African support might well decide that the advantages of exploiting its African territories outweighed any crisis of conscience. The assumption in both Lisbon and Pretoria is that the successor black states could not maintain order, prevent decay, or halt communist domination. To give in to the guerrilla would thus be a defeat for all Western civilization. Although there is in white Africa a deep-grained tendency to look north for the inevitable catastrophe, there is little doubt that the problems facing Lusaka or Kinshasa are immense, maybe beyond the capacity of the new governments, and that they give every indication of growing more desperate. The rising urban population of the partially educated and disgruntled unemployed is a nightmare. The ragged edges of tribal fears and jealousies have not been smoothed in the past decade and have in fact led to the wars in the Congo and Nigeria and to the edge of war in Kenya. The cold-minded and practical men in Salisbury or Pretoria can more easily envision—in the name of Western civilization—the necessity of intervention in Zambia or Katanga than a failure of will in Lisbon. Without either anarchy in Black Africa or revolution in Portugal, the future would appear to be lacking in surprises. A sudden Chinese presence or serious Russian involvement, an unexpected Western conversion to a total blockade, a return of South Africa to the *laager* while not impossible, are unlikely.

If prospects of exterior changes on a major scale are faint, the African nationalists still hope for a transformation of the masses within the white bloc. The more astute have, perforce, lost their enthusiasm for guerrilla-infiltra-

---

* One of the results of a liberal change in Lisbon, long discussed in Africa, might be a militarily aided UDI in Angola.

tion and have again turned to subversion. Naturally, it is difficult to judge the extent and efficiency of any conspiracy when there is no surface evidence. Either a highly successful network of cells is multiplying, drawing in the militants, converting the passive, preparing the basis for an indigenous war, or nothing or at least little is happening. There is no evidence of a middle ground: hundreds of arrests of unsuccessful conspirators, a high level of political crimes that can not be hushed up, or massive strikes and boycotts attracting world-wide interest— each of these has happened in the past. There are from time to time trials of a few militants,* occasional indication of sabotage, some arrests, some resistance to resettlement or the removal of tribal chiefs, and the Coloured electoral rejection of apartheid; but six years ago in Rhodesia or ten in South Africa the level of public subversion was far higher. Previously, there were obviously more assets in the hands of the African nationalists, more leaders on the ground, more public militancy in the masses, fewer mistakes and blunders to explain, apparently greater possibilities for progress. Logically the organizational difficulties are now much greater than before, the danger of complicity higher, the general hope for change lower. Thus logically, although revolutions are not always open to logic, the weight of evidence would be that a transformation of the situation as a result of a newly revolutionized black mass is improbable. For years all the counters have shown a decline in subversion. That a massive reservoir of frustration and anger exists to be exploited is undoubtedly the case; but so far it has not been, at present there is scant evidence that it is being, and

---

* In October 1969, there were two cases in the Rhodesian courts concerning subversive activity during 1968. In one a member of one of the guerrilla-columns was charged with giving training to local men and in the other the prosecution claimed a secret meeting of "a banned African political party" had occurred in 1969.

consequently the indications are that it will not be for some time to come.

Therefore, whatever the Black nationalists would like to see or in some cases hope to see in the future—an enfeebled Portugal with a liberal government or a mass rising—increasingly the atmosphere is one of stability. There is in some quarters at least a reluctant acceptance that there will not be a *deus ex machina,* that barring miracles, devoutly to be desired, the struggle will be fought largely on the same ground with the existing resources. On this level, the prospects for a collapse of all or part of the white African complex, while not hopeless, are slim indeed. As long as the dynamic economic expansion of Pretoria's interests continues, there will be more resources on the side of white Africa than the various liberation movements can hope to command.

The present possibilities of the various nationalist movements would, superficially, seem to vary greatly. Some, like FRELIMO or MPLA, are conducting relatively successful wars of attrition, while others, like PAC, appear to have faint hope beyond the acrimonious politics of exile. Yet the most vital factor for all is the continuing involvement of the Republic of South Africa in the areas north of the Limpopo. Whether overtly conceded or not, Pretoria has largely accepted this commitment to cooperate with Rhodesia in a defense line along the Zambezi; and since the most vital area in Tete, site of the Cabora Bassa dam, is in Portuguese Mozambique, this implies a commitment to support Portuguese Africa as well. Such a commitment is not formal and far from total, for within the South African Nationalist party there are those who would still prefer to let both the Rhodesians and Portuguese solve their own problems. The direction of South African policy, the involvement in black Malawi, the relations with Botswana, Swaziland, and Lesotho, the intimacy with Lisbon and Salisbury apparently become increasingly irrevocable as time passes. Thus the possibility of independent success by an African movement which would be tolerated by Pretoria has continued to decline. This does not mean that Pretoria might not opt out of Angola at some point if the depth of involvement indicated the possibility of a southern African Vietnam; but there is, so far at least, an escalating expansion, at least as much for economic as diplomatic reasons, which has increasingly tied South Africa to the exploitable marches to the north. The Cabora Bassa dam and the possibilities of investment in Portuguese Africa and Rhodesia are attractive. While neither the Portuguese nor the Rhodesians are delighted by the prospects of South African economic domination, this is increasingly the direction of events. Consequently, time appears to be solidifying white Africa into a bloc, albeit still a reluctant bloc, capable of realizing and responding to the pressure of terror and subversion.*

If the African nationalists had a cohesive policy, if the various alliances and pacts were a step toward a unified movement under the aegis of the OAU, if Black Africa were willing to place the southern African problem at the top of the agenda, then the present war would in reality be a general Black African crusade. For the fore-seeable future this possibility seems remote. With the partial exception of Zambia and Tanzania, Black Africa has continued to show little but vocal interest in the tribulation of the southern African movements. The schism and squabbling in Lusaka and Dar es Salaam have continued. The limited cooperation of ANC and ZAPU or FRELIMO and MPLA, while sound, has produced few

* The growing white cooperation has long been of serious concern to the various nationalist movements:
"Expansionist South African imperialism, in close alliance with Portuguese colonialism and the settler regime in Zimbabwe, and backed by world imperialism, constitutes a grave menace to the neighboring African independent countries, and ultimately to the independence of every African state"; *The Declaration of Khartoum* (January 20, 1969).

results when contrasted with the intimate cooperation of
the Portuguese and Rhodesians in the Zambezi valley or
the three-way involvement in the Caprivi strip. Consequently it is still necessary to examine the prospects
of each area—really each movement—and still largely in
isolation from the broader picture.

In Mozambique, the great strength and major weakness of FRELIMO is the secure tribal base of the Makonde.
As long as the Makonde remain committed to the revolution, a war of attrition can be waged in the north with a
loyal population supplying recruits, supplies, and security.
With a secure base in Tanzania, where over half the
Makonde live; a rough and inhospitable terrain for operations; and an opponent willing, or forced, to hold only
scattered urban centers, the war can go on until a failure
of nerve or resources on either side. What, so far, have
been impossible for FRELIMO are escalation of the tempo
and, more important, expansion of the largely Makonde
base. Within the northern provinces, FRELIMO is running a classic and highly successful operation. The Portuguese have not been able to prevent infiltration, to
control the countryside, or to damage seriously FRELIMO
strength. Outside the Makonde areas, FRELIMO has
had only limited success in the Tete area, and has made
only very limited organizational forays elsewhere. Essentially the Makonde are not universally popular with
the tribes to the south, who tend in many cases to view
the struggle in tribal rather than national terms, a failing
not unknown to the Makonde. While FRELIMO headquarters is quite justified in denying that the war is tribal,
claiming that half the combatants are non-Makonde, its
base remains tribal. This has caused stress elsewhere, for
the leadership tends to come from the south, to be more
Westernized, and in some very visible cases less "African":
for example, Mondlane was educated in America and
married to a white American. FRELIMO has seemed to
weather the leadership crisis rather well. In February and

March 1969, much of the anti-Mondlane, anti-West pressure was dampened down after his assassination. There were, however, still real strains at headquarters between advocates of Moscow or Peking or nonalignment, between pure Africans and the color blind, between the fighters and the writers. Even with the December split, FRELIMO seems capable of continuing the war at the present level, although, as yet, not seriously infiltrating Tete or expanding to the south. If—or when—this happens, the war in Mozambique will take on a new dimension. Whether at this stage, without Mondlane's vision and sophistication, the divided leaders of FRELIMO can respond on a plane beyond the tactical is unknown. The future of Mozambique is now integrated into the entire southern African problem and cannot be solved to the satisfaction of much of FRELIMO on a Makonde–guerrilla level nor probably on any other level if Pretoria decides otherwise. The long-held hope that the attrition will be too great for Lisbon or even Pretoria is rational, but until FRELIMO can raise the stakes beyond the Makonde the prospect is for the same bloody round of ambushes, air strikes, and refugees, rather than inevitable victory.*

On the other side of the continent, the possibility of escalation is probably greater but the opportunity for a united effort less. The presence of the COREMO competitor in Mozambique has so far played a small part in hampering FRELIMO and has been to a limited degree effective against the Portuguese in Tete. In Angola, the quarrels between the three major liberation movements, extended to open war, have had serious consequences indeed. Yet, on balance, the existence of three quarreling movements, each dedicated to the others' dissolution, has

* "The struggle will therefore be long and hard. Although we have not had long experience in armed struggle, we can see through the struggle to a successful conclusion. . . . It is inevitable that, in the whole of Southern Africa, foreign domination and racism will be eliminated once and for all"; José Monteiro: "Mozambique Revolution," *Sechaba*, Vol. 2, No. 9 (September 1968), p. 7.

been overwhelmingly advantageous not to the Portuguese but to the Africans. First, and for them fortunately, the major area of competition has been to seize the military initiative, to prove to the outside world in general and the OAU in particular that their movement is militarily more successful—the most successful. Thus, when GRAE seemingly peaked in 1964 and appeared headed into decline and exile politics, the rising star of MPLA goaded Holden Roberto to renew the war. Much the same sequence occurred when Savimbi created UNITA. His first, perhaps premature, decision was to enter directly into the armed struggle to prove his credentials. If some Africans have shot each other, or some host governments imprisoned the "heretics," the visible result still has been a heightening of the guerrilla-war through invidious comparisons that had to be made good in the jungle. Secondly, and tactically of equal importance, is the fact that the stumbling block of single-tribal or regional support that had so hampered FRELIMO has been sidestepped. Unable to compete in GRAE's area, MPLA was forced to open a second and a third front, broadening the number of ethnic groups involved. UNITA, also, had to go into a virgin area in eastern Angola, again involving a new and different support base. The result was that the three movements have been able to spread the war geographically, incorporate a wide range of ethnic sentiment, and consequently raise the cost to the Portuguese considerably—but as yet by no means prohibitively.

The other side of the coin in Angola is that the more effective the various guerrillas become, the more likely the competitive combat principle will be extended to one another. Consequently, the possibilities of effective political use of any military success will decline in proportion to that success. So far in Angolan revolutionary politics, neither coercion nor compromise nor self-interest has been able to produce unity, not even a patchwork front. If the first sweet scent of Portuguese frailty is wafted into the various liberation headquarters, there is ample evidence to indicate that the virtues of conciliation and unity will be even less in evidence. In any case, as in Mozambique, the level of attrition is still too low and the guerrilla-infested area, despite the exaggerated propaganda, still too limited to warrant serious discussions of the hereafter. Still, the prospects for an "independent" victory in Angola are somewhat brighter than in Mozambique, where South African involvement is great, and where the geographic threat to Rhodesia and South Africa is more serious. Although Angola is potentially quite wealthy and the oil strike there of considerable interest to South Africa, independent in all other resources, a black Angola might not pose too great a threat. The border along South Africa is rugged, relatively easy to defend; and, although there are tribal soft spots, these are a long way from the white *laager*. The difficulty is that a coup in 1961 or a quick victory in 1962–3 or a Portuguese collapse or conversion to liberalism might have been tolerated with equanimity in Pretoria, but much has changed in relatively few years. The war has revealed the potential wealth of Angola, has underlined the importance of white-African unity. "Not an Inch" is a valid concept rather than bloody-mindedness. Ambush by ambush, South African attention has been riveted. Thus the guerrillas will have to run faster and faster simply to stay in the same spot, and the spot is most certainly not past the point of no return. Hence the three movements must escalate the level of attrition rapidly enough to stagger the Portuguese and pre-empt a South African decision to intervene.

If the Africans are sustaining a war of attrition on the two flanks of southern Africa, the same can no longer be said for the center. The last commando-guerrilla raids during 1968 failed dismally, gobbling up not only a substantial number of the trained men controlled by ZANU and ZAPU but a great deal of already waning enthusiasm. The rather uncertain feedback of what was happening inside Rhodesia began to penetrate; essentially there was at best minimal support for the guerrillas and a considerable reservoir of bad feeling. The combined result of past failures, present inaction, and constant Rhodesian vigilance has thrown a considerable pall over the movements. The efforts to infiltrate agents and money across the Zambezi through open checkpoints have run into serious difficulties. Intelligence coming out of Rhodesia into the Lusaka headquarters is slow and often inaccurate. The result has been an erosion of membership, a decline of funds, and, quite important, a drop in morale.

By the beginning of 1970, ZANU had little more than a skeleton organization, although the leadership remained talented and articulate. ZAPU, with better international contacts and alliances, however strained, and with liberation groups, was in better shape but hardly remained a serious threat to Rhodesian security; the old days of "thousands of guerrillas" had passed. The capacity to send at least one more wave of men across the Zambezi existed; and in January 1970, following largely the same tactics, new intrusions were launched. The results appear no more promising. Even a change to piecemeal tactics could not counter the immense odds such adventures have entailed. The options remaining for ZANU and ZAPU are narrow and unattractive. Continued commando-guerrilla intrusions seem predestined to failure. Yet the remaining guerrillas cannot be kept in camps in Zambia forever, if for no other reason than that the Zambian government is quite aware of the danger of armed and disgruntled aliens to the fragile structure of the state. Secondly, if there are no signs of visible activity, the already frayed patience of the OAU and the various sympathetic governments may not take the strain. Both Nyerere and Kaunda in the past have expressed their lack of enchantment with the two exile headquarters—their constant squabbles, public blunders, and ineffectual policies. At least in December 1970, ZANU and ZAPU agreed to unite under the leadership of

Robert Mugdbe, former secretary general of the African National Union, but how effective the merger will prove is uncertain. Finally, the claims for the present stage of quiet, long-range subversion, certainly the most practical policy, are difficult to substantiate and have none of the attractions of violent action necessary to maintain international support and domestic morale. Vastly disconcerting to their advocates and perhaps even to the leadership is the evidence, even if largely discounted, that the African population in Rhodesia largely feels that ZANU and ZAPU are obsolete, that they bungled their chance in the internecine struggle in 1963–4, and that there is no point in becoming involved in a hopeless and discredited struggle. Thus, in 1970, the movements face the bleak prospect of continuing the futile guerrilla policies or beginning again at the beginning, trailing behind them a reputation for failure and the nearly insurmountable handicap of an exile base.

SWAPO has much the same problem but without quite as long a record of errors to expunge. The forays into South-West Africa, if misguided and undertaken with misplaced optimism, have, if nothing more, generated considerable interest, particularly in those areas habitually opposed to white domination. The difficulties of infiltrating men into South-West Africa are great but have not proven to be insurmountable. The basic error again, although not still, was to opt for guerrilla-infiltration before the ground had been sufficiently prepared. SWAPO has given up this tactic, really without any other option, and is firmly determined on the long, slow process of subversion. Fortunate in their present lack of competitors and, so far, in their ability to win friends and influence people in all camps while remaining unconverted either to the Moscow way or the Peking way, SWAPO is under less pressure to produce propaganda victories. The level of talent remains high and the future difficulties are viewed rationally. The blunt fact remains that SWAPO alone or in conjunction with its ANC and ZAPU allies remains quite incapable of transforming the basic facts in South-West Africa. The very best that can be hoped is that some time in the future a low-level war of attrition can be germinated. Even then, since Pretoria considers South-West Africa as an integral part of the country, such a campaign could only meet the most ruthless suppression without apology and without the limitations of "winning the hearts and minds of the people." The Afrikaners are interested solely in obedience, not the subtleties of African loyalty still stressed in Rhodesia or Portuguese Africa.

The obsessive South African advocacy of apartheid remains one of the few cards in the hands of ANC and PAC, for elsewhere in white Africa it is possible to be black and live as a full, if restricted, human being. In much of Africa few people participate in the governing process anyway, and many remain far outside the fringe of the ruling oligarchy; but in South Africa the Afrikaners' arrogance is a constant humiliation to the human condition—a black, despite intricate apologies and the nurtured ideal of separate development, is a different, a lesser breed to the Boer, outside salvation and probably civilization, eternally damned. Nevertheless, the South African black is economically better off than his potential liberators and will probably continue to be. He is also secure if not free —hardly the case in Nigeria or the Congo. Finally, after centuries of exposure to the Afrikaners and the previous two decades of struggle using Western political techniques, the black South African is only too aware of the brutal determination of Pretoria to crush any alternative, however mild, to the regime's policies. In the midst of a rapidly expanding economy with some dribble-down benefits, under the eyes of a vigilant security apparatus, the mass of black South Africans have had no option but resignation.

His vaunted numbers are of little use when the entire apparatus of security, intelligence, and intimidation awaits the least deviation from the required norm. With all the weapons and skills of coercion on one side and not even the basic educational skills to build a broad movement on the other, the real choice has remained a spontaneous rising leading to a massacre or reluctant acquiescence. ANC and PAC are probably correct in assuming that a potential for revolution exists in the republic, but neither has been able to organize it under far more favorable conditions than now exist. The attempt to do so by guerrilla-infiltration on the low level available to ANC aborted; and the hope of doing so by subversion from an exile base without the aid of a sympathetic segment of the white population, without an organization in place, and without the possibility of effective international intervention seems to doom ANC to growing futility. PAC has continued to divide into a bewildering number of factions issuing proclamations and seizing the mountaintops of new ideological positions but is in no position to act on the present.* Despite the traditions of ANC and the caliber of its leadership, a similar fate to that of PAC is not out of the question. For both, the history of the last decade has been a long, sorry tale of new strategies aborting, with each successive option offering less real possibility of success until, on the tenth anniversary of Sharpeville, little remained but a refusal to resign and an inability to continue.

The course of the war in southern Africa for the nationalists—limited success on the fringes and total failure in the core—has been the result of an accumulation of errors in timing and organization, interpretation and self-criticism, in the face of shrewd and implacable opponents highly motivated and endowed with vast material

---

* PAC's efforts to infiltrate a group of men through the length of Mozambique, a formidable undertaking even if no Portuguese security forces existed, failed. Three were killed and nine captured. PAC contends that Pogo is still carrying out sabotage actions in the Cape Province, but control from the exile headquarters could hardly be tight.

assets. Even if the board could be swept clean and black replay the game so far with the advantage of hindsight, the result might very well be much the same. If the original white assets were not actually insurmountable, the capacity of black to use his available pieces remains very limited and the value of those pieces was never as great as observers assumed. Thus, the various errors of timing might be corrected—most often the decision on the armed struggle—but the capacity to pursue such a decision would not have increased.

Once Malan took office in 1948 and consolidated the Afrikaners' grip on the government, the aspirations of the African nationalists, still very much limited, faced little prospect of fulfillment. Persuasion, propaganda, conventional politics were simply not going to work. The example of Gandhi's vision of the realities and the success of the Indian National Congress clouded the reality of the African situation. In 1948, the groundwork necessary for a mass revolutionary organization had not been done and perhaps could not have been done without embarking on a campaign of confrontation politics to revolutionize the mass, which would simultaneously have forewarned the government and exposed the leadership. When the Africans exercised their normal options one by one—United party toleration, a liberal-radical white alliance, a nonviolence campaign and then the threat of disorder—the Afrikaners crushed the maneuvers one by one by propaganda, by fear, by blackmail and bribery, and, when it was necessary as at Sharpeville, by open force. In 1961, when the African population might well have been ready to turn to violence, the option no longer existed—the potential allies had defected or been silenced, the militant leadership had been exiled or imprisoned, the formal network of organizations dismantled, and the state security apparatus elaborated. In Rhodesia, a similar error had been made as the Africans passed through, with increasing efficiency, the traditional steps to independence within British Africa without under-

standing, any more than London did, that Rhodesia was
not Zambia. When the level was reached where the
capacity for violence existed, even if the will as yet did
not, and the prospects of success or even forceful British
intervention might have existed, the leadership turned on
itself in a futile effort to seek control of a movement that
had lost sight of its real enemy.

Perhaps only in Angola was the decision taken in time
to catch the Portuguese sufficiently unprepared so that
momentarily it appeared they would be swept out on a
single, violent wave. The difficulty was that the organization to do so did not exist in 1961, nor did either UPA or
MPLA have sufficient control to take full advantage of
their opportunities. To have waited would have by no
means assured the Africans of a higher degree of readi-
ness, since the possibilities of organizing legally within
Angola were few and the difficulties of a small, untrained
group of quarreling leaders in doing so illegally were
huge. In Mozambique, if the Portuguese had been forewarned by Angola so then had FRELIMO; so that the
rejection of conventional politics was swifter but no more
effective. FRELIMO decided essentially that it was better
to make a start, however small, rather than to build an
elaborate organization which might prove as brittle as
those in South Africa, collapsing at the onset of the armed
struggle and leaving the movement scattered and isolated.
If FRELIMO could have called on greater resources, the
base of operations and the variety of support might have
been far broader and the Portuguese position far more
fragile; but the leadership was unwilling to take the risk.
Thus, all or nearly all of the movements waited too
long, playing out their options until the optimum moment
for violence had passed; or began too soon, when their
movement was unprepared to take full advantage of surprise.

Once the struggle had begun, all of the movements
assumed that their own long-range assets outweighed

those of white Africa. The basic premise which colored all else was that white Africa was doomed by the winds of change, was an anachronism in Africa, which would fall before the moral righteousness of world opinion, the opposition of its overwhelming black majorities, and the expanding power of independent Black Africa. Time, the remorseless logic of history, and justice were on the side of black nationalism. By the time of Sharpeville, the future seemed set, the continent was rapidly being colored with flags of new black nations, and the forums of the world resounded with the rhetoric of independence and self-determination. Disillusionment has come slowly—if at all.

Majorities have not ruled and don't in the Seventies rule just because they are majorities. Many a just cause has been buried in the sands of time. World opinion is a feeble prop and international support backed only by enthusiasm is of scant use in the jungles.

The power and unity of Black Africa soon evolved into the reality of a score of small, weak, often squabbling states barely capable of maintaining their existence, much less embarking on a distant crusade. With the growth of African problems and decline in visible solutions, additional time seemed likely to sap further the vitality of Black Africa. To the south, the winds of change died out. South Africa's economy grew by leaps and bounds, its influence snaked north into Africa and across the seas to influence world finance, trade, and industry. Rhodesia, with or without sanctions, was more secure, more prosperous than its neighbors to the north. Portuguese Africa, wars or no wars, remained a net asset to Lisbon and held the potential of incalculable wealth. South Africans did not dismantle the *laager* and go away no matter how often they were condemned as alien colonialists in Africa, and the Rhodesians did not crumble before British pressure or the Portuguese cut their losses when the defense budget and casualty figures rose. At the time of Sharpeville, not only the enthusiastic Black Africans but the supposedly astute observer in Washington or London or Moscow shared many of the same illusions. The awakening has been gradual and, for those with a profound abhorrence of the societies of white Africa, painful. Many in the West are still reluctant despite the accumulated evidence to accept that white Africa for the foreseeable future is an irrevocable fact. The militant African nationalists enmeshed in their various wars and warmed by the approval pouring in from abroad have closed their minds to the premise that evil will prevail.

For the black nationalists the struggle must go on, for the humiliations are too great, the frustrations too bitter. To a very real extent this was the attitude when, after all other alternatives seemed exhausted, they turned to the armed struggle. Whether or not the power of Pretoria could be eroded by the force of black arms, ANC and PAC had to make the attempt. Whether or not the Portuguese would eventually bleed to death in Mozambique and Angola, the struggle had to continue, for the alternative was unthinkable. Whether or not crossing the Zambezi into Rhodesia guarantees an early grave or a prison cell, someone should persist. Many, if not all, of the high hopes and easy predictions have gone; but the determination to wage war—the only war available—has not. Whatever their limitations in capacity and vision, the leaders of the liberation movements are determined to persevere. They have often played their other cards poorly or not at all; but this, their last trump—the guerrilla in the jungle—they have husbanded to the last. To discard it would be to reject their own identity.

CASE STUDY TWO

On the Road of the Sure and Inevitable Victory: The Palestine Fedayeen

"Falastine Arabiyeh"

You who usurped
Our homes and lands, our country,
Driving us into exile,
Displaced and dispossessed,
Know that your days are numbered!
Know that we shall return
As an army, strong and triumphant,
To wrest from you what is our own.
(Falastine Arabiyeh.
Do you hear us?
Battle-cry of our liberation,
Of our flesh and our blood
And our bone!)

—ETHEL MANNIN

IF THE CONFRONTATION between the Arabs and the Zionists over Palestine has not lasted as long as that in southern Africa, the level of violence and agony more than compensate for a lack of historical credentials. Jews and Arabs, of course, had lived more or less in peace side by side for well over a millennium*; but not until the

* One of the articles of faith in the Arab World is that the Jews were never so happy as during the long centuries of acceptance within the Islamic world. To a substantial degree and for a very long time, this was indeed the case; but for most of the Oriental Jews and recent immigrants to Israel from Yemen or Morocco or Iraq, the period before emigration was hardly halcyon and their memories of the "tolerant" Arabs are bitter.

injection of that new breed, the Zionists, into the Middle
East at the end of the nineteenth century did toleration
erode and polarization begin to occur. The limited number of Zionist settlers within the Turkish-controlled Holy
Land caused little impact until the Balfour Declaration
on November 2, 1917, and subsequently the British establishment of the Palestine Mandate made it clear that an
entirely new and, for the Arabs, totally unexpected situation existed. Yet, neither the British nor the Zionists felt
that the establishment of a Jewish National Home in
Palestine necessarily violated Arab aspirations—if anything, the contrary. To the hopeful, the Zionists' presence
was in no way incompatible with the indigenous Arab
population.* The new settlers returning home after a two-
thousand-year odyssey would make the desert bloom, and
surely the Arabs, long rutted in sloth, medieval poverty,
and narrow customs, would be able to gather some of
those blooms. In any case, the promised land worked by
the Zionists had long been barren and was usually sold
freely by the Arabs. Whatever their eventual hopes, the
Zionists soon found that immigration was less than spectacular: the process of creating a National Home, acre by
acre, orange tree by orange tree, could hardly threaten
the Arabs and would certainly benefit them and there
would be Arab modernization by osmosis. Most of the
Arabs, sunk in lethargy, deaf to politics except for the
rare penetrating call to riot in the streets, ill-led, undisciplined, continued the daily drudgery of seeking a living
in time-honored and self-defeating methods, only vaguely
aware of the Zionists' presence. Some—a few, the tiny
elite, the ultra-Islamic, the rare activist—saw, if dimly,
the dangers to the Arabs of rising Zionist immigration.
   In Palestine, Arab nationalist movements were few

* The most visible sign of this optimism was the Weizmann–
Hussein Agreement, signed on January 3, 1919, which welcomed
Jewish immigration to Palestine, conditional on Britain's honoring
the wartime pledge of Arab independence.

and feeble, the community divided into clans and cut across by ancient grievances. However, despite the difficulties and despite the relatively low level of Jewish immigration, the Arabs were by no means completely passive. In 1920 and 1922, there were outbreaks of violence, and a delegation was dispatched to London to advise the British government of Arab resentment to Zionist ambitions. Renewed Arab violence in 1929 led to the arrival of two Royal Commissions and reports on the continuing clash of Arab-Zionist aspirations. Even then the British did not see an unreconcilable conflict, and urged policies which would allay Arab fears without denying Zionist ambitions. But Arab fears were not allayed. Although the Jewish proportion of the population had risen to only 17.7 per cent in 1931, far less than the Zionists had anticipated, the dynamic drive and successes of the Jews' community, their more advanced economic and political institutions, their vast international contacts, their unity and dedication drove many Arabs to desperation. The British could not or would not see that the Zionists were gobbling up Arab Palestine orange grove by orange grove and the squabbling and divided Arab community could not prevent it.

Although the British grew more sympathetic to Arab grievances, the rise of Hitler led to a rapid growth in Jewish immigration, compounding the problem and driving the Arabs to desperate measures to persuade the British to intervene before the point of no return had been reached. Arab toleration for a Jewish National Home eroded rapidly as the eventual nature of the "home" became clearer. In 1936 the Arabs instituted a general strike and, for nearly three years, the "Arab Revolt," strikes, demonstrations, riots and brawls, terror and mass meetings, kept the Mandate in turmoil. In May 1939, the British issued a White Paper which envisaged a bi-national state with a permanent Jewish population of one third. The Zionists were outraged. To them, this plan was a violation of the terms of the Mandate and a denial of humanity, given the conditions in Europe. The Arabs were sullen, for they wanted an independent Arab Palestine, not a British-controlled, bi-national state. With the outbreak of war in September, both groups tended to postpone their ambitions until the outcome became clear. The Arabs were not averse to an Axis victory* but largely remained on the sidelines. The Jews were determined to defeat Hitler, even with Perfidious Albion as an ally.†

For twenty years the overwhelming majority of both Jews and Arabs had seen the dominant factor in their future as Britain. While intercommunal violence did exist, spontaneous frustration played a greater part in the clashes than rational planning. Both Arabs and Jews concentrated on persuading the British. Since the British government was otherwise occupied from 1939 to 1945, Palestine tended to wait out the war. The exceptions were the two Revisionist Zionist organizations, the tiny Stern Group and the slightly larger Irgun Zvai Leumi. Appalled by the news of the holocaust in Europe, they felt that the British must be forced to open Palestine to the remnants of the Eastern European Diaspora while there was still time.‡

* The Mufti, Muhammad Amin al-Husseini, head of the Supreme Muslim Council, was forced to flee the Mandate—leaving the nationalist movement in disarray, the Arab Higher Committee outlawed, and many of his colleagues in prison—and spent the war in Europe cooperating with the Axis.

† The enthusiasm of the Zionists for the British war effort was hardly disinterested. Most of the new Jewish recruits anticipated that British military training was going to be a most useful asset in establishing a Zionist state.

‡ Lechi (the Stern Group) had been all but obliterated in a series of gun fights with the police, with Stern killed in mysterious circumstances. The new leadership reorganized and continued the struggle, which included the assassination in Cairo of Lord Moyne, Churchill's Minister of State resident in the Middle East. The Irgun, however, had cooperated with the British. Its commander, David Raziel, had been killed on a British-directed operation. The operative factor in the decision to begin the armed struggle before Hitler had been defeated was the dreadful news from Eastern Europe.

But their campaign, although at times spectacular, had little more than nuisance value. The Arabs under the leadership of the Arab Higher Committee, established in April 1936, and the Jewish Agency, representing most of the Zionists, both continued to feel that the key to their aspirations lay in London and that diplomacy, not violence, was the means to turn it.

Once peace had come to the rest of the world in 1945, the Irgun brought a mini-war to Palestine. The British were not to be allowed to impose an undesirable solution. Sabotage, assassination, and terror were the weapons. Even the Haganah, the defense militia of the Jewish Agency, shifted back and forth between cooperation with the British and with the Irgun, uncertain as to the proper path to the Jewish Commonwealth. The Arabs once more watched from the sidelines. The crucial point remained the ultimate British decision, and there the Zionists seemed to hold most of the cards. In America and Britain, a vast, highly skilled campaign began, aimed at converting the influential. In Palestine the Irgun absorbed an increasing number of British troops and British funds, while the Jewish Agency insisted that it had no control over the extremists. Much of world opinion was sympathetic to the Zionists. The American government, London's closest ally, often seemed more than sympathetic. Increasingly, it became clear that the British probably could not impose a decision on the Zionists in Palestine, nor did they want to forego their position in the Middle East by imposing one on the Arabs. The Palestinians, still weak, still divided, without a Haganah or Irgun, without an effective political organization, had to depend on the good auspices of the new Arab states, a British sense of justice, and the validity of their aspirations. The British, trapped amid

Both groups saw Britain as the prime bloc to Zionist aspirations; but the Irgun foresaw, eventually, an Arab confrontation while Lechi felt an anti-imperialist alliance between Zionists and Arab nationalists was possible.

Zionist defiance, international pressures, domestic difficulties, and the call of self-interest, could discover no solution which would not deny the minimum desire of one side, no formula to extricate themselves gracefully. With the Mandate slipping into chaos, in February 1947 Foreign Secretary Ernest Bevin announced that the future of the Mandate would be decided by the United Nations.

The ultimate arbitrator had become the United Nations rather than Great Britain, and both the Arabs and the Zionists continued to assume that the ultimate solution would be achieved there, subject to their own efforts, not in a conflict on the ground in Palestine between the two communities. For months the battle for the diplomats' vote was waged in the world's capitals and the corridors of the United Nations. On November 29, 1947, since Arab–Zionist coexistence had become impossible, expulsion of either unthinkable, and absolute submersion of either unenforceable, the United Nations passed a resolution prescribing the partition of Palestine. Partition was the best that could be made of the situation in the Mandate. The Zionists took their half-a-loaf, albeit reluctantly. The Arabs refused to accede to what they considered to be an injustice, the theft of half their land by aliens sanctioned only by a majority of foreigners in a distant organization. For the first time, the Arabs in Palestine and the Middle East realized that their destiny lay in their own hands, not in those of the British or the United Nations. They would not acquiesce and so they would have to fight. After the euphoria of the partition vote, the Zionists too accepted that what the United Nations had granted would have to be defended by force. After thirty years, the Arabs and Zionists recognized that their aspirations were irreconcilable.

The first Arab effort to prevent the partition of the Mandate and the establishment of a Zionist state took the form of irregular guerrilla-attacks on isolated settlements and, particularly, on the fragile lines of communications. British forces gradually withdrew, leaving the field open to the two sides, which both scrambled to put together sufficient armed forces to impose their will. From December 1947 until early spring 1948, the Palestinian Arabs, reinforced by volunteers from elsewhere in the Middle East, sorely pressed the Zionists' hold on Palestine, all but isolating Jerusalem from the coast and attacking the kibbutzim. The response of the Haganah, which went over to the offensive before the proclamation of the state on May 15, was sufficient to persuade the Arab irregulars that their partisan warfare, ambushes, and hit-and-run attacks on kibbutzim would be insufficient to drive out the Zionists. The Arabs felt the real war would begin on May 15, when Israel was "created" and their regular armies intervened. Once again the Palestinians did not have sufficient local force to impose their solution; however, all assumed that the regular Arab armies would.

The month-long assault by the regular armies against Israel dispelled these Palestinian illusions. The Lebanese, Iraqi, Syrian, Transjordanian, and Egyptian armies not only failed to sweep the Zionists into the sea but also failed to hold for the Palestinians all the areas guaranteed by the partition resolution. Fought in a tangle of international resolutions and initiatives, by two weak and understrength forces, the war of four weeks revealed both the determination of the Israelis and the incompetence of the Arab armies. Sweeping into war on a wild wave of popular enthusiasm, the Arab armies had been committed for selfish reasons by men doubtful of their competence. There was no unity of purpose, no unity of command, only the unpleasant revelation of Arab weakness. Unable either to secure victory or admit defeat, the Arabs in July tried a second round after the cease-fire. In ten days, Arab offensive efforts aborted and the Israelis picked up additional slices of Arab Palestine. Still, the Arabs would not recognize the substantial growth in Israeli strength or the danger of standing exposed to a counteroffensive.

In October, the Israelis struck at the Egyptians in the south, driving them out of the northern Negev. In the north, Galilee was cleared of the volunteer Arab Liberation Army. Again in December the Israelis attacked in the south, and under a series of lightning strikes the Egyptian Army crumbled. In Cairo King Farouk, who had personally ordered his unprepared army into the war to create an Egyptian presence, was forced to heed the call for an armistice.

The Palestinians were shattered by the rapid pace of events. There was no victory parade to Tel Aviv nor a free Palestine. Instead, Israel, having defeated both the irregulars and the five Arab states, controlled vast new areas. Hundreds of thousands of Palestinians huddled in jerry-built refugee camps. The dream of Arab unity lay in pieces. The reputation, even the honor, of Arab leaders had been soiled. The defeat was too great to be absorbed and too great to deny. The Arabs began the agonizing reappraisal. Defeat, in this case, had many fathers: disunity, egotism, self-interest, primitive or incompetent institutions—essentially, Arab society as constituted was feeble, noncompetitive, incapable of waging a modern technological war.* Most agreed that the Arabs could win Palestine only if they could transform their society. As obvious and axiomatic as this conclusion was, it gave scant comfort to the confused and bitter refugees, to the maturing generation alienated from its natural home, to those who thirsted after revenge or for their rights. The transformation of the Arab World was clearly a lengthy operation, so that the Palestinians would have to wait. Having no choice, they waited.

The West Bank was absorbed into the Hashemite

---

* All of these were proposed by various Arabs, accepted by a great many, particularly the young, and served as a rationale for the series of coups and changes over the next decade. After June 1967, the self-criticism scanned like a rerun of the previous generation's analysis.

Kingdom to become the major part of the new Jordan. Egypt administered the refugee-jammed Gaza Strip. Palestine appeared on no maps, only in the hearts of the Arabs. Every Arab spokesman, Palestinian or not, insisted vehemently that the Palestinian entity must be preserved, the Palestine personality perpetuated. Much of this remained oratory as the various regimes went their own way transforming their own societies; but there was a real feeling that Palestine must not disappear, a reluctance to "solve" the refugee problem at the expense of a future return, and a feeling that the entire Arab World was diminished and poorer for the loss. There were great changes in the Arab Nation but still the prospects of a *jihad* to throw the Zionists into the sea came no closer.

In July 1952, the Free Officers gained control of Egypt and haltingly set about modernizing not only the army but the economic and social bases of the state. Britain agreed in 1954 to evacuate the Canal Zone, and elsewhere the dependence of the Arab states on Western guidance faded. Increasingly, there was a feeling of momentum, which culminated in the Egyptian–Czech (Russian) arms agreement in September 1955. By then, Nasser had finally reopened the Palestine question by more than rhetorical intervention. For years, tiny groups of Palestinian conspirators had existed—frustrated, desperate men without coherence, plotting vengeance. There was still no single coherent leadership, no rational program, not even an agreed direction. Most Palestinians by necessity had to depend on the good auspices of the existing regimes; and Nasser, the most militant, the new Messiah of Arab nationalism, did not disappoint them. The Egyptians sponsored, armed, and trained the "Palestinian" fedayeen in the Gaza Strip in 1954. The fedayeen undertook a series of sabotage and terror raids. In February 1955, one group reportedly penetrated nearly as far as Tel Aviv. The fedayeen campaign, backed by the might of the new Egypt, far more than all the futile blockades, boycotts, and firefights on the border, indicated to many Palestinians that the day of the return was at hand. By the spring of 1956, even the conservative Arab states were impressed with Nasser's emergence as a nationalist Messiah. The parades of T-34 tanks and the fly-overs of MIG-15 jets symbolized the transformation of Egypt, so devoutly desired. The arrival of Soviet technicians symbolized the new independence of the Arab World. Radio Cairo, echoed by every Arab voice in every bazaar in the Middle East, trumpeted the shift in the scales.

Growing isolation, harsh austerity intensified by the Arab boycotts, the shrill voice of Arab vengeance, and, above all, the insecurity created by the fedayeen raids had placed Israel in a state of siege. The Israelis' search for a way out coincided with Anglo-French determination to undo Nasser's nationalization of the Suez Canal on July 26, 1956. The result was the Israeli blitz through the Sinai, orchestrated with the Anglo-French descent on Suez. The ignominy of the collapse of Nasser's new army in Sinai disappeared under the clouds of oratory that brought Nasser a stunning diplomatic victory over the British and French—the force of Arab justice had triumphed over the power of imperialist aggression. Radio Cairo claimed total victory: Egypt had intentionally withdrawn from Sinai, the air force had never been committed, and in light of the crushing defeat of the imperialists nothing else greatly mattered. Most Arabs, including Palestinians, agreed. Nasser stood amid clouds of glory, praised by his bitterest rivals, adored by the masses, the symbol of a new and better future.

For some Palestinians, nevertheless, the present remained grim. They had been forced to square one; in fact, for some time the Israelis had even occupied Gaza. Whatever the verdict of Sinai, the Egyptian Army would have to be rebuilt. The Arab World was still not unified. Cairo might claim victory, but little had changed in Gaza or on the West Bank. The chain reaction of revolution and change in the Middle East, revolutionary regimes in Iraq and Syria, then the creation of the United Arab Republic, the Lebanese crisis—these created a feeling that all the pieces might suddenly fit and Arab unity would at last be realized. But for the Palestinians nothing changed. Arab unity did not come. The revolutionary regimes proved as self-interested as their predecessors. For the Palestinians, the more things changed—the more coups, revolutionary programs, arms deals, and international conferences—the more things remained as they had been. And all they were offered was the pabulum of patience. It was very hard to accept the dictum of Nasser, the savior, that the time was not ripe.

> When I initiate war I want to be able to achieve one, and only one, result and nothing less—namely, decisive victory. Anyone can bring about war, but on the victory can terminate it according to his desire. I know that the Arab nation does not want an adventure unless I am capable of developing it into an all-out war against the enemy and against all support which may be sent to him, and achieve sure victory.[1]

Year followed year and the time was never ripe. Children grew up to be men in the refugee camps. Wandering in the Palestinian Diaspora, a man might have a position, wealth, prestige, but never a real home. They were all men without a country, and for many the dream faded and the accommodation was made. More than any other Arab people, the Palestinians pursued education with a vengeance, mastered the sophisticated skills of modern technology, and found a welcome in the universities of the West or the oil fields of the Gulf or the classrooms and counting houses of Beirut. Perhaps it was true, as Hussein said, that "without Palestine, Arabs cannot possess real freedom and genuine unity or even a good life"; but most of their Arab brothers seemed sufficiently content and many lost hope. Perhaps the day of reckoning would come, but the bleak, soul-killing refugee camps still sat on the fringe of the homeland and the best of the new generation was scattered and the Palestine entity less real than ever.

One small band of brothers had lost patience. A young Palestinian, Yasser Arafat, had, like many of his generation, migrated to Cairo to study engineering at Fuad I University. There he became involved in Palestinian student politics and dabbled in the Moslem Brotherhood. In 1954 the latter connection made it necessary for him to move on, and in 1956 he was in Gaza during the Israeli occupation. For Cairo, 1956 might have been a year of victory, but to Palestinians in Gaza it was not. Arafat gathered around him some of the militant members of the General Union of Palestinian Students. After long hours of analysis and recrimination, they founded the Movement for the Liberation of Palestine, known in Arabic by its reversed initials as al Fatah ("conquest"). Arafat spent the next years as a salesman of liberation, moving through the Palestinian Diaspora preaching the gospel of action. Al Fatah for a long time was as much a state of mind as an organization. In many places, the seed fell on rocky ground, for only the mad would assume that "action" by a handful of rebellious young men could succeed or even aid success when even the might of Nasser's Egypt was still insufficient. Yet in Kuwait, in the Arab student organizations in German universities, among the unrepentent and unreconstructed apparently comfortable in their new jobs in Beirut or Damascus, the spark caught. The Algerian FLN, which for al Fatah had become a glowing example of what could be possible, encouraged the young men. A few Palestinians left for military training under the FLN guerrillas. In Damascus, Syrian intelligence expressed sympathy and then offered more practical aid. Al Fatah opened a Damascus office, but the young men still represented no one but themselves, had formal backing from no one, and had only a desire to begin the armed struggle to win a free Palestine from the alien Zionists.

A Palestinian organization eventually was formed which did have backing, did claim to represent all Palestinians, and did produce a formal "reasonable" program. This was the Palestinian Liberation Organization (PLO), established on May 28, 1964, by six hundred representatives of the Palestinian community. Led by Ahmed Shukairy, a convert to extreme nationalism from Acre and a bombastic orator, the PLO announced the establishment of a Palestine Liberation Army (PLA) which would cooperate with the other Arab armies in the liberation of the homeland. In September 1964, the Arab League recognized the PLO as the only representative of the Palestinian people, discarding the moribund Arab Higher Committee and ignoring the underground al Fatah. To members of al Fatah, Shukairy and the PLO were simply Nasser and delay written small. Increasingly, in the internecine wrangles of Arab politics, the PLO appeared to be shifted by strings pulled in Cairo, Shukairy mouthing Nasser's words, and the PLA little more than a form of outdoor relief for the discontented refugee. Al Fatah, in its monthly, *Our Palestine,* first published in Beirut in 1959, had long insisted that time was not on the Arab side, that the armed struggle must begin without the long, elaborate preparation Nasser urged, that to wait was to betray Palestine and to doom another generation to the Diaspora.

Few in the higher reaches of the Arab power structure took note of what was felt to be an irresponsible, marginal dissident group, a nuisance, not an alternative. Only the Syrians, who used the fedayeen alternative as a club to beat Nasser, expressed any public sympathy.*

* At the first Arab summit meeting, in January 1964, the Syrians had called Nasser a traitor because of his unwillingness to attack Israel immediately. The Syrians, having read Mao and Che and

When four young men of al Fatah did begin the armed
struggle on the night of December 31, 1964, blowing up a
water pump at El Koton, all the agencies of the Arab
World, the summit meetings, the Arab League, the Arab
Unified Command, government spokesmen, condemned
the campaign as a dangerous provocation which might
bring war before the Arab Nation was prepared for the
final campaign to victory. Al Fatah had heard it all before
and paid no attention. If war came, all the better. If
Israel won, all the better, for more Arabs would be involved, more Israelis would be tied down as occupiers,
and more opportunity to wage a successful war of national
liberation would exist.* It was not war which frightened
al Fatah but the debility of a peace that sapped the soul
of Palestine.

The advent of armed struggle on January 1, 1965, by
only eighty-two men hardly transformed the Middle
East. The campaign remained on a very low military
level, ineffectual even as sabotage, pursued by the dedicated but incompetent. Despite the enthusiastic battle
communiqués, the raw and uncertain fedayeen of al
Fatah often placed their mines in the wrong places or in
the right place, without activating them. Their targets
were minor and isolated: pumping stations or irrigation
installations. Little damage was done. From January to
March, only seven sabotage raids were undertaken. Al
Fatah recognized many of the problems, but it had decided that it was preferable to make a bad beginning than

---

observed the Algerian success, advanced the slogan of the popular
liberation war. At an Extraordinary Congress on April 1, 1966, the
Syrian Ba'athists accepted the People's Liberation War as the central doctrine of its ideology: Damascus was to become the Hanoi of
the Middle East.

* There is every indication that later, in 1967, the leadership of
al Fatah, like that of all other Arab groups, was swept along in the
orgy of optimism, anticipating a glorious victory. Certainly, there
can be no doubt that Ahmed Shukairy and *his* Palestinians expected
to be in Tel Aviv.

none at all. Without a beginning and without a record of combat, the mobilization of material and moral support to expand the campaign could not be achieved. By the end of the year, al Fatah's military "campaign" had achieved, on paper, no visible military results; however, a great many ripples had been sent across the uneasy waters of the Middle East. The Israelis, for example, felt convinced that the Syrians had seized on al Fatah as a means to pursue their traditional border harassment but without assuming responsibility.

As for the Arab states, with the exception of the Syrians, particularly the Deuxième Bureau, who continued to see very considerable possibilities in manipulating al Fatah, they felt that the "armed struggle" was irresponsible, potentially inviting massive Israeli retaliation against the innocent.

> Naturally we see the Revolutionary Road, which *Our Palestine* has chosen, as an unwarranted one, because it is built on improvisation, excitement and spontaneity. . . . Smashing Israel cannot be done by Fedayeen's attacks because of the completeness of her preparations and arms. . . . Why should we suppose that the Israeli Army will stand with its hands tied in the face of Fedayeen's attacks? The Israeli Army will destroy Arab villages, and cities, and even may take a decisive step, and, for example, occupy the whole West Bank.[2]

The aspirations of the Palestinians could best be served through the PLO and by the regular Arab governments. Egypt remained particularly suspicious of the influence of the Moslem Brothers within al Fatah, seeing the whole movement as an anti-Nasser ploy to erode the influence of the pro-Egyptian PLO. All the Arab rulers, Left and Right, had grave doubts about the loyalty and intention of their Palestinians, who often seemed more concerned with their own grievances than the stability of their host state.

During 1966, the capacities of al Fatah—its level of

training, competence in the field, and its financial and human resources—grew substantially. The new Syrian government came to a formal understanding with al Fatah in February and diverted considerable effort and funds to improving the fedayeen-guerrillas. Between February and August the Israelis reported ninety-six shooting incidents, mainly along the border. Five Israelis were killed and twenty-four wounded. Under any normal criteria, this was less than a pinprick, although it far exceeded the al Fatah record of 1965. The Israelis, however, do not use normal criteria. For them provocation, however minor, must be answered by retaliation if the asp is to be killed in the egg. For Israel, the responsibility was Syria's and Jordan's. The independence and aspirations of the Palestinians of al Fatah were a most minor side issue. Without Arab complicity, there would be no al Fatah operations. Thus, to the Israelis, their jet attack on the Syrian Baniyas River diversion project on July 14 during which a MIG-21 was shot down, a second jet fight which cost Syria another MIG-21, and a MIG-17 downed by patrol boat fire were integral parts of the hard border policy against Syria, rather than a response to the new factor of al Fatah. The same was true for the more direct Israeli retaliation against Jordan in May and September and against Lebanon in October. Both Jordan and Lebanon grew increasingly concerned, for neither had collaborated with the fedayeen nor approved of their raids.

With the exception of the Syrian Ba'athist regime, the Arab states feared that Israeli retaliation might not be limited to a few raids but could lead to massive attacks on innocent Arabs under the principle of collective guilt. This was the immediate concern of Jordan and was a real factor for Nasser, who still did not favor a premature confrontation. The result, for al Fatah, was that simultaneously with their growing effectiveness in the field and within the Palestinian communities they faced increasing repression by Arab security forces. Their agents and spokesmen were imprisoned, potential sympathizers or suspected members put under surveillance. In public, speaker after speaker, time after time, stressed the orthodox Arab line. The aspiration of al Fatah for a free Palestine, supposedly the common goal of all Arabs, could not be achieved by fedayeen action but only through Arab unity or by means of conventional Arab diplomacy or broadened Arab military forces. If the young men wanted action, let them join the PLA under the aegis of PLO. If the impatient saw no movement toward the ultimate goal, let them compose their souls, for the return to the homeland would be long and hard and there were no short cuts.

For the young and impatient of al Fatah, this was hypocrisy. In twenty years no one had done anything for the Palestinians but proffer promises and urge patience. Where necessary, al Fatah went underground; wherever possible, the recruiting and proselytizing continued. During 1966, operations often had to be carried out in defiance of Jordan and Lebanon. In July al Fatah and Jordanian troops fought a pitched battle and four fedayeen were killed. But they persisted in using Jordanian territory despite Hussein's efforts, and the Israelis continued to insist on Hussein's responsibility. In November the Israeli Army carried out a massive retaliatory raid on an al Fatah base in Samu, Jordan, which resulted in a four-hour battle with the Jordanian Army. Many Arabs felt that Israel, fearing to take too great risks, had struck at Jordan, "the innocent," rather than at Russian-supported Syria. The Samu operation seemed to be the result of weakness rather than strength. Most important, public reaction nearly threatened to topple Hussein's moderate government. To all, the crisis emphasized the instability that al Fatah could introduce in the Arab World. The uneasy Arab governments intensified their repressive measures. Without Syrian support during 1966, the fragile al Fatah net would undoubtedly have been broken in the name of prudence and unity. With the Syrian base, offered, as both sides realized, for purely Ba'athist purposes, al Fatah persisted.

The first real break for al Fatah within the Arab World came as a result of worsening Jordanian–Egyptian relations, which meant a rise of tension between Shukairy's PLO and Hussein. To confound Amman, Shukairy came to Damascus in December and agreed with the Syrians that the PLO and al Fatah would cooperate. As such, this was meaningless, since Nasser had no intention of allowing fedayeen operations from Gaza, the PLO base, nor did al Fatah have much faith in Shukairy's conversion to the armed struggle. What mattered was that, along with Damascus Radio and the Ba'athist press, the Egyptians now opened the floodgates of publicity. For the first time in the Arab World at large, the name of al Fatah became common currency. Nothing else revealed the shift more than the sudden proliferation of fedayeen organizations, such as the Heroes of the Return to the Homeland or the Abd el Kader al-Hussaini commandoes—over a dozen shifting and emerging coteries without military capacity or, in some cases, members. If still a minor factor in the Arab kaleidoscope, al Fatah had become fashionable.

Both Shukairy and al Fatah sought to exploit Hussein's dilemma, not merely to achieve freedom of operations but also to replace him with a more radical regime, a policy encouraged if not guided by the benevolent regimes in Damascus and Cairo. Hussein closed down the PLO offices and Shukairy's people went underground, setting up a revolutionary council. Al Fatah carried out small sabotage operations within Jordan from Syrian bases. At the same time, Damascus and Cairo broadcast the regular series of al Fatah battle communiqués claiming victory for al Fatah operations within Israel—operations which the Israelis discounted or denied entirely. However, behind the exaggerated propaganda, directed as much against Hussein as anyone else, there was a nugget of truth. Al Fatah had not given up the armed struggle against Israel. Inter-Arab complications, however, had drained off much of its energy so that the level of the campaign remained low if the provocation to Israel was relatively high. From January until June 1967, al Fatah killed 14 Israelis and wounded 72, initiated 122 acts of sabotage, 45 of which failed, and made life along the Israeli border uncertain but hardly intolerable. In the spring of 1967, al Fatah intensified the campaign. Al Fatah communiqués became even more inflated and grandoise. An Israeli jet strike into Syria on April 7 deterred neither the fedayeen nor Damascus. On May 11, in a closed speech to Mapai leaders at the Yahdav Club in Tel Aviv, Prime Minister Levi Eshkol noted that "in view of the fourteen incidents in the past month alone, we may have to adopt measures not less drastic than those of 7 April."[3] Eshkol and the Israelis were still thinking in terms of retaliation but the chain reaction that was to lead to the confrontation in June had begun.

Events overtook the fedayeen. Their operations against Israel and squabbles in Jordan were overshadowed as, step by step, the Middle East shuffled toward war.

Early in May, the fragile Syrian government seemed to be tottering before rising internal opposition. The Russians were concerned about their protégé's survival and felt that perhaps Nasser should be brought in as a stabilizing force. The Syrians were, as usual, proclaiming an imminent Israeli attack, partly because their continued provocation made it likely and partly in desperation to divert their domestic critics. The Russians prodded Nasser, hopeful that a strong Egyptian stand in favor of Syria would pull the Ba'athists out of the crisis. Nasser, who had been strongly criticized by his rival Hussein for refusing to respond to the April 7 Israeli air strike, was not adverse to playing an active role. His prestige had suffered

a series of setbacks and if the Syrians felt really threatened
—even if they were not—a bold gesture might burnish
his image.*

On May 15, Nasser began a military build-up in Sinai
and on the following day the Egyptian Chief of Staff,
General Muhammad Fawzy, telegraphed the commander
of the United Nations Emergency Force demanding that
his men be withdrawn from their posts inside Egypt's
border. This may have been sufficient answer to Nasser's
critics that the Egyptians lived in safety behind the United
Nations wall; but Nasser went further. On May 22, he
announced the closure of the Straits of Tiran, garnering
wild acclaim, first from Arab radicals and then from his
bitter conservative opponents. The enthusiastic support
culminated in Hussein's arrival in Cairo on May 30 to
sign a military pact. Arab enthusiasm reached fever
heights. The issue suddenly became not Syria or the Straits
of Tiran but the existence of Israel. Both the PLO and
al Fatah were delirious at the thought of a break in the
long-frozen Palestinian issue. Shukairy's speeches grew
more violent: the Jews were to be thrown into the sea.
"Zero hour has come. This is the hour our people have
been awaiting for the last nineteen years."[4] In Gaza thousands of Palestinian refugees appeared on television at
great rallies, screaming, shouting, waving banners emblazoned "Death to the Jews" and "We Shall Return." The
moment of Armageddon seemed at hand, when the years
of injustice and humiliation would be swept away by the
united might of the Arab Nation.

During the first week of June, the Arab World lived
in an almost unbearable delirium of enthusiasm. All the
hopes and dreams of years hovered on realization. Every

---

* Apparently Nasser felt that his army was, if not prepared for
victory, prepared to prevent defeat. Consequently, to gamble on a
confrontation with Israel would not be a "political swindle," for
in event of war the Egyptian Army could hold out until international diplomatic intervention arrived.

Arab, everywhere, glowed with the high fever of certain victory. Never before, even on the evening of the invasion of the Mandate in 1948 or the morning after the Anglo-French debacle at Suez, had so many felt so certain that tomorrow was the sure day of retribution. Tomorrow came on June 5, when in a few hours the Israeli pre-emptive strike wiped out Arab air power. In less than a week the armies of Egypt, Jordan, and Syria had been reduced to blackened hulks and stunned, unbelieving men wandering on the hills or in the deserts. The Israelis had occupied Sinai and stood on the banks of Suez, Jerusalem and all the West Bank were gone, the Golan plateau had been lost. Nothing lay between Israeli tanks and Damascus, Amman, and Cairo but the traffic jams of shattered and defeated armies. From the Jordan River on the west to the Suez Canal on the east, from the tip of Sinai in the south to the Golan Heights in the north, the Israelis stood easy with as swift and as total a victory as seemed possible in the mid-twentieth century. All has changed. The disaster for the Arabs was complete, total; the shock, the humiliation, the horror beyond bearing.

Amid the burned-out glitter of yesterday's incandescent hopes, only within al Fatah did the fire of resistance still burn. Admittedly, al Fatah too had been as naïvely optimistic, as foolishly arrogant; but more than any others they had publicly doubted the orthodox might of Egypt and alone had stressed the ultimate importance of the Palestinians' winning their own destiny. After the June War, the Palestinians had a choice only between al Fatah's war of national liberation or accepting another generation of despair. Amid the welter of resignations, recriminations, the inchoate coups, and the calls for regeneration, al Fatah alone foreswore the shopworn clichés and discredited programs of the past. The young men in Damascus grasped the nettle of resistance—the fedayeen would lead the Arab World out of the valley of despair. The fedayeen would not permit the Arab Nation to sink into despondency and resignation. Al Fatah not only had a program but also an obligation, not only a high purpose but also a certain remedy for the dagger held to the Arab heart by Israel. In the past discredited, derided, buffeted by condescending experts, by the experienced, the wise, and the practical, al Fatah alone in the summer of 1967 retained the faith and possessed the one true doctrine for victory. Everywhere there were prophets of doom, and only al Fatah offered certain victory. And for the first time, they found ready listeners and then a trickle and next a stream of converts.

In the late Fifties, al Fatah had not been overburdened with an extensive ideological infrastructure. A call to act in the field against Israel, as Palestinians untied to the policies of any Arab state, had at first largely proved sufficient. The ultimate nature of Palestine remained vague, the means beyond the onset of the armed struggle unclear, and detailed discussions of "politics" unwise. Once the early ideas of al Fatah saw the light in *Our Palestine*, a more detailed defense against the criticisms of the conventional forced a rapid elaboration of basic principles. By the spring of 1967, al Fatah had developed a relatively coherent corpus of doctrine. While many of the tenets of the faith had been defined in response to Arab criticism, the core had evolved over the years in response to the lessons of Palestinian history. The publicists of al Fatah produced a view of the nature of their enemy, the Zionists, an analysis of the strengths and weaknesses of the Arab Nation, a doctrine of action which would achieve their ultimate goal, and a vision of what victory would mean for the Palestinians and the Arab Nation. Although influenced by the success of national liberation movements elsewhere, particularly in Algeria, by the most militant ideas of Arab nationalism, by the dicta of Mao, Giap, and Guevara, the overriding factor for al Fatah was the impact of twenty years of Palestinian history. Thus, more often than not, the ideas of al Fatah seemed to Cairo or Damascus both parochial and alien, a combination of mini-Palestinian bazaar nationalism and fashionable international sophistry.

Whatever their ideological difference, the one basic, bedrock area of agreement between al Fatah and much of the remainder of the Arab World was and is the integral nature of the state of Israel. Israel was an alien, artificial pseudo-state imposed upon the Middle East by the West as a means of controlling and dominating the Arab Nation, denying it unity and justice. Without repeated injections of Western aid and Western gold, Israel, which had no true nationalism—only Zionist illusions—would collapse before the united power of the Arabs:

> Israel has never had, and never will have, a natural sovereign existence that can easily and quickly adjust itself to the changing atmosphere. Israel has been, and still is, an artificial state composed of poor-quality, brittle material, something like plaster, which can only change when it breaks up.[5]

Al Fatah perceives Zionism as an unnatural creed, avowedly racist, which has clouded and corrupted Jewish minds, an alien ideology even to the Jews of Israel, who have been manipulated, misinformed, and "converted" for the benefit of a few unscrupulous power seekers. Once the blinders of Zionist prejudice are removed from Jewish eyes, loyalty to the artificial Israeli entity will evaporate. The older generation of Zionists may be beyond redemption, but al Fatah is certain that the young Jew and particularly the Afro-Asiatic Jew possesses only a skin-deep commitment to Israel. It is inconceivable to al Fatah that a rational Jew—a fellow-Semite—could truly believe, could actually commit himself without reservation to so blatantly unnatural an ideology. For al Fatah, Zionism is, of course, not only an artificial theory but an evil practice; for Israel is racist, dominated by a single religio-ethnic elite who would and have excluded all but members of their own tribe from full participation. Employing the very methods of the Nazis—"big-lie propaganda, international blackmail, and the use of brute force"[6]; even "race-extermination"—the Zionists have, as agents of international capitalism, created a new Nazi state in the Middle East:

> It is our duty also to expose Zionism for what it really is, an international racist movement synthesized of religious prejudice, intellectual dishonesty and capitalistic greed. This anachronism of a movement is much more inhuman than the Nazism it purports to have opposed.[7]

And like the Nazi state, Israel is innately aggressive, driven by the false logic of Zionist theology to expand, an unnatural cancer planted in the Middle East by the power brokers in London and Washington. For al Fatah, and much of the Arab World, this, then, is Israel. A superficial patina of arrogance and power disguises an evil, unnatural, and foredoomed philosophy of racist aggression in the service of imperialism.

In place of the abomination of Israel, al Fatah offers instead a secular, bi-national, democratic Palestine, open to all who foreswear loyalty to racist Zionism, open to all religions but in the service of none, open to all Palestinians so long denied their rightful home. If, as al Fatah contends, Zionism is only skin deep, all but the few hopelessly deluded Israeli citizens can find a home in the Palestine of the future, for by then they will have seen the error of their ways. From time to time, statements have been issued that might indicate that only the "real" Jewish inhabitants should be permitted to remain, but whether this means those present before a certain date, indicates a specific sum total, or really means a substantial exodus of the unrepentant remains unclear.

Al Fatah feels it sufficient to offer an open, free, democratic Palestine in contrast to the misguided aspirations of some Arabs to drive the Jews into the sea. The nature of the political and economic institutions of the new state remain, by intention, vague. Adopting the Algerian FLN policy of postponing until tomorrow those issues which would inevitably divide today, al Fatah has refused to become involved in the internecine, ideological quarrels of the various Ba'athists, socialists, Marxist-Leninists or followers of the Arab National Movement as to the structure of Palestine; the existence of Palestine is sufficient unto itself. To a degree, however, both spokesmen and some publications have indicated that al Fatah is not fighting to return the old landlords, petty capitalists, and exploiters of the recent past. In the Middle East of the Sixties this is hardly very radical, and has proven insufficient for most of the ideologically dedicated who feel al Fatah should eschew the Front philosophy and define its war aims more specifically. Al Fatah, despite the competition from other Palestinian fedayeen movements waving alluring doctrines, has remained steadfast against becoming too involved in hypothetical institution building.

If the enemy is clear and the goal ill-defined, the "means to victory" has been the aspect of al Fatah ideology which has produced the bulk of analysis and become the target for major criticism. For al Fatah, the guerrilla campaign of the fedayeen waging a war of national liberation became the core: guerrilla-war was no longer a tactic, a means to wage war, but a strategy. All the aspirations of the Palestinians could be accomplished, except perhaps the last decisive battle, solely through fedayeen action, which on the battlefield would simultaneously bleed the Israelis dry, transform the Arab masses, and without recourse to exterior interests or institutions create the decisive conditions for ultimate victory. Such a guerrilla-war of national liberation would, as it always had elsewhere, succeed.

Israel is undoubtedly engaged in a losing battle as the forces of the Palestine liberation movement acquire experience and achieve the strategic depth provided by the Palestinian and Arab masses. However long it takes, their struggle represents another historical example of a people's inevitable triumph over colonialism, racism, and oppression.[8]

Although voluminous elaborations of the basic theory were churned out first in the pages of *Our Palestine* and then in mounds of pamphlets, press releases, and statements, the key to the theory remained the all-encompassing results expected of fedayeen action which *alone* would lead to an Arab Palestine, which *alone* would transform the masses in a Pan-Arab revolution, and which *alone* would secure the unity of the Arab Nation, so long denied by imperialist intervention and national self-interest.

After the June 1967 debacle, the Palestinians insisted that fedayeen action was not so much the last alternative but rather the true road, long ignored. In this position, they had on hand ample evidence that all the conventional alternatives had aborted, leaving in their wake the hopes of a generation. Israel, under attack by traditional means, waxed and grew fat on new Arab lands, more arrogant, more successful, more secure than if from the first the Arabs had surrendered or cooperated. Palestinians' dependence on Arab diplomacy led to the partition in 1947. Dependence on Western good faith led to intervention in Suez and Lebanon. Dependence on the United Nations produced sterile resolutions, barren negotiations, and permanent refugee camps. Even dependence on Soviet Russia in the end had left the Arabs with rusting tank hulks, burned-out jets, and the sour memory of bombastic Moscow oratory but no help when it was needed. When the Palestinians put their faith in Arab armies, the sword had splintered and they had only the defeats of 1948 and 1956 and 1967. When they turned to the Arab states, they found vocal support but private treachery; no one made an effort to unite in the face of Zionist aggression, everyone urged over and over the need for patience, the

need for time. And yet all the patience, all the waiting
had been frittered away in six days in June. If in twenty
years, with massive injections of sophisticated weaponry,
with vast and highly visible development schemes, with
a new generation of technologically educated Arabs, with
for one brief moment a unity of purpose, the only result
was the catastrophic humiliation of June, then it was no
wonder that al Fatah held tight to the fedayeen war of
liberation as the true road. The Palestinians were not to
put their trust in princes but in themselves. For a just cause
could not be denied, a whole people could not be exiled;
therefore, there had to be a means to ultimate victory.
And the one long proffered, and the one remaining, was
the way of the fedayeen. Consequently it was the true
way, heretofore ignored by the proud, blind men in Cairo
and Amman and Baghdad.

According to the new gospel, once fedayeen action
had been initiated on a sufficiently broad scale, all of
Arab society would find dissensions melting, contradictions
fusing, and mass mobilization inevitable. This was, of
course, an act of faith; but it raised the significance of a
series of commando raids to the central fact of Arab life.
There could be no comfortable, proud life for any Arab
as long as the Palestine issue went unresolved. There
could be no unity in the Arab World without a Free
Palestine: Liberation of Palestine was the road to unity.
As the Palestine fedayeen movement went from strength
to strength so would the revitalized Arab masses, and
from these masses would evolve the united, revolutionary
army of the future which would apply the *coup de grâce*
to Zionism. A true people's army would be irresistible,
for people—not machines—win victories; spirit—and not
technology. This new spirit would spread out from the
battlefields of Palestine, crumbling the old ways, sapping
the old politics, undermining the old leaders and their
sterile panaceas. Naturally, as with all wars of national
liberation, this was to be a long process, although an

inevitable one; for by their operations in the Occupied Zone the fedayeen were creating the new Arab as well as the new Palestine.

The fedayeen strategy would not only harass the Israelis, cutting one by one the artificial roots of Zionism in the Middle East, but also day by day, operation by operation, mobilize the Arab masses. In the still distant future, when the Arab masses were ready to strike with the fedayeen, Israel, undermined by anxiety, uncertainty, and frustration, would collapse. Such a war of national liberation could not be limited by major-power intervention, East or West, and could not be crushed by the temporarily superior Israeli armed strength. If Israel were provoked to the point of massive retaliation or to the decision to occupy more Arab lands, the fedayeen would only gather more recruits to continue the struggle against a more extended, more vulnerable aggressor. Furthermore, the fedayeen strategy had more than tactical, military advantages over the old, conventional war programs in that the liquidation of Zionist society could only be achieved by a war of national liberation: "classical war may achieve a decisive military victory but it cannot liquidate a society in its entirety."[9] Only the Palestinian could be the vanguard of the struggle, and only through the armed struggle could the Palestinian become a full man.

> Violence will purify the individuals from venom, it will redeem the colonized from inferiority complex, it will return courage to the countryman.
>   Blazing our armed revolution inside the occupied territory is a healing medicine for all our people's diseases.[10]

The fedayeen way, and only the fedayeen way, would achieve all things, all the long-denied aspirations of the Arab World; unity, freedom, pride, and justice would be won in the hills of Samaria and the streets of Jerusalem.

The attraction of this apocalyptic vision of a heroic struggle for the Arab World in the months after the June War was undeniable. The conventional response of the conventional regimes held no charms. The élan, the charisma, the panache of the fedayeen flittering through the Arab World preaching just aggression, the battle of vengeance, the revolution of the moment gave hope even to the despondent. Men who had denied the al Fatah philosophy, root and branch, set about appropriating it for their own uses. Fedayeen movements multiplied like mice. Soon after the end of the June War, the Arab National Movement of George Habash sponsored a new group, the Popular Front for the Liberation of Palestine (PFLP). Previously the ANM had felt al Fatah parochial and that Arab unity was not to be found in mini-Palestinian nationalism; now Habash accepted the premise that unity lay through the Palestine gate. However, he and the PFLP insisted that the "Front" policy of al Fatah was mistaken, that the future Palestine must be defined in the terms of the Arab Nationalist Movement. Much the same was true for Palestinians committed to the ideas of the Syrian Ba'athists, who formed Sa'iqa. Others less ideologically motivated simply rushed into the fray creating "vanguards" and "fronts" and "commando" columns until nearly two score organizations existed, on paper at least. By early autumn, practically every national or ideological current in the Arab world had sponsored some sort of fedayeen organization. Some came together in fronts one month, only to hive off the next over an issue of principle or a clash of personalities. Even the discredited PLO did not fold up its tents but forced Shukairy to resign and embraced the fedayeen philosophy. On December 20, the Organization for the Liberation of Palestine called for a union of all fedayeen.

On January 20, thirteen groups, many little more than personal splinters, collected at a meeting in Cairo called by al Fatah. Only the PLO was not present. Refusing to be dominated by al Fatah, the PFLP withdrew, but the others agreed on a policy of joint action—"we believe only in guns." Even if unity within the fedayeen movement was as illusive as in the Arab World at large, the Palestinians made several points crystal clear. First, they were not simply interested in erasing the aggression of June. The United Nations resolution of November 22 calling for withdrawal was insufficient. The fedayeen were fighting for all of Palestine, not a makeshift compromise, not a *modus vivendi*, and most particularly not to pull Egyptian or Jordanian chestnuts out of the fire. On February 19, al Fatah announced that the fedayeen would allow no one and no regime to prevent operations. Such efforts had already been made. As early as September, Hussein had warned against terrorist attacks. Other regimes, Syria excepted, showed no more enthusiasm. Because of the growing popularity of the fedayeen, repressive measures had to be circumspectly applied; nevertheless, restrictions were applied, and as late as March Jordanian spokesmen in Amman publicly criticized fedayeen excesses. For the old regimes, the fedayeen—the new heroes—posed a difficult problem. Their wildly romanticized activities absorbed the attention of the Arab people, reducing the domestic demands for retribution and vengeance but at the same time greatly complicating and preventing any conventional solution, any diplomatic overtures. Their all-or-nothing philosophy, so congenial to the Arab mind, became once more the fashion. Since they could not achieve anything tangible, the Arab regimes were left with nothing: no Sinai, no West Bank, no Golan Heights. They could take no initiative without risking revolution. They could not renew the war and they could not tolerate existing conditions and they did not quite dare close down the fedayeen operations. Thus, even without unity the fedayeen had largely secured their first objective: the Arab Nation could not deny, even if it did not yet fully support, the Palestine dream.

To grasp the dream, the fedayeen continually sought unity, inevitably the first item on any Arab agenda. On March 20, 1968, the PLO, cleansed of Shukairy, al Fatah, and the PFLP—the big three—agreed to unify politically and militarily. Beyond agreement, little was forthcoming until the meeting of the Palestinian National Assembly on May 30. By then the PFLP had split over the arrest of George Habash and two other leaders by the Syrian regime. The Ba'athists, with some reason, regarded the ANM as subversive. Not until July did the National Assembly announce its intention to set up a coordinating council with military experts from each organization, but even then unity remained an aspiration. All the fedayeen movements continued to suffer internal strains. In August the PFLP barely avoided a Left–Right split, and the new commander of the PLA was arrested by his own officers and whisked off to detention in Damascus. There was another council in November, closer cooperation was pledged by al Fatah and PFLP; but there was no visible change. In the same month, another pro-Nasser group of the PFLP, under the leadership of Ahmed Jibril, split off to form the PFLP-General Command B, later in turn the parent of the Palestine Arab Organization under Colonel Ahmed Za'arur. In January 1969, at a Cairo meeting, Arafat and al Fatah took over the domination of the fedayeen movement. Arafat became chairman of the PLO Executive Committee, composed of four al Fatah men and seven others of various persuasions. The mercurial PFLP remained on the outside, as troublesome as when there had been a joint policy. On February 23, the PFLP split Left and Right, with Naref Hawatmeh leading off the pure Left to form the Democratic Popular Front (DPFLP). Habash, holding to the true way, soon sounded even more revolutionary than his Marxist competitor Hawatmeh.* Although Arafat

---

* The PFLP's troubles were by no means over with the defection of Hawatmeh, for two more groups split off, each retaining the parent title. Habash, however, has kept the core group together

and al Fatah gradually brought most of the fedayeen under one roof—the Palestine Armed Struggle Command was founded on April 2—Habash and the PFLP went their own way, not to return until ten fedayeen groups united briefly in Amman in February 1970 in response to restrictions imposed by Hussein. On May 7, the ten major fedayeen organizations, including the PFLP, agreed to participate in a new Central Committee, but not until June 9, during renewed fighting in Jordan, did the agreement come into effect. Even then the PFLP pursued an almost totally independent course, making it difficult for observers to discover how much control the new Central Committee actually exerted. Not only were the ideas of the PFLP difficult to control within a Front organization, but Habash also insisted on pursuing a military policy of spectacular coups, terror attacks, and airplane hijackings that did not fit in with al Fatah's guerrilla-strategy. Eventually the airline hijacking of the PFLP in September 1970 brought the wrath of the Jordanian Army down upon al Fatah and all the fedayeen, whether or not they disagreed with Habash's strategy.

Although the Armed Struggle Command and, later, the Central Committee presented a façade of unity, essentially the various organizations retained considerable independence. In the case of the PLA, Arafat's control of the PLO made cooperation, even integration of effort, feasible; but Sa'iqa, DPFLP, and the others maintained their identity. Except for the PFLP and the possible exception of the Ba'athist Sa'iqa, all the fedayeen movements inside or outside the al Fatah camp were tiny and their chances of initiating independent—i.e., harmful—action small. Often the movements existed so that the host country could

---

despite the overt or latent opposition of practically every government or party in the Arab World. It is reasonable to assume that without the fedayeen aura of immunity most of the leadership of the Arab National Movement would find themselves in jail as dangerous, self-proclaimed revolutionaries.

control the potentially subversive fedayeen, favoring its own and excluding competitors. Thus there was a Cairo-based Arab Sinai Organization, the Iraqi-backed Arab Liberation Front, and, of course, the prototype, Sa'iqa. For a time there had been groups funded, if not organized, by the conservative monarchies, but gradually Kuwait, Saudi Arabia, Libya, and the oil sheiks gave up their puppets and supported the larger groups. Given the bitter ideological divisions, the interference of the various regimes, the old feuds, and the intense personal ambitions interacting on the fedayeen scene, the central position of Arafat and the Armed Struggle Command was a considerable accomplishment. Yet the separate existence of so many groups, the wildly independent tactics of the PFLP, and the willingness of some Palestinians to place the charms of the Iraqi Ba'athist ideology or the Arab National Movement before Palestinian unity gave scant support to the theory that fedayeen action alone would prohibit the old separatist mistakes of the past.

The tendency of the fedayeen leaders was to brush aside the little, domestic divisions and to point to the victories on the field of battle. According to al Fatah, the First Stage after the June War had been one of organization and preparation; then in September, strikes across the border began again. Inside the Occupied Zone, new networks were set up to replace those shattered during the June War. On March 21, the Second Stage started, with a heavy Israeli raid on the village of Karameh. With considerably less indirection and elegance than they normally employed, the Israelis sent in an armored brigade to wipe out the Karameh base. Caught in the village, the fedayeen instead of running stayed and fought. As the battle proceeded house by house, with the Israelis methodically wiping out Arab resistance, the Jordanian Army lost patience and in violation of orders opened heavy artillery fire on the Israeli columns. The result of the long battle was that the Israelis, as they had intended, wiped out Karameh, killed

170 fedayeen, and withdrew across the border. Their casualties, however, were far heavier than the Israeli Army likes to take, in this case approximately one per cent of the attacking force. For al Fatah, however, Karameh was a glowing victory. The fedayeen had stood and fought, and fought well; the Israelis had been hurt, and had shown that they were not immortal and indestructible:

> The Jordanian Army and the Popular Resistance in Karameh have, beyond any doubt, shattered the "invincibility" of the Israeli forces . . . a myth so naively widespread in and out of Israel.[11]

The Arabs, with their vast populations, could absorb huge losses in order to inflict far smaller ones on the Israelis—and there in Karameh were the burned-out Israeli armored cars, and there in the Israeli papers were questions as to whether the raid had been worth the cost. After Karameh everything seemed changed. Despite the vast publicity given to al Fatah and the deep concern in the Arab capitals, the organization had until Karameh controlled only a few hundred trained fedayeen. After Karameh recruits flooded Amman headquarters. Funds poured in, forcing the fedayeen to hire accountants to handle the flow. Weapons, hospital equipment, reporters, and well-wishers descended on Amman. The stage of confrontation, initiated at Karameh, produced intense enthusiasm not only in the Middle East but within al Fatah.

While hit-and-run attacks across the border continued, al Fatah continually insisted that pitched battles were regularly being fought between the fedayeen and Israeli security forces. There were occasional terror-bomb attacks within Israel, a technique espoused more by the PFLP than by al Fatah; but the main thrust of the campaign was the commando confrontation. The Third Stage, according to al Fatah, began on May 2 when a three-pronged, ninety-two-man al Fatah column seized the town of El Hamma in the Golan Heights for three hours. The Armed Struggle

Command communiqué claimed the destruction of nine Israeli military posts, a Patton tank, five half-tracks, the killing and wounding of scores of enemy soldiers, and the destruction of Israeli military headquarters, twenty-eight houses, a hotel, and a swimming pool. The Israelis admitted the occupation of El Hamma but indicated casualties and damage were considerably less than al Fatah claimed. In point of fact, the Third Stage showed little significant difference from any of the other stages. The fedayeen continued, as they always had, to attempt to penetrate the Israeli border defenses, plant mines or set up ambushes, and then withdraw into Jordan or Lebanon. Secondly and almost daily, the fedayeen moved up to the border and unleashed a rocket or mortar attack, withdrawing before retaliatory Israeli fire zeroed in. Finally, extensive efforts were made to establish al Fatah cells on the West Bank and in the Gaza Strip to relay intelligence and carry out sabotage attacks, most of which took the form of indiscriminate grenade tossing. The Armed Struggle Command generally acknowledged that operations originating within the Occupied Zone had remained at a low level, although there had been spectacular results such as the rocket attack on Jerusalem. Al Fatah claimed that the failure of large-scale armed resistance within the Occupied Zone was an intentional tactic rather than the result of incapacity. The fedayeen wanted to be able to orchestrate the internal resistance with the actions of guerrillas when the time became ripe. By the end of 1969, al Fatah and the Armed Struggle Command expressed considerable satisfaction with the course of the campaign. They admitted losing a few hundred fedayeen, the exposure of several resistance organizations, and the growing effectiveness of Israeli counteroperations, but claimed that they had inflicted immense losses on the Israeli Army, many, many times their own losses. Arafat and the Armed Struggle felt that the war of national liberation was going well, if not spectacularly well.

If al Fatah and the others stuck rather steadfastly to guerrilla-war, the PFLP did not. With limited manpower and tight finances, the PFLP chose the path of terror rather than attrition. On July 23, 1968, three PFLP men hijacked an El Al airliner between Rome and Israel and forced the pilot to fly to Algiers. On December 26, the PFLP attacked an El Al airliner on the ground at Athens with automatic rifle fire and grenades. This attack so outraged the Israelis that they descended on Beirut airport on December 28 and demolished thirteen planes worth fifty-six million dollars. On February 18, 1969, the PFLP attacked an El Al plane on the ground at Zurich. Three days later, PFLP headquarters in Amman claimed credit for a bomb attack in a Jerusalem supermarket which killed two people and wounded nine. On March 6, twenty-nine people were wounded in a bomb explosion in the cafeteria of Hebrew University. On May 25, the British Consulate in Jerusalem was bombed.

The PFLP was by no means intimidated by the howls of outraged indignation not only from Israel but from the international press and more "mature" Arab spokesmen. On August 29, a TWA Boeing flying from Athens to Israel was diverted to Damascus.

The PFLP felt that each of these coups further lessened the Israeli sense of power and security—not even in the air was an Israeli safe, and even the American imperialists of TWA faced retribution. There was much to be said for the hijackings, despite orthodox Arab criticism; for a great many Arabs apparently felt as did the PFLP that the operations were spectacular successes provoking the Israelis to self-defeating retaliation, as in the Beirut raid. Consequently, the PFLP continued the strikes against the airways: attacks on El Al offices in Brussels and Athens, firing on El Al passengers in the Munich airport, and a second, unsuccessful strike in Zurich. Emulating the PFLP, the tiny Popular Struggle Front was credited with a bomb attack on an El Al airliner in Athens in February and the hijacking of an Olympic Airlines plane in July so that the passengers could be used to win the freedom of fedayeen being held in Greece. No one wanted the responsibility for the destruction in the air of a Swissair jetliner over Austria en route to Israel, with the loss of forty-seven lives. The most recent and greatest PFLP spectacular was the almost simultaneous hijacking and subsequent destruction of four airliners in September 1970. This coup provoked more than simply criticism and moral outrage: the Jordanian Army intervened even before the completion of the bargaining for the release of fedayeen prisoners in Europe and Israel. Some other of the PFLP coups to the uninitiated seemed not so much ruthless as almost mindless in their inanity. The most notorious was the sabotage of the Aramco Tapline where it crosses the Golan Heights, which resulted in blocking 440,000 barrels a day of Saudi Arabian oil and the loss of transit fees to Jordan, Syria, and Lebanon—all at no cost to the Israelis, previously tolerant of the existence of the pipeline in their Occupied Zone, and possibly to the advantage of their own Iran–Europe oil trade. The PFLP, however, has as little time for the oil regimes as it does for the Israelis. The organization has managed a far greater impact in the war of national liberation than its small size would have indicated. Even more than al Fatah, the PFLP has no time for the existing regimes and no compunction about bringing down a massive retaliation on its head. Even full-scale war or an Israeli invasion would suit PFLP, for without responsibility they have been without restraint. What the PFLP provoked in September was a serious effort by Jordan to curb all the fedayeen, even at the risk of open war. And there has followed more or less open war, interrupted by truces and peace missions, ever since, as the Jordanian Army has sought to crush the Palestinian state-within-a-state.

Despite the intra-Arab turmoil, to the Arabs in general and to most Palestinians the war of national liberation has gone not only well but spectacularly well. The Israelis have suffered heavy casualties, so heavy that they have hidden the death tolls in automobile fatality statistics. Israeli prestige has been as shattered as has El Al airlines. Even the imperialist West has been brought to heel by the PFLP tactics. Israel is in a state of siege and it is only a matter of time, albeit a long time, before the false, plaster ideology of Zionism cracks.

> The morale of our enemy is falling down every day, his economy is perplexed, immigration is almost at a standstill and his main force is tied down. . . .
>   He is becoming increasingly contradictory and with no poise, in spite of the victorious and all-powerful faces he is putting up to cover up for an inherent weakness known only to usurpers who like to look respectable and act naturally.[12]

In the meanwhile, even if the military victories have not been quite as substantial as the glowing battle communiqués indicate, the fedayeen can certainly claim other undeniable successes. First and foremost, the Palestinian entity has been saved. The Palestine issue is alive and well. Palestinians are for the first time not the odd-man-out in the Arab Nation but the central heroes. "On the National level, we have regained our rightful place in the community of Arab peoples as the vanguard working for a dignified Arab future."[13] Not only have the Palestinians taken over the spiritual leadership of the Arab World but the armed struggle has transformed and purified their own character, with "armed revolution" being the promised "healing medicine."

> Our people have been able to throw away the yoke of bondage and break away from their chains. They are regaining their self-confidence and self-respect and taking their fate into their own hands. The vision of regained homeland has become real and a daily in-

spiration. The solidarity of our people after years of decadence and disintegration is being consolidated and strengthened.[14]

This transformation has been recognized not only in the Arab World but further abroad, as for the first time the Palestinians "have made a break-through in the propaganda siege imposed by Zionism upon the Palestine question."[15] In the West, al Fatah has become the new hero of the New Left and for the first time young, articulate Western spokesmen speak for the Arab cause in the place of dubious oil companies and self-interested big-power strategists. To the East, Soviet Russia permitted an Arafat visit and even blessed the fedayeen organization—Ansar ("Partisans")—formed by the illegal, Moscow-oriented, Communist parties of Lebanon, Syria, Iraq, and Jordan. As foreseen years before by Arafat and his little band, the armed struggle has created a Palestine entity, has transformed the Palestinian people, and has written Palestine into the conscience of at least part of the world.

Also the fedayeen popularity and influence apparently had given Arafat and the rest very close to a veto power over the actions of the Arab nations on the Palestine issue. Little by little the overt opposition of Hussein and Nasser had to be cloaked in kind words. Under pressure Hussein shifted out his "repressive" politicians, announced that all Arabs were fedayeen, and watched as al Fatah set up a state within a state. Every Israeli retaliation raid rebounded to fedayeen advantage. Every glowing battle communiqué underlined the frustration and helplessness of the regular Arab armies to reverse the "set-back" of June. In Cairo in January 1969, even Nasser—or particularly Nasser—lavished praise on the fedayeen, "at whose disposal the UAR unconditionally places all its resources." In Libya and the Sudan, coups have brought new regimes deeply dedicated to the Palestinian cause. At the Arab summit at Rabat, Arafat sat not as a supplicant but as an equal. Even

the Saudi Grand Mufti, little versed in revolutionary politics or wars of national liberation, issued a *fatwa* allowing
part of the *zaka* to be paid to fedayeen. In Lebanon in
April 1969, when the government tried to hold down commando activity, the streets of Beirut suddenly boiled with
demonstrators, mobs of Palestinians, leftists, students, la-
borers, and school teachers. The regime barely scraped
through April only to fall into the same pit in October.
Once more only skilled negotiations, a little discreet use of
force, good luck, and the auspices of Nasser kept civil war
at bay. Hussein, too, came close to the brink in February
1970, when fighting broke out between his army and the
fedayeen. Again a compromise treaty was negotiated. Then
in June a minor incident sparked off another round of fighting that may have cost the fedayeen more men than they
have lost to the Israelis since 1965, but it seemed to reveal
that Hussein could not risk full repression. In September,
as a result of the strains caused by the multiple hijackings,
the mini-civil war began in Jordan; but as yet it is uncertain
if this has evolved into a protracted showdown between
Hussein and the fedayeen that neither "truce" nor "agreement" can patch up. Both Syria and Iraq have taken the
most stringent precautions to keep "their" fedayeen under
control in order to prevent the same unwanted confrontation. While there is no love lost, to be mild, between the
fedayeen and the old regimes, the official fedayeen policy
remains that there is not, now, any conflict of interest as
long as guerrilla-operations are permitted. There may,
almost certainly, be a conflict of interest, particularly if
any Arab states indicate a willingness to accept a less than
total solution to the Palestine problem. But the fedayeen
hope that, by then, the Arab masses will have been mobilized and that it will be possible to shrug the old regimes
off into oblivion as relics of a disgraceful past. Thus, when
Egypt and Jordan accepted the American-proposed ninety-
day cease-fire, the fedayeen broadcast pleas, over the heads
of Nasser and Hussein, urged the masses to continue their

support of the fedayeen. At the moment, however, al Fatah at least does not seek a test of strength; but the Palestinians know there is strength on their side and that the Palestinian issue cannot be settled without reference to the Palestinians. And this, too, is a great accomplishment. So great that just possibly—as an interim stage—al Fatah could even consider a less than complete Palestine: a temporary compromise accepted from a position of spiritual strength.

From the Israeli side of the hill, the "accomplishments" of the fedayeen seem quite different. The Israelis have great difficulty in recognizing, even as a caricature of reality, the fedayeen communiqués and analyses. What seem so real and obvious to the Palestinians often appear to Israeli eyes the baleful dreams of desperate men who have withdrawn from the real world into a fantasy land. For Israel the "stages" of the "War of National Liberation" do not exist; the Arab victories on the battlefield are largely the figments of overheated imaginations, the Nazi-Zionist-Imperialist conspiracy is the old Arab Devil Theory —all our troubles have been caused by the British or the CIA or someone—burnished by lies and exaggerations. Obviously the PFLP has attacked El Al planes, the fedayeen of al Fatah do creep across the border, grenades are thrown in Gaza and Hebron, and Israelis are dead and the Arab governments intimidated.

Yet on any rational scale, the fedayeen war of national liberation hardly merits serious military consideration. Fedayeen operations have been poorly planned, poorly executed, and subsequently inflated into "confrontations" unrecognizable to the Israeli participants. Other "victorious and highly successful" fedayeen attacks have remained invisible, making it difficult for Israel to refute a nonevent: nonexistent assassination attempts on Prime Minister Eshkol and General Dayan, an attack on the Independence Day military parade in Jerusalem that no one saw, the destruction of General Rabin's garage where one does not exist, and the regular loss of dozens of Israeli soldiers no one has missed.* And all the new Arab theories—the incredible identification of Israel and Nazi Germany, the glib denial of Zionism as a real ideology, the wild exaggerations of the potential of a war of national liberation when, to the Israelis, there is no nation to be liberated—appear twisted meanderings of bitter minds.

For Israel, the fedayeen campaign has in reality had specific stages. Until September 1967, all the heralded victories of the guerrillas came to nothing but highly irritating border incidents, never a threat to Israeli security and only a minor strain on the nerves of those involved. The escalating campaign revealed only an increase in the number of raids rather than any quantum leap in efficiency. The first stage of the Israeli response was to clear up the Arab resistance networks in the Gaza Strip and the West Bank. Here, with the benefits of long years of careful intelligence work and captured files, particularly of Jordanian security forces, very few fedayeen agents escaped the round-up. Secondly, the new Jordan River border was heavily patrolled and then protected with a barbed-wire fence and a variety of mechanical detection devices. Since total prohibition is almost impossible to achieve, the Israeli armed forces struck back at the fedayeen bases close to the border. After Karameh, admittedly not a highly successful operation, the guerrilla-bases had to be moved deeper into Jordan. Unwilling to become involved in another land operation, the Israeli Air Force took up the task of responding to infiltration by hitting the new bases. When the traditional psychological retaliation did not result in a noticeable lessening of incidents, tit-for-tat retaliation was discarded and the air force struck regularly at the guer-

* One of the most exotic of all fedayeen claims was that President Banda of Malawi had sent troops to aid Israel. Some of the claims may represent a combination of optimism, confused intelligence, and a nugget of fact. Our men are supposed to be there and this is the kind of thing they should be doing; therefore, we will claim credit.

rilla-bases and Jordanian military targets in a continuous
campaign of punishment. The center of operation remained the Jordanian front; then, in response to increasing
intrusions in the north, raids were also directed against
Lebanon and Syria. To some degree the Israelis have
discarded the theory that heavy retaliation will force the
host regimes to control the fedayeen and now concentrate
instead largely on a continuous air strike campaign to
erode Arab military capacity.

In summary, in Israeli eyes the greatest potential
danger and consequently the most glaring failure has been
in the occupied zones. Efforts to establish a real resistance
network in the West Bank and the Gaza Strip to act in
harmony with the cross-Jordan raids have not had impressive results. Despite the almost optimum theoretical
conditions in places like Gaza, the fedayeen have not been
able to build a permanent resistance network, to maintain
an escalating level of violence, nor to harness and use the
seething Arab resentment. Consequently, in the Arab
areas—the real and only base for a war of national liberation—the Israelis through their intelligence, first-rate
police work, intimidation, and retaliation have kept the
lid pretty well on. With each blown net, each arrest, the
prospects for effective Arab action in the future declines;
so that if Arab actions are consciously being held to a
minimum then the chance of widespread resistance declines through the present use of their obviously limited
assets in holding operations. Yet, despite the obvious attractions of West Bank resistance, the fedayeen movement has always stressed the guerrilla-column as the
key, rather than civil disobedience or random terror. For
the Palestinian it is the fedayeen in the hills with his
camouflage uniform, his AK-47, his hit-and-run tactics
who is the real hero.

There are very few fedayeen in the hills and there
never were many. Once the Israelis had cleaned up the
West Bank—and Gaza was too isolated to serve as a base—

it became increasingly difficult for fedayeen to find secure houses. They could, if they escaped detection, hide in caves or dugouts; but constant Israeli sweeps and intelligence leaks make it imperative that most, nearly all, operations be run in the course of one night, of two at the most. Even the swift raids across the Jordan have become more difficult since the Israelis systematically destroyed the guerrilla-bases near the river. Regular Israeli patrols, the fencing and electronic devices, close air support, excellent prior intelligence, and the nature of the terrain have made successful forays, or *any* forays, very difficult. Once a column does manage to penetrate the border, the chances of a counterambush are vastly higher than the chances of the fedayeen reaching their objectives. Attacks on secure and fortified areas can be little more than brief demonstrations of sound and fury. Ambushes can be kept up for only limited periods, and the placing of mines has had to be substituted. Even the sneak-over, fire-a-few-rockets and rush-back tactics often result in the same appalling casualties. Except for a few of the more rugged border operations, fedayeen raids are really an elaborate form of suicide. Intrusions attempting deep penetration have produced an almost unbroken string of small massacres. Increasingly, "operations" have had to be limited to night fire-fights from across the border or the placing of mines or rocket launchers after the most elaborate preparations by cells inside the Occupied Zones. None of this seems to deter fedayeen headquarters from trying again, from issuing elaborate battle communiqués, and, most significant of all, from clinging to the basic assumptions that tactics-as-strategy is an approach that is working and that the Israelis are losing in the field.

Putting aside what the fedayeen claim they are or are not doing, the results for Israel have still not been particularly satisfactory. Despite their appalling casualties, the fedayeen still attempt to cross the border. In the two years after the June War, Israel reported 468 fedayeen

border crossings, although in over 400 of these the feda
yeen penetrated only a little over a mile. Despite the
heavy repressive measures in the Gaza Strip and on the
West Bank, the fedayeen still manage to put together
sabotage networks. Even more distracting than the abor
tive resistance movement in the Occupied Zones is the
evidence that some of Israel's Arabs have joined the resistance. Essentially the Israelis have made border penetration
difficult, painful, and largely ineffectual—but not impossible. In the Occupied Zone they have used a variety
of repressive measures to minimize Arab resistance, but
they have not eliminated it. The air strikes into Jordan
and Lebanon have made Arab shelling operations more
costly and have complicated fedayeen operations, but have
ended neither. The cost to Israel in time, effort, funds, and
blood has been considerable, but—given all—not excessive. By January 1970, the total cost in Israeli lives, the
most important commodity of all, due to fedayeen activity
including shelling has been given as 138 soldiers killed,
575 wounded, and 73 civilians killed, 523 wounded. The
total was less than the losses from the war of attrition along
the Suez Canal (244 killed and 669 wounded) but still
an unpleasant and unwanted reminder that not all of the
wild fedayeen claims are without substance. During 1970
the Israelis admitted another 182 Israeli soldiers killed and
639 wounded, but again most as a result of military and
not fedayeen operation. The Israelis feel, however, that
the situation is largely in hand, that militarily the fedayeen
have failed and are failing, whatever their political successes in the Arab World. To maintain their security and
their frontiers, the Israelis contend they are willing to live
with the casualty lists just as they are willing to live with
the toll of traffic deaths. In time—this year, next year,
the year after—the Palestinian Arabs will recognize that
"the war of national liberation" has been, is, and will be
a fruitless pursuit and the fedayeen will go away.

For a small country, mindful of the value of each life,

this is an unpleasant decision. The losses are painful; but they are not clear and present to the state. Israel is, in fact, more secure than ever before. Given the hundreds of thousands of Arabs under Israeli military occupation, particularly those in the wretchedly crowded Gaza Strip, there has still been no effective civilian resistance movement, no real underground, no indication of a collapse of control. Given the bombastic threats and claims from the Amman headquarters of the fedayeen organizations, the reports of thousands upon thousands of armed guerrillas hovering on the borders, there has still been almost no serious penetration of the border, no evidence of Israeli retrenching or moving out of the new kibbutzim— much less the old settlements—and no serious fighting, only skirmishes. By January 1971, the Israelis claimed to have killed 1,828 fedayeen, and several thousand other Arabs have been arrested, imprisoned, or interned inside Israel. The relative losses of both sides have been small, the damage done slight, the level of the war of national liberation very low indeed. The real threat to Israel remains: Russia-and-Egypt, first; the other Arab states, second; international intervention, third; and the fedayeen, a very bad fourth. The very best that can be said is that the fedayeen military successes have been mediocre, simply no threat to Israel, while an effective resistance campaign would have posed most serious problems.

The fedayeen are aware of the Israeli claims that the "war of national liberation" has been a series of military failures, pocked by ineffectual terrorism and the odd propaganda coup. In Amman, however, Zionist "propaganda," Zionist "evasions," Zionist "lies" have had little effect on the endemic optimism. Fedayeen headquarters *know* that Israel has been painfully mauled, that, whatever pro-Zionist and Western journalists say, their war of attrition bleeds Israel. There is an awesome gap between the fedayeen communiqués, issued with absolute, unyielding conviction, and what independent observers can determine. The vast number of Israelis claimed as killed or wounded boggles the imagination. Most of the fedayeen believe implicitly in the Armed Struggle Command's casualty figures—once specific, now more general—even when it is clear that no one could possibly have reported from the operation site.* The PFLP, for example, remains absolutely convinced that their fedayeen inflict twenty casualties for one loss. And neither logic, sweet reasonableness, nor independent evidence can sway the leadership. The totals claimed for all the fedayeen would indicate a level of success many times that of any previous guerrilla-operation and far greater than could be covered up by a guileful Israel.† The magnitude of exaggeration is so great that the whole fedayeen movement becomes suspect. Yet in their communiqués, in private conversation, in interviews and on platforms, the fedayeen unvaryingly and without qualification maintain that not only are their figures accurate but that they are winning the war of attrition. While it might be understandable to the Western mind that a man can hold faith in a future yet unrevealed despite the opposing odds, the inability of the fedayeen to grasp the present reality passeth all understanding. The fantasy world of thousands upon thousands of dead Is-

* For a considerable length of time specific casualty figures were given, but eventually the fedayeen spokesmen under attack even from their advocates in the Arab press reluctantly began announcing only "serious" Israeli losses. To everyone—but the fedayeen leadership—it had long been obvious that the numbers game was doing untold harm; but the fedayeen themselves *believed,* and could not then and do not now understand why their communiqués were so regularly discounted.

† One of the more rational fedayeen advisers out of Beirut has estimated that the fedayeen have claimed to have destroyed very nearly the recognized strength of the Israeli Army. The need to impress potential supporters has been one of the reasons for the "communiqué campaign" between various groups, but most largely believe their own estimates. Even the contention that casualty figures are hidden in traffic deaths by the Israelis would require highway mayhem far beyond the very considerable competence of the Israeli driver.

raelis and the invisible victories and mysterious battles that form the core of the fedayeen life are far beyond rational logic. The fedayeen, like other Arabs before him, sees clearly things denied less committed eyes. If, then, the casualty figures are imaginary, and there is every evidence they are, then a shadow is thrown over all the other optimistic Palestinian predictions and positions. Instead of closely reasoned analysis and scientific interpretation, much of fedayeen explanation begins to resemble wish fulfillment, creating a world that never was.

In fact, the whole vision of the Palestinians is self-centered and self-controlled. They have transformed the world into the image they so devoutly desire. Not only is it just that the power of Israel is an illusion, its citizens fragile papier-mâché tigers, but also that in the larger Arab World Palestine occupies the central position. That Palestine is not now and that it has not in the past been the first priority of the Arab leaders should be self-evident. The maneuvering and hedging in the Arab capitals, the promises without substance, the betrayals and lies are common currency among Palestinians. Each new savior has proven faulty, each new movement has degenerated into sinecures for incumbents. If Palestine is not the center of the conventional Arab World, then it must be the center of the "real" Arab World. With no more heroes (Nasser was as hopeless as is Faisal), no more valid ideologies (the Ba'athists are as unreliable as are the Monarchists), the Palestinians have placed their faith in the strategic depth of the mystical masses, who will turn from their narrow ways and frugal poverty to help save sacred Palestine. It is not the dry, upper crust of the Arab World that will bring salvation but the rich, seething masses who will crush Zionism. This dream at least does have supporting evidence. The growing enthusiasm for the fedayeen cause can be heard not only in the mouths of the new rulers in the Sudan or Southern Yemen or Libya but in the gossip of the marketplace. That the fedayeen are the new Arab heroes is obvious, but the Arabs have felt strongly about other heroes without sacrificing excessively. Even if the Arab masses are in the process of mobilization, whatever that may mean, very little thought has been given to the means by which the masses might be applied to the Palestinian problem. Are the masses to be a new army, untrained and unequipped, rushing to battle with only justice as a weapon? Are the masses to create new regimes different in kind so that victory without preparation can be seized? What does it mean for Palestine to be the central concern of the masses?

It is not in their articles of faith, in their views of the "brittle" Israel or the militant masses, that the Palestinians' grasp of reality is the most feeble, for there proof lies in the future; it is in their elaborate evasion of the present. That Israel is objectively stronger, controls more territory, has not collapsed under attrition, answers provocation by massive retaliation has to be interpreted away as a virtue along with the misery of the new refugees, the ambivalence or open opposition of the Arab governments, the confusion and schism within the movements. Faith says that victory in a just cause—"the people's inevitable triumph"[16]—is assured, so that all present failings are at worst the building blocks of the future. Because it has been so predicted, Israel must be increasingly unstable, immigration must be declining, the economy must be weaker, the tourists fewer, agriculture disrupted, the contradictions in its society widening.

The fedayeen continue to insist on their vision, adjusting and altering as reality intrudes. They contend that Israel cannot suffer the exaggerated losses they inflict, cannot stand the drain, cannot compensate for the dead. Buttressed only by the illusions of Zionists, the Israelis will quit. Time, once an Israeli asset, is now one for the fedayeen. Given the history of Zionism, the history of Israel, this must be more than an article of faith. The great failing of the Arabs is simply that, as in the past, their analysis of the nature of their enemy is hopelessly inaccurate. The Zionists dug into the Promised Land, watered with the blood of the long war for survival, under the shadow of the holocaust, do not feel and will not act as the transient, misguided, alien colonists the Palestinians insist on describing. Israel may be "artificial," but how much more so is the heralded Free Palestine, an aspiration and not a reality. And whether or not Israel is "artificial" by Arab definition, the Israelis have given every indication, over twenty years and in three wars, that their artificiality is awesomely effective on the field of battle.

The Palestinians have followed too much the devices and desires of their own hearts, have out of their desperate humiliation and need created a new "reality." Scathing in their indictment of the past, they have offered their people a fresh vision but repeated the old error of shaping the world to their own image. There is to be unity and yet there is not. Dozens of movements seethe and split over minor heresy and narrow ambition. Arabs shoot each other in the streets of Beirut and Tripoli. The real enemy is Hussein or Nasser. There is civil war in Jordan always, always the road to Arab unity seems to lead first to the door of civil war. There are glorious victories in the field as the invincible fedayeen sweep from one brilliant confrontation to another. Yet no one else can see the heaps of Israeli corpses, the shattered Israeli jets, the panic-stricken Israeli masses. The Arab masses are mobilized but nowhere to be found. Israel is destroyed but is not. The Arab Nation goes from strength to strength and Israeli jets circle over Damascus and Amman. The world, East and West, clamors for the Palestinian cause, for justice, decency, and honesty, and then as usual tends its own distant garden. And once more and always, the cause of failure, the elusiveness of victory, is to be found elsewhere: in plots and betrayals, in international collusion and machinations, in others' egoism and others' failings. The new men have led their people far down the garden path, vaulting over imaginary barricades and throwing open invisible doors. At the end, as always, the way lies barred by the adamant, military might of a united and dedicated Israel. The realization that the only real progress of the *jihad* has been in the minds of the Arab and not on the battlefield may prove an awesome awakening. So far, the war of national liberation has followed the pattern of the classical Arab *rassia*: a great mock battle, sound and fury, roiling clouds of dust, the roll of drums, the rare clash of swords, the horses turning and prancing under the swirling black and green banners, howls of exaltation, honor satisfied, glory gained, and no one the poorer. The Israelis play a different game, march to a different drummer. Not for them the symbols of success but the hard, cold sinews of power. Once the dust settles and sound and fury fade, the Palestinians may, most assuredly will, find dug in opposite them on the hills of Samaria and the slopes of Golan the same stern, unchanging, perhaps unchangeable, fact of brute Israeli power—hard, cunning, adamant, flexible in diplomacy, defiant in war, magnanimous never. Then, in desperation again, the Palestinians may turn on themselves or on the other Arabs or on an enemy that can be taken by storm and oratory rather than face the ruins of this last, most seductive illusion of all—the inevitable victory of an undeniably just cause.

CASE STUDY THREE

Don Quixote and El Cid: Che Guevara in Bolivia

To risk all means that, having risen
in the mountains, the fighters must wage
a war to the death, *a war that does not admit*
of truces, retreats, or compromises.
To conquer is to accept as a matter of principle
that life, for the revolutionary,
is not the supreme good.

—RÉGIS DEBRAY

ON NOVEMBER 7, 1966, Che Guevara arrived at the Calamine House near the Río Ñancahuazú in southeastern
Bolivia to take personal command of the first guerrilla-
foco—the mother cell—which was to breed another Vietnam in the cordillera of the Andes. He arrived trailing
clouds of excitement and contention, with fame as a halo
and a name on the tips of many alien tongues. Few small
wars would ever start with such a big name. To the hard-
line imperialists, to the schismatic revolutionary Left, to
the naïve, the impressionable, and—most of all—to his
old and faithful comrades of the Sierra Maestra he was—
then in Bolivia, as he had been in Cuba—Che: the embodiment of permanent revolution, a dedicated and ruthless practitioner of war, a military thinker linked with Mao
and Giap, a comrade without fear and without reproach.
To the hard-faced realists in Moscow and Havana, he was
a failure, an embarrassing and clumsy symbol who could
not be discarded gracefully. To them, his ideas on revolution were infantile romanticism. His military capacities
had proven minimal and his guerrilla-program an un-

relieved litany of failure. As a revolutionary planner and administrator he had been an unalloyed disaster. His industrialization policy had been revised and his presence in Cuba only complicated the new direction. Guevara's allies in Bolivia may have neither known nor cared for this appraisal. But Guevara did—for he acepted the indictment. And this is vital to an understanding of his final and most complete debacle of all: the Bolivian campaign.

Guevara had thrown himself once more into revolutionary action to expurgate his sins, to resurrect, despite the evidence, his theory on revolutionary war, to hone his strategy into tactics and his own life to a keen and final point, to succeed on his own discredited terms or fail. Success, always a chimera, was never more distant, for without a revolutionary miracle Guevara—knowingly or unknowingly—had written his own ground rules in such a way as almost to guarantee failure. He was playing open-ended Russian roulette, and in time, unless someone else changed the rules, the end was inevitable.

The last adventure had really begun in the middle of March the previous year in Havana, when Guevara returned from a three-months' world tour. After a grueling forty-hour conference with Fidel Castro, Guevara had become convinced that his continued participation in the Cuban Revolution was impossible: his presence distracted, his politics confused, his contribution was no longer needed. No sleight of hand could cover the ruins of Cuba's economy, largely a result of Guevara's inexperience coupled with excessive zeal. Nor could the increasing irritation of Moscow with Guevara's criticism of the Soviets as Marxian Revisionists be papered over any longer. Castro's old and exceedingly loyal comrade Che was doing more harm than good. Great as a gunman in the Sierra Maestra, Che—like so many old gunmen—had outlived his time; however, unlike so many other old revolutionary gunmen, Che was to be allowed to fade away. Guevara, apparently shattered, went into seclusion from March 20 until late July, an isolation so total that he did not even know his mother had died.

Once he had recovered from the trauma of expulsion, Guevara sought, with Castro's blessing, an acceptable revolutionary vocation. The obvious avenue for a graceful exit was the path of world revolution, which would remove him from the Cuban scene but not the camp of world revolution. Even before the ultimate "Marxist" nature of the Cuban Revolution had become apparent, the Castro regime had become deeply involved in exporting the Sierra Maestra experience. Essentially, the first steps had been to encourage potential revolutionaries—"The Revolution Is Not Limited to Cuba"[1]—but, as time passed, the degree of Cuban involvement deepened as the need for a friendly Latin American frontier to break Cuba's growing isolation grew. But the breeding of another Cuba had proven more difficult than had been anticipated.

On April 18, 1959, an expedition led by Pedro Albizu Campos had landed in Panama. Albizu held on for only a few hours. On May 28, a new guerrilla-*foco* opened in Nicaragua. After a few months of lessening activity, it collapsed. On June 14, two landings were made in the Dominican Republic. The prospective guerrillas were wiped out within a few hours. On August 14, a landing was made in Haiti. Within days the revolutionaries were eliminated. During 1959 and 1960, efforts at internal subversion rather than overt intervention bore few useful results. On December 8, 1960, for example, the Cuban ambassador was expelled from Bolivia—the one South American country with a valid social revolution. The following year a Cuban-Peronist plot was revealed in Argentina. Ultimately, Cuba was expelled from OAS in January 1962. Guevara had in no way been disheartened either by the isolation from Latin American orthodoxy or the recurrent failure of the plots and rebellions. He had by then developed his own theory of revolution, based largely on the Cuban experience and partly on revelation.

Essentially the Cuban Revolution had been similar to a typical *pronunciamiento,* which entails the proclamation of the rebels' demands and then a pause while—in theory—the opposition coalesces, the government falters, and then with a minimum of fighting the control center falls to the rebels. Castro's second *pronunciamiento,* quite different from the coup or a war of national liberation, obviously failed. The naïve and inexperienced Cubans landed from the *Granma* and stumbled into Batista's army. In the first clash, the rebels were decimated. The fifteen survivors of the first battle fled into the mountains and, by necessity, began a war of attrition. Guerrilla by default, militarily impotent, Castro did begin to coalesce the widespread opposition to Batista. He neutralized potential United States opposition, tranquilized the middle class and much of the wealthy, corrupted Batista's army and benefitted from the terror and sabotage in the cities with his slowly expanding columns in the hills. At the end of December 1958, Batista, with his support crumbling visibly, fled the country. The *barbudos* came down out of the hills into Havana. They were only five hundred, and Batista had once commanded fifteen thousand men.

In the Cuban crucible Guevara felt that three alterations in the mechanisms of Latin American revolutionary theory had been revealed.

1. The people's forces can win a war against the regular army;
2. It is not necessary to wait until all conditions are favorable to start a revolution; the insurrection itself can bring about those conditions;
3. In the underdeveloped nations of America, the basic field of action for armed struggle must be the countryside.[2]

The first radical alteration was hardly radical, although the defeat of a regular army by "the people's forces" was hardly the normal form of unconstitutional change in

Latin America. Cuba itself had two long experiences with "people's forces" in the nineteenth century. At this stage, in any case, Guevara did not clearly define what he meant by the people's forces, although his third premise implies that they would largely be peasants. In time, this became axiomatic; the Cuban experience had revealed to Guevara the power of the peasant. It had been the eventual conversion of the local peasants that had made possible the growth and ultimate success of Castro's fifteen isolated young men. The second proposition simply underlined the apparent hopelessness of the Castro attempt, the desperation of the period of isolation in the mountains, the enormous odds against success. Any objective, pragmatic analysis of Castro's chances, before or after the first disastrous battle, would have quite reasonably advised the rebels to wait for more favorable conditions, to hesitate before so adamant a foe, to consider the futility of the previous attempt on the Moncanda Barracks on July 26, 1953. Guevara knew, however, from his own experience that a revolution generates its own momentum, that, once the people have been won over, the odds have shifted—no matter how desperate the situation may seem to "objective" observers. Certainly, he admitted the possibility of failure—the small early mother cell was very vulnerable and even Castro had failed at Moncanda—and that certain Cuban conditions, especially Castro, were unique; but with some adjustments there was no reason why the Cuban formula could not be applied throughout Latin America.

There were obviously ample reasons not at first apparent. The efforts of 1959–61 aborted, often early on. More carefully considered guerrilla action in Guatemala and Venezuela foundered, and in Peru collapsed. A few guerrilla movements struggled on or revived under other leadership. Most disappeared or remained so isolated from both the people and reality that they posed no threat. During this period, Guevara was a recognized prophet as a result of his little book *La Guerra de Guerrillas,* the obvious success of the Cuban campaign, and his wide-ranging tours to the sites and symbols of world revolution: Mao and Moscow, Ben Bella and Cairo, Tito and Accra. The rapid shuffle of Cuba through democratic liberalism into the socialist camp—the consummation of the revolution which only Guevara and Raúl Castro had so devoutly desired from the very first—brought adulation of Guevara as well as aid to Castro. Cuba along with China and Algeria and then Vietnam, became a classic liberation struggle, to be not only admired but emulated. Yet the strategy of Cuba persisted in failing on the Latin American field of battle. The techniques foundered in the most brutal banana republics and before the most incompetent Caribbean dictators. The vast misery, the seething dissatisfaction, the high level of frustration, the potential insurrection in South America could not somehow be exploited. That the formula had not worked was for Guevara immaterial. He continued to elaborate the lessons of the past in speeches at international conferences, in interviews with sympathetic journalists, and in the endless private conversations with the leaders of the Third World.

Basically, as many of Guevara's old friends knew, and probably Castro as well, the Cuban Revolution had been misinterpreted. As is often the case, the guerrillas had not won a revolutionary war—they had failed to lose. They had persisted, allowing full scope for the brutality and inefficiency of Batista to be revealed. Castro's use of publicity, particularly in the United States, had been superb. The alliance with the educated middle class, the organization of youthful idealism, the elaborate network of support and sabotage in the cities had been masterfully used to exploit the guerrilla menace in the hills. The peasants—and the educated guerrillas—had played a major part but hardly the sole part. The complexities of Cuban politics had escaped a Guevara isolated in the guerrilla milieu, and the very special aspirations of the peasants of the Sierra

Maestra had been generalized into a universal axiom. What was in reality a most complicated revolution was simplified and revealed in traditionally clumsy Marxist analysis. The "people's forces" contained a great many people not visible from the Sierra Maestra; the number of conditions favorable to the little band in the hills was far greater than their desperate day-to-day existence indicated; and the basic field of action was not so much in the mountains as in Batista's response to his eroding control. Thus, the injection of little bands of guerrillas in other Latin American countries without close consideration of a variety of factors had revealed to Guevara only that the initial difficulties were greater than he had assumed, not that the Cuban strategy was unique or, at least, highly complex and difficult to export intact. While Che accepted that "we cannot export revolution. Only those who have no freedom should fight for freedom . . . everything must be done by the people themselves,"[3] he remained convinced it was Cuba's revolutionary duty to sponsor and support with material and moral assistance those who would follow the example of the Sierra Maestra. Cuba continued to do so even if it "remains that revolutions cannot be exported."[4] Criticisms, particularly from the Left, only hardened Guevara's conviction.

Much of the carping from the Left that the Cuban Revolution was unique was in time adequately answered by Guevara or his apologists. The general strike, beloved by the Trotskyists, was a proven failure, particularly in Cuba. The conventional conservative tactics of Latin American Communist parties, no matter how pragmatic, had also failed to produce revolution anywhere. As Régis Debray pointed out, the theory of seizing an area, a revolutionary base, and defending it against the onslaughts of imperialism—reformist self-defense—had been futile in Colombia. And "if Fidel Castro was necessary to our revolution, more Fidels are not necessary for the other revolutions"[5] was the answer to those who insisted revolution must wait on a revolutionary savior. If these revolutionary alternatives were unpalatable to Guevara—proven failures—the record of his own strategy was by 1965 still no more promising.

> There have been many experiences in armed conflict in Colombia, Venezuela, and Guatemala. Everywhere there are accounts of failure, and these should be made known so that profitable lessons may be drawn for the struggle of the future.[6]

The lesson Che seemed to be drawing from the list of gutted hopes was the need to stress the world-wide nature of the struggle. His extended travels had brought him into contact with national liberation movements in Asia and Africa which seemed to share his own goals and the adamant opposition of the United States of America—"the great enemy of mankind."[7] The revolution that his vision had largely limited to Latin America now had a broader scope: ". . . imperialism is a world system, the last stages of capitalism—and it must be defeated in a world confrontation."[8] In such a confrontation, all men of the Left had a part to play, and it mattered little on which stage they played.

> To die under the flag of Vietnam, of Venezuela, of Guatemala, of Laos, of Guinea, of Colombia, of Bolivia, of Brazil—to name only a few scenes of today's struggle—would be equally glorious and desirable for an American, an Asian, an African, even a European.[9]

Admittedly the beginning would not be easy—had not been—but the key was to strike at the United States again and again. For Guevara, the most relevant task of the Cuban Revolution should be the creation of a second or a third Vietnam. Imperialism would bleed to death in the Andes as Batista had in the Sierra Maestra. The expanded vision of the world strategy reflected, however, no particular broadening of his immediate strategic vision. If the masses in Guatemala or Venezuela had not yet been converted, they soon would be by the catalyzing effect of the guerrillas. "The great lesson of the invincibility of the guerrillas taking root in the dispossessed masses"[10] remained for Che the ultimate truth. Repeated failure had only taught that the war would be long—a cruel war—but it was the only hope for victory to achieve the revolution:

> . . . rivers of blood will have to flow. The blood of the people is our most sacred treasure, but it must be spilled in order to save more blood in the future. What we affirm is that we must follow the road to liberation, even it it costs millions of atomic victims.[11]

This apocalyptic vision of the violent future may have had a certain charismatic charm within the world of the Far Left but it engendered only suspicion in the cold men in Moscow, who began to hear the voice of Mao in the mouth of Che. Castro was increasingly embarrassed by Soviet concern. Guevara seemed to be developing a dangerous cult of permanent revolutionary violence: ". . . violence is the midwife of the new societies."[12] So far, like Michael Bakunin, he had too often mistaken the third month of revolutionary pregnancy for full term, leaving behind him a series of violent abortions for the more pragmatic to clean up. The Communist parties of Latin America, supported by Moscow, could not see themselves as the inevitable martyrs of the next stage of world revolution. To many practicing revolutionaries what seemed simple to Guevara on world tour appeared very complicated on the ground. Everyone could see the temptations of the vision. Some were willing to sacrifice themselves or their vested interests in the good cause if a rational chance of success existed; but few felt impelled to join so idealistic a crusade when past experience had proven Che a failed prophet.

When Guevara at last confronted Castro in March 1966, and found that his leader felt the requirements of Cuba outweighed a total commitment to world revolution, that the pragmatic politics of the Eastern bloc moved him more than revolutionary idealism, that the real world was quite different from the world revolution, he felt that the supreme practitioner of his ideology, his ideal, his revolutionary father had betrayed him. Guevara, eventually and predictably, decided that he would not betray his vision. He would go where his experience and his intentions would be welcome, rather than settle for honored retirement or placid exile.

> It is not a matter of wishing success to the victims of aggression, but of sharing this fate; one must accompany him to his death or to victory.[13]

Excommunicated by Castro, exiled from Cuba, Che turned to the rebellion in the Congo for fulfillment—in his revolutionary act his theories would be made manifest.

Supported by Castro and accompanied by over a hundred of his comrades from the Sierra Maestra, Guevara embarked on the Congo adventure. He had met Gaston Soumialot, leader of the Congo revolutionary force, and his aides, Pierre Mulele and Laurent Kabila, in Cairo in February and had been attracted by their reports on their anti-imperialist struggle. Once Guevara arrived in the Congo the reality of the struggle proved at odds with his briefing. Whatever revolutionary illusions Guevara had husbanded had to be discarded by his exposure to the institutionalized anarchy of the Congo, the brutalisms of tribal war, greed, corruption, cowardice, betrayal. However pure the cause of the revolutionary government, the tribal guerrillas performed atrocities as a matter of course. Men who ate the hearts of their slain opponents simply did not fit into any of the pigeonholes of revolutionary theory. The ideals of Marx and Lenin—even of Mao—had no

place in the Congo. What had been clear in his Cairo conversations collapsed in the nightmare reality of the African
jungles.

Only his Cubans seemed seriously interested in fighting. The Africans ran before a handful of white mercenaries. They accepted neither orders nor discipline, took
neither prisoners nor indoctrination. They reverted to
barbarism at the slightest opportunity. There was constant
intervention and interference, with little respect for the
aspiration of the Congolese leaders. Agents abounded.
There was not so much a struggle for liberation as manipulated chaos. The Brotherhood of World Revolution was
revealed starkly in the Congo as no more than a slogan to
sell pragmatic policies made in distant cities. Guevara and
his Cubans stuck it out, but his presence in the Congo was
an ill-kept secret. The Russians insisted that he was doing
more harm than good. Moscow put pressure on Havana.
Castro had to bring his wandering and unwanted Knight
Errant back. The idealism which had glowed so strongly
guttered low. After nine months, Guevara returned to
Havana with few illusions and less hope.

There was, of course, no peace and still no place in
Cuba for Guevara. For lack of options, he clung to the old
dream of the armed struggle, for himself and for the world:
"I believe in the armed struggle as the only solution for
people who are fighting for freedom, and I act according
to this belief."[14] He still believed, even if Liberty or Death,
the only alternatives for a revolutionary, had nearly
merged. He would play out his flawed hand where, if death
came, it would be welcome, "provided that our battle cry
may have reached some receptive ear."[15] Once more he
mounted Rocinante, lifted his shield and began another
journey as the most famous twentieth-century *condottiere*
of revolution. This time the objective was Bolivia.

In some very specific ways Bolivia was not the ideal,
textbook target for a revolution that was to be based on the
peasant. In April 1952, after a three-day struggle, a con-

servative junta had been overthrown and the Movimiento Nacionalista Revolucionario (MNR) swept into power determined to transform Bolivia. In October 1952, the tin and zinc mines in Oruro and elsewhere were nationalized. On August 2, 1953, an extensive agrarian reform was instituted by decree, giving legal recognition to the seizure of the land by the agrarian syndic ites. Although the nationalization of the tin mines ultimately brought little change in the brutal working conditions, the redistribution of land reform did siphon off considerable peasant pressure. Thus, while the miners remained sullen and militant, the Indian peasants had achieved many of their immediate ambitions. After thirteen years of declining vitality, the MNR was removed from power in a military coup led by General René Barrientos Ortuno and Alfredo Ovando Candia on November 4, 1964. As President, Barrientos, dynamic and spectacular, proved not unpopular, particularly with the Indian peasants. Still, from Guevara's point of view, his government was an imperialistic pawn and by necessity discontent must be seething out of sight. In Havana, intelligence concerning actual Bolivian conditions was read through pink spectacles. Most important, the "people's forces" would have to be recruited from peasants who were Indians—a formidable undertaking at best. The difficulties of mounting a revolution on the crumbling foundations of the quarreling Bolivian Left were largely discounted. Still, the lure of the Andes, the driving necessity for a suitable site for action overcame the obstacles—"It is not necessary to wait until all conditions are favorable."

By 1966, many of the special conditions included in Guevara's theory—the pointlessness of attacking a democratic government, the overriding importance of the peasant's hunger for the land, and the impossibility of exporting revolution—had been discarded by the impatient. Now, detailed by the French journalist and philosopher Debray in his *Revolution in the Revolution,* written in 1966 and published in January 1967, the whole revolution

had to germinate in a guerrilla-*foco*. The importance of a
political apparatus, urban terror and sabotage, a support
and intelligence network, international publicity, and
internal alliances had been minimized or entirely discarded. For the revolutionary, it was sufficient to begin, to
move into the hills, to act in what would be a long and
hard struggle, but one which would generate other *focos*,
spread across boundaries, involve the United States, and
entangle imperialism in another Vietnam. With recent
failures to the theory's credit in northern Argentina and
southern Peru, Bolivia under dictator General René Barrientos, nevertheless, appeared from Havana as an acceptable target. Castro, still motivated by old gratitudes and
present realities, agreed to support the Bolivian adventure
despite the risks.

The most serious consideration for Castro was
whether or not to suffer again the inevitable strains that
another Guevara adventure would assure. The money was
of no matter and the score of persistent comrades from
Che's old campaigns were—to be kind—easy to spare.
Guevara received permission to begin recruitment and set
up the preparatory base in Bolivia. The feedback of indignation began early, for the Bolivian Communist party,
feuding with both the Maoist splinter and the persistent
Trotskyists, needed no imported violent revolutionaries—
particularly when led by a man already a legend in his
own time. In September, the Bolivian Communist party
discovered that their country was to be the site of the
"next Vietnam." Horror, confusion, wounded pride, doubt,
and concentrated self-interest bubbled up on the Bolivian
Left. Guevara and his agents plodded on ahead, little
interested in alliances and compromises. No effort was
made to unify the schismatic and quarreling Bolivian Left,
no serious effort was made to contact potentially friendly
exiles of the National Revolutionary Movement. A primitive intelligence and support network was set up with little

recourse to proper channels. The overriding urge seemed to be to set up the *foco* as quickly as possible and let the subsequent details sort themselves out. In November, once in place in the *foco*, Guevara showed little interest in the support and intelligence net in Bolivia. His radio and courier contact with Castro in Cuba seemed sufficient.

By the time Guevara arrived, the Bolivian Left had been permanently seized on the whole issue. The charismatic appeal of Che and his call to action could not be ignored. Yet formal acceptance would almost certainly result in violent persecution by the government of Barrientos, which would not bother Che in the *foco* but would disrupt, if not shatter, the entire movement. The Bolivian Communist leader Mario Monje flew to Havana to consult with Castro in December, but with little result. In January, he met with Guevara at Ñancahuazú, now the magnet for every schismatic Leftist in Bolivia.

When Monje arrived in camp on December 31, to try and hammer out some sort of arrangement between the guerrillas and the Bolivian Communist party, Guevara rigidly held to his position. "Che was also a very authoritarian man. In the guerrilla-camp he would simply say, 'That is the way it will be.' Che did not support discussion."[16] Monje, hoping to find an honorable compromise, was—along with the Bolivian Communists—off the hook. Guevara, an Argentinian backed by Cuba, insisted on being the only *jefe* of the Bolivian revolution, a revolution of which the Bolivian party had been innocent until so informed of its existence and then barred from its planning or execution. When Monje left, the following day, Che was left with his own ragtag support operation pieced together with schismatic Left militants, Marxist heretics, the dubious and the doubtful, opportunists, single and double agents, and was isolated in his *foco* in the jungle. Once the first stage had passed and operations began, actual contact was going to be even more difficult; but

Guevara continued to show no real concern except to keep the lines open to Havana and whip his men into shape for the approaching ordeal.

As the site of the mother cell for the Bolivian Revolution, the Ñancahuazú was singularly unappealing. In the midst of an extensive uninhabited quadrangle, the *foco* was isolated from the few urban areas in the province; Camiri, the nearest center, was ten miles away, and only the village of Lagunillas with six hundred people could be called neighboring. The area was a maze of rugged escarpments; twisting, unmapped, torrential rivers, gullies covered with impenetrable thorn trees, cacti, tangled liana, and spiny brush which tore the flesh, pierced shoe leather, and restricted vision to six feet. All movement was difficult, usually painful, and occasionally dangerous. There were as an added bonus: chiggers, mosquitoes, ticks, and several unknown voracious insects. For guerrilla purposes, most important, there were almost no peasants in the isolated areas—which meant no food supply, no potential recruits, no information, and no easy contact with the urban support apparatus.

In any case, the peasants in the fringe areas were Indians, speaking not Spanish but Quechua or Guarani. They, like most Bolivian Indians, were impenetrable, suspicious of the strange, apparently without curiosity or ambition, a cold, closed circle largely isolated from the movement and aspirations of Latin America. If the Bolivian Indian had any particular involvement in the system, it was a mild show of interest in President Barrientos, who knew Quechua, had traveled widely, spoken often, and made a serious effort to reach the Indian peasant. Thus the *foco* was isolated in a wild forest area without really convenient targets, with difficult communication and supply lines, and on the fringe of a strange and hostile population.

The situation was by no means in violation of

Guevara's basic theory concerning the initial stage of guerrilla-war:

At the onset there is a more or less homogeneous group, with some arms, that devotes itself almost exclusively to hiding in the wildest and most inaccessible places, making little contact with the peasants.[17]

Gradually, during December and January, local recruits drifted into Ñancahuazú; but the influx remained a trickle and the *foco* largely a Cuban affair. Ultimately the Bolivians serving under Che in the *foco* would number thirty-six, to eighteen Cubans, two Peruvians, two Argentinians, and two of unknown background. The experience and capacities of the Cubans were impressive indeed. Many were officers in the Cuban Army who had served in the Sierra Maestra with Che; several had been through the Congo expedition; four belonged to the Central Committee of the Cuban Communist party; one, Acuna Nuñez, had directed a guerrilla-school in Cuba and served nine months in Vietnam. With the exception of Guido Peredo Leigue—"Inti"—trained in Cuba, the Bolivians were not of the same ilk, although some had also been trained in Cuba. In this stage, a camp in the jungle, away from the Calamine House, was constructed, caches were established, and intensive training route marches were undertaken.

The first extensive route march, scheduled to last twenty-five days, began on February 1. It stretched out for forty-eight days. The going was laborious. Men fell sick, even Che: "A black day for me; I made it by sheer guts, for I am very exhausted."[18] The maps were useless. The column wandered about in unknown country. Some guerrillas straggled off and had to be hunted down. There were mosquitoes, hunger, wrong turns, miserable weather, and accidents—on February 26, a guerrilla drowned crossing one of the innumerable jungle rivers. The rare contacts with the local Indians showed only that they were not willing to join the guerrilla-band. The men grew increasingly discouraged. There were discipline problems. Another guerrilla drowned fording the flooding Río Ñancahuazú. A raft of supplies was lost, leaving many without clothing. Finally, on March 20, the column—exhausted, demoralized, ravenous, and discouraged—stumbled back to base. There was clearly much to be done before the *foco* was ready to move on to the next stage.

Unknown to Guevara, the second stage had already arrived. The balloon had at last gone up and the Bolivian Army was on the move. After nearly four months of coming and going in the isolated Ñancahuazú, accidental contacts with the local Indians, the curiosity of the neighbors, and the seething rumors within the Bolivian Left, the discovery of the guerrillas' existence should hardly have come as a surprise. Revelation had come in several ways. Earlier in February, the army had received unconfirmed reports from local Indians of suspicious activity. Bolivian intelligence quickly built up an uncertain picture of what was going on in the southeast. By March 9, General Robert Porter, Commander of the United States Southern Command headquarters in the Panama Canal Zone, arrived to be briefed. On March 1, Guevara's liaison contact in La Paz, Tania (Laura Gutiérrez Bauer, or Haydee Tamara Bunke Bider), a double agent attached to the Russian intelligence operation, had brought Ciro Roberto Bustos, who was to be part of the primitive support apparatus, and Régis Debray to Ñancahuazú as ordered. She had left a jeep parked in Camiri. Although Guevara was still on the training march, all three remained at the camp with the jeep in Camiri, where inevitably it attracted attention. Then, on March 11, two of the Bolivians deserted. Arrested on March 14, they revealed the existence of the *foco*. By March 17, when the Bolivian Army attacked and destroyed the Calamine House, losing one man and capturing one guerrilla-sentry, most of the details of the *foco* were known in La Paz. The guerrillas under the Cuban major Antonio Sánchez Díaz, without orders to stand and fight, pulled back from the Calamine House into the base area, leaving the Bolivian Army a clear trail to follow. The hunt was on.

Conditions were grim. Morale in the camp was low. Guevara reintroduced rigid discipline, expelled four of the Bolivian guerrillas, and criticized Díaz's conduct. His basic decision was not to withdraw without a fight, regardless of the condition of the guerrillas. He ordered an ambush manned by five men set up on March 22. The next day a Bolivian Army patrol walked into the trap. Seven were killed, four wounded, and fourteen captured. The guerrillas captured sixteen Mausers, three mortars with sixty-four shells, two Bz-30 machine guns, two thousand rounds of Mauser ammunition, three USIS's with two clips each—one thirty-caliber with two belts of ammunition. It was a highly successful beginning. Two days later the National Liberation Army of Bolivia was formally established. Even without a secure base, a detailed knowledge of the area, a functioning support organization, and any indication of peasant support, the battle had been joined.

On the other side of the battle lines, the Bolivian Army was almost as ill-prepared for the campaign. Most of the soldiers were inexperienced and inexpert. Their equipment left much to be desired, their training was nominal, their diet less than satisfactory, and their motivation uncertain. On a command level, there was no functioning centralized control, no real understanding of the nature of guerrilla-war, and considerable administrative confusion and cross-purposes. There was bitterness that the Americans, who had shown little previous interest in supplying the Bolivian Army with what La Paz wanted, were determined, as the United States ambassador said, that "this must be kept a strictly Bolivian operation."[19] Washington was willing, and had given aid and comfort, had for some time urged Barrientos to accept a training mission for the

Bolivian Rangers, but was not interested in sending jet planes and tanks. Most significant, the United States had no intention of blundering toward Che's dream of another Vietnam. On March 23, United States rations and arms, as well as further anti-insurgency training, were promised La Paz. On April 1, the first C-130 flew in, but the actual involvement remained low. The maximum number of United States experts sent in from Southern Command in Panama was less than one hundred and never many more than fifty. The most important contribution was the four-months' training course, already in the pipeline, for the Bolivian Second Ranger Battalion, which began on May 1. In the meantime, the burden of the campaign would rest on the regular army supported by aircraft and helicopters. For some time, it would be a mismatch; for whatever his strategic omissions, Guevara remained a shrewd and ruthless commander in the field, a man of iron will capable of inspiring a group of previously discontent and quarreling men to repeated feats of endurance and persistence.

Tactically Guevara and his column were superb. The Bolivian Army was slow, uncertain, low on initiative and spontaneity, but increasingly dogged. In La Paz a crisis atmosphere developed. The prisoners released after the March 23 clash exaggerated the strength of the guerrillas and despite other hard evidence were believed. There were indiscriminate arrests throughout the country and exaggerated rumors seeping out of official quarters. In the meantime, the army moved in two thousand men and attempted to throw a ring around the Ñancahuazú area. Ill-prepared for the rugged country, the army units began carrying out heavy patrols; clumsy in concept and uncertain in execution, the operations did isolate the guerrillas in a still-porous ring. On April 10, at Iripiti, a fifteen-man Bolivian Army patrol, taking minimal precautions, moved along the banks of a river directly into an ambush. In a burst of fire, one soldier was killed, three wounded, and six taken prisoner. Later a sublieutenant was killed, although four soldiers escaped. Two of the wounded prisoners soon died. Those who didn't gave Guevara sufficient information to keep the ambush in place for the expected arrival of another patrol. They too walked into the ambush. Surprise was total. Seven were killed and five wounded. Guevara gives the final totals for the day as "ten dead, including two lieutenants; thirty prisoners, including a major and some lesser officers, the rest soldiers; six were wounded, one in the first fight and five in the second."[20] The column lost one killed and had two wounded. Another highly successful day; but unless it could be exploited politically in the country at large, the Iripiti clash would be a sterile exercise in violence. However narrow his vision had become within the *foco,* even Guevara recognized the danger of continued isolation.

Neither Bolivian Communist party, pro-Moscow, or pro-Peking, would support the guerrillas. Guevara made no further effort to contact either. Early in April, ex-President Paz Estenssoro from his exile in Lima denounced the guerrillas as alien communists. With both the conventional and revolutionary Left in Bolivia alienated, Che's only option remained Cuba or perhaps Argentina. The obvious couriers were Debray, Bustos, and Tania, and on the evening of the Iripiti clash Guevara insisted that they make their way out of Bolivia. Debray wanted to stay, but Guevara valued his potential worth as a propagandist far more than his uncertain military contribution. Bustos, who had been involved late and with some doubts, had already been critical of Guevara's approach, particularly the timing of the operations and the state of preparations. In 1963–4, Bustos had been one of the few men to escape from a disastrous guerrilla "campaign" in northern Argentina led by Jorge Masetti, an advocate of the Guevara thesis, and he could see the same faults being repeated in Bolivia. Guevara, never one to suffer criticism gladly, had accepted Bustos's two objections that too little information existed about the surrounding countryside and that there was lack of regular supplies. If Debray had to be persuaded to leave and Bustos accepted the decision with grace—perhaps enthusiasm—Tania refused, and managed to convince Guevara.* Debray and Bustos, entrusted with various messages and instructions and accompanied by an English journalist, George Andrew Roth, who had managed to break through the army encirclement, left the column on April 19. The following day they were arrested at Muyupampa. The only link with the outside world was the shortwave radio.

In order to expedite the departure of Debray and Bustos, Che had made what proved to be an unfortunate tactical decision to split his forces. Seventeen guerrillas, including the four formerly expelled but still drifting with the column, were left under the command of Major Juan Vitalio Acuña. Included in the group were Tania, whom Guevara still hoped to smuggle out to make contacts in La Paz, and the Peruvian revolutionary Juan Carlos Chang, who might regain touch with the Peruvian revolutionary movements. This group lost contact with Guevara; and the two columns, wandering and twisting through the rugged, unmapped country, never managed to regroup during the next three months. Even a brief separation could be fatal, as one of the Bolivian guerrillas found out a few days later when he ran into two army sentries, shot both, and rushed into the jungle to stumble about alone until he was wounded and captured. With his forces split and out of contact, with his secure base at Ñancahuazú blown, Guevara was forced to give up the initiative and react to the Bolivian Army's pressure.

The pressure kept up. There was a clash at El Mesón and the army suffered two casualties. Two weeks later a skirmish at Taparillas cost the security forces two killed.

---

* Tania had already worked for both the Soviet KGB and the East German Ministry of Security while in Cuba since as early as 1961. Che's unorthodox behavior was causing concern in the orthodox East.

At almost the same spot, the guerrillas hit again the following day, killing three more and wounding several. Meanwhile Acuña's group circled back into the Ñancahuazú area to unearth a few old caches; but as far as Guevara and the main column were concerned, they had vanished.

In his diary Guevara's regular monthly summary, despite detailing the difficulties, still ended on a hopeful note, more hopeful than conditions seem to warrant:

> . . . our isolation continues to be total; various illnesses have undermined the health of some comrades, forcing us to divide our forces, which has reduced our effectiveness a great deal . . . our peasant base is still underdeveloped, although apparently a programme of planned terror will succeed in neutralizing most of them, and their support will come later. We have not had a single recruit . . . the army . . . has improved its techniques; they surprised us at Taperillas and were not demoralized at El Mesón . . . we have also cut our communications with Cuba (Dantón) and we have lost our plan of action in Argentina (Carlos).
>
> To sum up: a month in which everything has evolved normally considering the standard development of a guerrilla war. The morale of all the combatants is good because they have passed their first test as guerrilla fighters.[21]

Everything was evolving normally in Guevara's eyes, because his standards were remarkably different from those of conventional commanders. In six months, not one of the vital peasants had joined the *foco* and the general hostility was so great that Guevara considered the use of terror. Still, it had taken nearly a year before the first Cuban peasant had been converted. His outside couriers, Debray–Dantón and Bustos–Carlos, had been arrested, his alternative choices, Tania and Chang, were—along with his other column—lost. Still, contact with Havana by radio had not been lost. The Bolivian Army was more efficient and, although his losses had been few during the month—three—these were irreplaceable. Nevertheless, things had been far worse in Cuba during the early days.

Early in May, Guevara pushed on, delayed by the sick and as worried about the lack of food as the presence of the Bolivian Army. On May 8, in a series of clashes, the column hit the army, killing three and capturing ten prisoners, two wounded, along with some arms and, most necessary, food. The column moved out again, wandering uncertainly, always on the outlook for food, increasingly hampered by colic, vomiting, and diarrhea in a cycle of fast and famine. In the middle of the month, Guevara fell seriously ill; and, when he partially recovered, it was the turn of someone else. On May 18, he radioed one of his regular messages to Castro, which detailed some of the problems—particularly the isolation from La Paz—but insisted that morale remained high. Actually, despite the deteriorating physical condition of the guerrillas, there was ample room for elation if their long-range prospects could be ignored. Repeatedly on the ground the guerrillas had proven superior to the army. Army patrols were still clumsy, Bolivian intelligence was poor, and the guerrilla-ambushes regularly effective. On May 30, a two-hour battle occurred around a grade crossing on the railroad from Yacuiba to Santa Cruz. The army walked into yet another ambush and had two men killed and four wounded. Thus, at the end of the month, Guevara felt that by his success in the series of clashes, by army pressure on the peasants which might lead to their conversion to the guerrilla cause, by the publicity as a result of Debray's arrest, and by the continued incapacities of the Bolivian Army his cause was hopeful. But the isolation remained. And the slow, painful, and so far sterile task of winning the peasants seemed no nearer completion.

In June the situation remained stable: the guerrillas on the run, exhausted, and sick, Guevara forced to ride everywhere on a mule. Yet the *foco* was deadly. Despite a new commander for the Bolivian Fourth Division and the initiative of the full-scale Operation Cynthia, army casualties were several times guerrilla losses. The army could, of course, afford nickel and dime losses, the guerrillas could not. Guevara's column was down to twenty-four men by the end of June and there was no contact with Acuña, who also found his strength whittled down in the clashes with the army as well as through desertion. Under the tightening pressure of the Fourth Division, Guevara was gradually squeezed north, short of food, isolated, and most of all suffering badly from violent asthma attacks without appropriate medicines. Then came a startling guerrilla victory. What seemed from La Paz to be a nasty defeat carefully inflicted by Che was actually a desperate attempt to acquire food and medicine. The column on July 6 seized and held the town of Samaipata on the Santa Cruz–Mataral road, well north of previous operations in the area of the unprepared Eighth Division.

The brief seizure caused considerable journalistic flurry, for a variety of factors seem to indicate that by July the tide had turned in favor of the revolutionaries, as in fact it might have if there had been a Bolivian Castro in the *foco* instead of Guevara. The *foco* had continued to exist, even if not expand, despite army pressure. The continued presence of the guerrillas in the hills and the magnetism of Che's name had created an atmosphere of considerable anxiety in La Paz and truculence in parts of the country. There was world-wide interest in the arrest of the theorist Debray. On June 24, the army in a fit of enthusiasm opened fire on a demonstration of militant miners. The Massacre of San Juan cost the lives of forty miners, with over a hundred more wounded, and the confidence of two of the three parties supporting Barrientos. Both withdrew from the coalition. If there had been an orchestrated rise of sabotage and terror in the cities, if there had been a focus of discontent which did not ideologically alienate so much of Bolivian nationalist opinion, if there had been a prospect of an alternative reform regime tolerable to the United States, if there had, in fact, been anything resembling a rational strategy based on effective mass support, Barrientos might have been in a shaky position indeed. Dramatic and dashing, he was hardly indispensable; his bases of support, the army and the peasant, were open to subversion; and his American connection was not immutable. As it was, the Massacre of San Juan, the coup at Samaipata, the international sympathy for Debray, the hints of political turmoil remained isolated. There was no control from the center. The *foco* remained a little group of desperate men, isolated and on the run. Barrientos maintained his nerve, the army its persistent willingness to track down the guerrillas, and the regime's hopeful successors their discreet retirement. In fact, the corner had been turned.

During the rest of July and on into August, the two guerrilla-columns continued to evade the army, scavenge for food, and suffer the low, slow losses of attrition they could ill afford. Acuña's column barely evaded a trap in the Iñaú hills. At the same time, the effect of regular training, improved diet, and months of practice was beginning to show in the mobility and tactics of the Bolivian Army. Under Major Ralph Shelton, sixteen men from the United States Eighth Special Forces Group had begun a four-month training program of the 650-man Second Ranger Battalion. Although formal graduation did not come until September 16, by mid-August some elements were already in action. Day by day the army ran patrols, tightened the picket loop around the area, tenaciously harried Guevara, who was often lost wandering back and forth through the same rugged area seeking to find his other column. On August 31 elements of the Second Ranger Battalion eliminated that problem. In really dire straits, Acuña's strength had declined to ten men and Tania. Morale was shattered. Tania was constantly on the verge of hysterics. Nearly everyone was sick. All were exhausted, starving, constantly quarreling without hope or prospects. Captain Mario Vargas, acting on detailed intelligence, set an ambush on the Masicuri River at Vado del Yeso. The guerrillas straggled into the river directly into the clear field of fire for the thirty-one Rangers. A prolonged burst of fire tore through the guerrillas. Tania was one of the first cut down. Only two lived to be taken prisoners and neither survived captivity.

After the Vado del Yeso ambush, La Paz knew it was only a matter of time. In September the Rangers were fully committed to winkling out Guevara, now down to twenty men and sealed into the same sterile area. Guevara approached September—even before the first rumors of the Vado del Yeso ambush reached the *foco*—considerably less enthusiastic, since August "was the worst month we have had from the point of view of the war. . . . We are at a low moment in our morale and in the legend of the revolution."[22] Throughout the month, the same wandering routine of scavenging for food, setting ambushes, moving up ahead of army patrols with the odd loss of a cache and, more rarely, a man. The area of operations declined day by day. On September 22, the column seized and held the village of Alto Secco. Some remained for two days before moving back into the jungles. The army was now very close on their heels.

On September 26, the column ran into an army ambush near La Higuera. Three guerrillas were killed and two separated from the column. During the next days, the army patrols were all around them. One tense day followed another. The peasants were openly hostile. The guerrillas were too exhausted to move swiftly and there no longer seemed to be any secure areas. They evaded the patrols until October 7, when, as Guevara had feared, a peasant woman reported their exact presence to the circling army. The seventeen-man column was again reported on the night of the seventh by a wandering peasant. On the following day, they straggled directly into a carefully laid ambush. Trapped in a ravine, the column was raked by army fire. Most of the guerrillas were killed in the fire-fight. Guevara was hit in the leg, his rifle smashed by a bullet. Wounded and unarmed, he was captured. After eleven months the *foco* had finished. The mother cell of the Andes had dissolved into three or four men fleeing back into the jungle.

Guevara was bundled into a blanket and carried by four soldiers seven miles to La Higuera. With their prisoner lying on the floor of the town schoolhouse, Captain Gary Prado Salmón, commander of the Second Regiment of Rangers, and his commander Colonel Andrés Selić contacted La Paz. Che had at last come to the end of the road. The Bolivian government wanted no show trial, no mesmeric prisoner. On the next day, October 9, he was executed without formality as he waited for the inevitable on the schoolroom floor. The last adventure was over. Che Guevara had already written his epitaph in his April 1967 message to the Tricontinental Conference:

> Wherever death may surprise us, let it be welcome, provided that this, our battle cry, may have reached some receptive ear, and another hand may be extended to wield our weapons and other men be ready to intone the funeral dirge with the staccato singing of the machine guns and new battle cries of war and victory.[23]

Less romantically, without the flourish of singing machine guns, he had much earlier written the final analysis of the Bolivian adventure as well:

> The guerrilla fighter needs full help from the people of the area. This is an indispensable condition. This is clearly seen by considering the case of bandit gangs that operate in a region. They have all the characteristics of a guerrilla army, homogeneity, respect for the leader, valor, knowledge of the ground, and

often good understanding of the tactics to be employed. The only thing missing is support of the people; and, inevitably these gangs are captured and exterminated by the public force.[24]

The weight of evidence indicates that the Bolivian attempt as directed by Guevara never—at any stage—had a chance of success, that the operation was programmed for failure, perhaps in Havana but certainly in Bolivia. Castro at first may have thought that the gunman par excellence had a chance of success; but once Guevara got into Bolivia, cut the apron strings and took only his own advice, even in Havana it was clear that this time something more serious was involved than a man "who risks his skin in order to prove his convictions."[25] When he had wandered off on his Congo adventure in 1965, he had written to Castro that, "If my final hour comes under distant skies, my last thoughts will be for this people and especially for you."[26] And to his family that, "perhaps this will be my last letter. It is not my intention, but it is within the realm of logical probability."[27] In 1966, even before the struggle had begun under the distant skies of Bolivia, Guevara had raised this logical probability to a near—but not an absolute—certainty. If shallow and naïve as an ideologist, Guevara was no fool, particularly tactically, for he had been a professional revolutionary for a decade, participated in two campaigns, and discussed others with experts. Yet he had Masetti's Argentine example before him. He had the analysis of the Bolivian situation from people in Cuba on the spot and whom he respected. They thought him hopelessly misguided and he knew it. Why then flirt with death, bet his life with hopelessly high odds and keep only a few chips in hand? Why skirt so close to the ultimate heresy defined by his old hero José Martí?

Anyone who starts a war that can be avoided in a country is a criminal, as is anyone who does not start the inevitable war.[28]

As is often the case with a certain variety of Latin American intellectual, Guevara was undertrained in his own discipline and overextended in too many others. While not necessarily shallow, his grasp of the tenets of his faith was limited and his interpretation often based on personal needs rather than close reasoning. It was not that he was incapable of understanding Mao or Giap but rather that he wanted Mao and Giap to reveal what he already believed—and of course they did. Such strictures as the three stages of revolutionary war, from the guerrilla to the army of national liberation, or the necessity of the local origin of revolution, or the uselessness of a vanguard alone were in Guevara's mind fudged over or misread or evaded. Thus, even a cursory reading by the disinterested would clearly reveal Guevara's heresy, but—even more curious— the heretical gospel according to Guevara was repeatedly and blatantly violated during the year of the Bolivian *foco*.

1. "The absolute cooperation of the people and a perfect knowledge of the ground is necessary."[29]

   Not one local Indian peasant joined the movement. In fact: ". . . the peasant mass aids us in nothing, is turning into informers." No one in the *foco* knew the country. On the first long training march, the entire column wandered in the jungle, lost for a month.

2. "The best age of the guerrilla fluctuates between twenty-five and thirty-five."[30]

   ("Generally the maximum age of combatants in the completely nomadic stage of the guerrilla struggle ought not to exceed forty years . . . although there will be exception."[31])

   At the maximum limit, Guevara was an exception—a remarkable one—driving himself with an iron will; but while inspirationally he was an immense asset, physically he was a drag.

3. ". . . he needs an iron constitution."[32]

   Repeatedly Guevara's asthma in Bolivia handicapped the column—the need for drugs became a tactical consideration.

4. "The guerrilla soldier should preferably be an inhabitant of the zone."[33]

None were and, furthermore, the Cubans from the first dominated the *foco.*

5. "Fundamental characteristic of a guerrilla group is mobility."[34]

After the early contacts with the Bolivian Army the guerrillas made no attempt to go over to the mobile, long-march stage, but remained stationary.

6. "As soon as the survival of the guerrilla band has been assured, it should fight; it must constantly go out from its refuge to fight."[35]

Once the army contact had been made on March 17, it was clear that the "base" was not secure, yet Guevara chose to stay in place and set an ambush.

7. "The importance of a suburban struggle has usually been underestimated; it is really very great. . . . If from the first moment of the war, thought is taken for the future possibility of this type of fight and an organization of specialists started, a much more rapid action will be assured, and with a saving of lives and of the priceless time of the nation."[36]

From the first nothing was done.

8. ". . . the struggle of the people for reforms is aimed primarily and almost exclusively at changing the social form of land ownership, the guerrilla fighter is above all an agrarian revolutionary."[37]

Bolivia has already had an agrarian revolution —in point of fact, the Barrientos government's propaganda suggested to the peasants that the Guevara-Communists might try and take away their lands.

9. "The guerrilla band [is] . . . the fighting vanguard of the people. It draws its great force from the mass of the people themselves."[38]

If the other omissions and violations are

minor, the principle of The People, the Sea for the Fish, is the basic axiom. Such support or toleration may be secured in a variety of ways, terror according to Giap or good works according to Mao, but it must exist. Nothing could more starkly reveal the awesome gap that separated Guevara from The People— the indispensable base for a valid revolution— that not only could he not speak the language of the local Indian peasants, but he did not even know what that language was.

What revolutionary logic, which immutable law of Marxist-Leninist doctrine could explain in dialectic terms an Argentinian out of Cuba by way of the Congo in the wilds of the Bolivian jungles memorizing the verbs of the wrong Indian language in order to convert a people, already possessing land, whose vision for endless centuries had turned inward?

Seldom has the gap between revolutionary theory and practice been so striking. A variety of excuses have been offered. The most comforting to the idealist is the Devil Theory: Che was betrayed by Tania, a Soviet agent, or by the Bolivian Communist party, or even by Castro. It was a plot or treason or both. Guevara, of course, was betrayed by himself. Some of his blunders can easily be excused by the effect of exhaustion, the pressures of time, bad luck, poor advice, perverse allies, even fate; but no catalog of apologies can erase the repeated series of decisions made, after contemplation, by Guevara alone against the advice of his colleagues—they led, step by inevitable step, to the floor of the schoolhouse in La Higuera. It is not even possible to suggest that Guevara remained innocent of the possibilities of his decisions, that a series of mistakes culminated in disaster, that an alternative decision in November or a reappraisal in March might have tipped the balance. Guevara was intimately familiar with and repeatedly reminded of the fate of the exactly parallel *foco* created by his friend Masetti in Argentina.

In April 1963, Masetti and Che in Cuba had agreed on an attempt to set up a guerrilla-*foco* in Argentina as part of an Andes chain of mother cells. By June, Masetti had arrived in Bolivia with three members of Guevara's Iron Guard. By July, the hopeful objective conditions examined in Cuba had vanished. The only other viable *foco*, Hugo Blanco's in Peru, had collapsed. In Argentina the "imperialist junta" had resigned and the moderate Arturo Illia won the presidency on July 7, 1963. None of the conventional parties was interested in playing games with Masetti—and he did not ask. His recruits came from the radical student movements and dissident communists. The conventional Left of all shades had no use for an ill-timed adventure. In September 1963, when Masetti's little band had crossed over into Argentina, there were only the most fragile links with individuals in the urban areas, and none with either the militant Left or mass movements. On arrival at the base camp near the Pescado River, Masetti composed an ultimatum using the name Major Segundo, which was eventually published in the relatively obscure weekly *Compañero* and had no visible effect except to warn the Argentine secret service that something was going on in the north.

A few recruits—no peasants—were attracted and a great many security people. The jungle around Salta was grim, conditions in the *foco* poor. Several guerrillas were violently ill and many were discouraged. A potential deserter was executed, and morale dropped. The country was so rugged and so isolated that there were no inhabitants to convert and, as yet, no army to attack. There was more trouble, and in February another guerrilla was executed. The isolation and decay continued until two recruits showed up on March 2 and proved to be informers. With the army on their track, the column tried unsuccessfully to break out of the tightening ring. Supplies ran out and three died of starvation. In mid-April the guerrillas ran into the army. One soldier was killed in a skirmish, the only "battle" of the Salta Campaign. The security forces immediately closed in on the column and killed two, capturing fourteen. Masetti fled into the unmapped, impenetrable jungle of Yuto. He never returned. Che had learned the details while he was in New York in December 1964. He was repeatedly reminded of them in the Bolivia *foco* by Bustos, who had escaped Masetti's fate in the Salta adventure only to be dragged into the rerun in Ñancahuazú. And still, one by one, Guevara repeated by rote Masetti's errors.

There can be little doubt then that Guevara knew exactly what he was doing and where the path could take him. His 1965 letter to his family that he could "once again feel Rocinante's bony ribs beneath my legs"[39] was not purely literary. The windmills of Bolivia were very real indeed, but the communist Quixote carried only a blunt lance. He had come to live once more the life of an active revolutionary—"the highest state of the human species."[40] He had lost his faith in his friends, in the future, in the dream. He had come not to the field of Armageddon but to the end of the road. Surrounded by friends who would and did follow him into the jaws of death, there he would fight the good fight coolly, rationally, stretched beyond his capacities, dependent on his own iron determination. He was not in the pursuit of power—"the purpose, indivisible and unavoidable for every revolutionary"[41]—but rather for the daily intense stimulation of living beyond his means. And so he did. And so he died, not as Quixote but as El Cid. And an archbishop praised his character. And fifteen thousand copies of his book on guerrilla-war were sold in a month in Italy. A bomb was placed in the Bolivian Embassy in Bonn. In Paris, the pop song "Che" was a hit. In Argentina, Arturo Illia proclaimed him a martyr. And his picture was posted on a thousand walls in a hundred universities. And the silent Indians come now to stand outside the schoolhouse in La Higuera and to buy his photograph and take it to the church in Valle Grande to be blessed. In death he has become something to all men; for, as is given to few, nothing in life so became him as his death. His end was his beginning.

CONCLUSION

The Myth of the Guerrilla

Yes comrades; revolution is the only way left open
to our people: Let us recognize that our brother peasants,
neglected and exploited for centuries, are telling us
the great truth of our time, they are on the march.
With their drums and pipes, their banners and their slings,
their women and their children, their early yet heavenly voices
are proclaiming the beginning of the epic which
will end with the mass descent of our victorious people
from the ageless slopes of the Andes.

LONG LIVE THE PERUVIAN REVOLUTION
—Luís de la Puente Uceda, Plaza
San Martín, Lima, February 1964

GUERRILLA-REVOLUTION, so easy to instigate, so difficult to terminate, successfully or unsuccessfully, has clearly dominated great segments of political and military policy notwithstanding its all too evident limitations. Despite the long and often bloody list of failures, despite the frailties of theoretical justification and the clear and present evidence of practical futility in the field, despite the very substantial cost in casualties and very minimal return in power, for a decade the guerrilla has maintained a central role in the minds of men who—logically—should have been more independent of mind. That the lay preachers of revolution hold to the true faith, safe in pulpits isolated from the realities of the battle, is to some degree understandable if not particularly admirable; but that the watching men on the edge of battle insist on denying the evidence, however tinted by spectacles of optimism and commitment, requires an explanation beyond the conventional. Clearly, most guerrilla-leaders are not fools or knaves, although some have been both, and yet their persistence in a course evidently doomed to failure or at least to long, perhaps indefinite, protracted action cannot be fully analyzed in orthodox political or military terms. The whole complex of illusions, assumptions, and misinterpretation, wrapped in the seamless garment of theory, have become articles of faith. In recent years many men, in many places, outwardly sane, sensible, sound, hardminded, and dedicated to victory, have accepted this particular course, inexplicable in logic but highly satisfactory for the troubled and desperate. For them, the new myth of the guerrilla must fulfill a need beyond the orthodox tactics and strategy of revolution. That to the blind or uninitiated, the coldly pragmatic and the purely rational such a faith is based at worst on tenuous illusions and at best on optimism is immaterial to the believer. For him, the Myth has a comforting reality, fulfills a need in a world which denies his dearest hopes. What to others are illusions are verities without which life to him would be continual humiliation and despair. Within the context of the faith, the Myth cannot be seriously questioned, the need it fills is too great to accept alien analysis.

For those lacking in true belief, the varied strands that make up the myth of the guerrilla can be handled as if they were of coarser cloth, a self-woven cloak to ward off despair. Perhaps the most central of all the facets of the Myth is the belief in the ultimate triumph of justice. The true cause—Black Africa, Arab Palestine, or a socialist Bolivia—is so undeniably "just," so truly "right" that failure is quite literally inconceivable. Justice must triumph because it is Just. Even to their opponents the appeal of their just cause has some attraction. Some few Zionists do deeply feel the agony of the Palestinians—men without a country—just as some Latin American oligarchs genuinely admired the charismatic vision of Guevara. Yet, for those not intimately involved, the world is full of just causes, each arguable on its real merits even when contradicting an equally just cause equally arguable on *its* real merits. There have, in fact, been few just causes which have led to war that did not contain a germ of legitimacy for those outside the crusade. Just causes, however, solely on their moral merits have not necessarily triumphed. At the beginning of the seventeenth century, a small group of alien colonists landed on the shores of North America and for over two hundred years, by dint of brute force and devious diplomacy, with novel diseases and advanced arms, destroyed one after another the societies of the American Indians. With a just cause painted on his shield, where now is that last of the Mohican? Justice—it should be obvious—does not always triumph in a flawed world. Again and again in pamphlets and books, on the public platform and before intimates in the privacy of the night, the true believer insists—maintains without qualms—that justice, largely alone, will triumph. Justice is sufficient, for the believer is the chosen child of history. And the Myth makes him so, for it emboldens the desperate to take up arms for justice in a cause that "logic" would deny, that the prudent would avoid. For the guerrilla-revolutionary his very act, sanctioned by the Myth, is a triumph, partial perhaps but a triumph nevertheless.

The depth of the commitment to the inevitability of victory is, for men engaged in war, hardly unique. Even in the bunker Hitler held to some hope of a miracle. Men cannot apparently live or fight too long on despair alone. What is curious about the myth of the guerrilla is that the illuminated path to victory has led so often only toward the grave. The key, therefore, is not in the hope that the grave may be evaded and victory seized but in the path itself. For men possessed of a just but denied cause, the activity of the guerrilla salves their wounds, absorbs their energies, makes the present bearable. The options perceived are, if not quite Victory or Death, at least Victory or the most wretched humiliation. For some, such humiliation is intolerable. If one cannot have Victory, at least as a guerrilla one can avoid the humiliation, be not wretched but proud, live as a man, a man of action and decision; one can evade or postpone the numbing reality of defeat, and perhaps, just perhaps, by taking arms snatch history's prize.

To follow the way of the guerrilla it is necessary then to have time so that the lip of the grave remains sufficiently distant. Time is the second great strand woven into the guerrilla-myth. Time is on the side of the Just. We have not won today because we will win tomorrow. We have not won here because we will win there later. Since we will win in time, time is an asset. Each day we grow stronger, more skilled in war, more dedicated in spirit, more capable of determining our destiny. Time is an ally and change a trusted colleague. Guevara believed that in time the intractable peasants would be mobilized, and as time passed they instead became more alienated. The fedayeen feel that in time the Zionists will crack from within; but from the time of the First Zionist Conference each decade has seen a greater Zionist presence, a greater Zionist power, until by 1970 the combined might of the Arab World could not even defend its own heartland. The African nationalists feel that in time the Portuguese will crumble, the Rhodesian will emigrate, even the South Africans will come to terms; but in a single decade the battle lines have moved into central Africa, the vast political organizations within the bastion have been broken and scattered, and even the Portuguese glacis are being tied into the infrastructure of the white fortress.

For men dependent, as are the Africans and Arabs, on the support of host states which in turn face a desperate rise in population and a decline in the capacity to cope with divided societies, time would seem to hold little promise. At least for the Latin American revolutionary, the oligarchs must bear the weight of discontent; but (even with superficially frail instruments of control) time, and the increasing weight of deprivation have not seemed to work for anyone in Bolivia or Brazil but rather against the poor and exploited. Time appears neutral, allowing man to work out the future largely in terms of the immediate past. For the guerrilla who accepts the actual difficulties of the immediate future (a relatively rare phenomenon), there remains not only the hope in the cause but also the possibility of the unforeseen intervention of a novel and favorable factor—in other words, a minor beneficial miracle. Time will permit the contingent and fortuitous; time, therefore, remains an asset. Tomorrow may be too soon but next year or the year after that will become the golden moment when the tide of oppression at last begins to ebb. Time serves justice.

Justice in time will triumph because the enemy is perceived as a paper tiger, outwardly awesome but inwardly rent with contradictions: the third strand. Mao had found imperialism a tiger but in twenty years converted it to paper. So shall it be everywhere: Portuguese colonialism is atavistic and doomed by history, South Africa contradicts itself, Zionism is brittle, American imperialism in Latin America the last gasp of a doomed class. When imperialism or Zionism persists, the reason is that as yet the inevitable contradictions, the hidden faults, have not fully matured but will—in time—do so. Justice and history are the possessions of only one side and therefore the other must, by definition, fail—and failing, must be inwardly more feeble, more rotten, than superficial analysis would indicate. The oppressor must be feeble because he must collapse; therefore, he is feeble. And there is the evidence of China or Vietnam or Algeria to prove the syllogism of hope.

Thus victory goes to the just, the cause of the guerrillas is just, victory will be theirs. But it is not. In time victory will be theirs. It has not. The exploiter must collapse but does not. Therefore the strategy for the present is to persist. Since guerrilla-revolutions are inevitably successful, the proper, the only valid course of action, the only credible alternative to defeat is to act so as to secure the future. Yet even in time the capacity of the guerrilla to secure victory remains visibly limited. Beyond the years of hide and seek must lurk an ultimate weapon to counter the might of oppression. Not only by their own efforts in the field will the guerrillas triumph but because of the support of the people, the mass.

Next is the key strand of the mass. Obviously there must exist a hidden but irresistible asset, a terminal counter in a game of rising stakes, to be played at the proper time in the service of the cause. With or without a future minor miracle, the mass will in the fullness of time provide the ultimate weapon. We are many and they are few: the illusion of numbers. The spirit of the mass will crush the machines of exploitation. Mere mechanical power can never stand in the way of the vitalized mass. The blue ants of China and the black pajamas of Vietnam, the people as an army, the army as the people, have proved this for all time.

Mere masses, much of the time, are mere mouths to feed, not assets but responsibilities. Mere masses, much of the time, are collections of people busy with the minutiae of their overpoweringly important daily lives. People have a reluctance to sacrifice for a distant grail, a distaste for a duty seldom properly understood, and they rarely live a life so intolerable that death is preferable. True revolt by the discontented and frustrated who are nevertheless fearful of change or opposed to it has often occurred, often unreasoningly but seldom without reason. To articulate the reasons for revolt, to persuade the masses to the necessity for action, to organize them with the capacity to act —to transform fear and frustration into an instrument of revolution—this has proven an awesome task. Even to seize upon and direct the spontaneous revolt into organized resistance to the regime has proven difficult, often impossible. The mass may at pressure point erupt, but the steady flow of lava that would bury the system is seldom forthcoming.

People—not only the Chinese or Vietnamese—have been mobilized, politicized, committed in battle, and from the caldron emerged victorious. They have not done so, however, on cues given by little groups of men in the hills or the simultaneous and spontaneous birth of a ripe idea but as a result of a variety of most complicated historical factors and contemporary pressures largely well beyond the control of the guerrilla-revolutionary. At some optimum moment, it cannot be denied, the mass might unexpectedly reach mobilization point, thereafter to be manipulated by the guerrilla-revolutionary, but this is an apparently rare phenomenon. Some movements seem to be content simply with a belief in such a mobilization; however, others have gone beyond the production of slogans and have invested years in working for and among the people without reaching the critical mass point. Time and the immutable processes of history may do the job for them, but meanwhile faith in the power of the masses has offered only comfort not aid. The masses seem to be a bomb without a known detonator, a very large and potentially powerful bomb but, without a more detailed book of instructions than exists at the moment, a dud.

An additional major strand is that the very length of the guerrilla struggle—year after year of aborted hopes—is an undeniable virtue. A quick bright coup, a sudden popular upsurge, a surgical campaign of terror—a revolt not a revolution—would grasp only the husks of power, not transform the people. The transformation of the Myth into reality requires time for the struggle. The guerrilla as he fails at first lives in an agony not of aborted hopes but of the birth pangs of the new revolutionary personality. The battle will breed a new generation, proud Palestinians, real black nations, transformed Bolivian Indians, new men whose spirit has been tempered during the bleak years of the campaign. These years so empty of visible victory will not be without their reward. Since in many cases the successful conquest of political power has proven so difficult or at least so protracted and the gestation period for the new generation unduly extended, for some the emphasis has been shifted to the supreme importance of the battle itself. Beyond the Myth, in the analysis of fantasy, the act of war, isolated from the goal, has become for here and now an end. The laurel of life has been won, is being won —not will be—by participation in the highest form of human existence, that of the active guerrilla-revolutionary. The Myth, however, is not a matter of fantasy. Struggling against an injustice not only intolerable but intractable, the only relief is the guerrilla-act, the most violent, the most visible, the most viable alternative to continued humiliation. But such an act must have a rationale beyond the pragmatic, must be impregnated with a higher purpose than military expediency, than desperation clothed in a camouflage suit. Consequently, the guerrilla-act becomes a means of spiritual transformation, turning the wretched of the earth into the inheritors of the future.

Most of the wretched of the earth—the humiliated and the desperate—do not in fact seek recourse by revolution. Most remain engrossed in the daily struggle for existence, in the frugal comforts of their home and family, in their own narrow but supremely important lives. They may draw some minimal comfort, some small measure of pride, from the actions of the men in the hills but still do not choose to abandon their own well-trod path. Why some men are not for the quiet life, refuse to adapt to the system, will not suffer poverty, humiliation, oppression, and misery in silence, remains largely an unanswerable question. Love of glory, hope of power, an excess of pride, unexploited talent, ambition, some deep psychological drive, fate, or friendship with the dedicated—each may play a part for the rebels. The revolutionary often perceives the world through a peculiar form of tunnel vision, blocking out all but the two alternatives, Liberty or Death. The young often think in absolutes, and there can be few commitments as absolute as armed rebellion against tyranny or oppression. In time the existence of other alternatives can be recognized; in time the purity of vision fades and the complexities of the world intrude; in time most men accept the imperfect world. Revolution, guerrilla-revolution included, is largely a young man's vocation and not solely, or mainly, because of the physical demands of the battlefield. Some men—the hard dedicated core—somehow can, decade after decade, maintain the vision of their youth; but old practicing revolutionaries are rare indeed, if for no other reason than that even protracted war seldom lasts forever. Then the high dream of the struggle is transformed into the real power of success or into the nightmare of undeniable defeat. Until that distant day, some few men, for whatever reason, hold to their single course buttressed by the power of the new myth.

It would be arrant nonsense to suggest that many of the guerrilla-revolutionary leaders have lived solely in a world of dreams and sublimations, that the Myth has become for all such revolutionaries a unique example of mass delusion—a fantasy. Most men of war have always believed in the justice of their cause, in its ultimate success; have hoped that time was on their, the angel's, side; have had faith in their people, if not the masses; have even at times felt that better men and better nations came out of the crucible of battle. The guerrilla-myth is different only in degree, not in kind, from many previous strategies of conflict. The illusions of the guerrilla-revolutionary are merely more demonstratively invalid and more remarkably long-lived in the face of disappointment. Even so, the illusions may determine a guerrilla-strategy that, given the objective conditions, may by no means be inappropriate. For FRELIMO in Mozambique, with no hope of Portuguese compromise, the guerrilla option did and does have much to offer. Portugal must pay a high price to stay and Portugal is a poor country. FRELIMO has a near-monopoly on nationalism and may be able to vitalize the masses and escalate the war; and if not, attrition is still a potent weapon. Time may not necessarily be a FRELIMO asset, given South African involvement; but it is not clear that Portugal has been consequently favored, given the risks Pretoria might face in a mini-Vietnam. If FRELIMO is to win an independent Mozambique, guerrilla-war is surely a feasible means. On the other hand, the leadership of PAC and ANC persists not because their abortive guerrilla campaign is a feasible means but simply because all other means have failed. If the South African Republic is not to be allowed to maintain power by default, then someone someplace must attack with some weapons, however bent and futile. ANC and PAC have no other means to maintain their opposition to the intolerable, while FRELIMO has no better. For the latter, the Myth is a comfort in troubled times; for the former, the only avenue of escape from an intolerable reality.

In Angola, with the revolutionaries' general illusions about the fragility of imperialism, the armed struggle appeared as effective a means as any to secure independence. In Mozambique, after the Portuguese reaction in Angola had been analyzed, a guerrilla campaign appeared not only potentially effective but perhaps the only feasible alternative, a course of action offering considerable promise. The decision by ANC and PAC to begin the armed struggle only after any chance of success had evaporated within South Africa was futile when taken, and increasingly so when the only mode of resistance became exile-based.

Guerrilla-war, the last option of the weak, the most costly and protracted route to power, has been offered as a conscious choice by the revolutionary among other options. In many cases it is not. Some, like ANC, have tried every alternative avenue first. The "logical" if horribly painful course would be apparently to accept what "appears" irremediable: the triumph of apartheid and the emasculation of the black man, the existence of Israel and the exile of the Palestinians, or the authority of the Latin American oligarchs and the misery of the peasants. Surrender to oppression is for some men unthinkable. Thus some means of change, some course of action, some strategy of revolution is for them at least essential. A guerrilla-revolution may be a valid option, as it has proven elsewhere. It may also be the only option, so secure is the power of the oppressor. It may also be a futile option—so weak are the revolutionaries—but notwithstanding still "valid" as an alternative to surrender. The Myth offers an alternative to the "logic" and "appearance" of the pragmatic and an alternative that has elsewhere emboldened men to strike and win. The Myth, however, cannot replace reality but only illuminate it. If the guerrilla-revolutionary believes that simply by following the undigested dictum of the theory, simply by being a revolutionary guerrilla, victory will come, then the vague border line into fantasy will have been crossed. Then, given the aims of the revolutionaries, guerrilla-war may not even be a futile option in that such a campaign may be counterproductive, engendering conditions even more intolerable or strengthening the power and refining the strategy of the opponent.

Guevara's *foco* altered the Bolivian government, frightened the oligarchs elsewhere into action, disrupted the orthodox revolutionary base, and made the prospects for the next *foco* in Latin America less promising. Still, Bolivia seemed to be a viable target, while the same could not be said about Israel. Putting aside the possibilities of the Arabs negotiating an Israeli withdrawal or seeking to coerce Israel into a major compromise in return for secure boundaries, the fedayeen strategy of attrition has not only been futile but has nearly eliminated a strategy of provocation, manipulating Israel into another round of open war and overexpansion. The fedayeen's low-level, commando activities have in fact by constant repetition raised the Israeli level of toleration month by month,

incident by incident, so that the prospects of massive retaliation grow fainter. The fedayeen have only hardened
Israeli hearts, improved Israeli security techniques, eliminated their own strategic options, and made certain that
the Palestinians can no longer secure even half-a-loaf. For
the Palestinians the guerrilla option was by no means the
best choice or the last choice but a poor choice. For the
fedayeen, dedicated to the elimination of Israel, it was not
necessarily the best option, discarding as it did the tools
of internal terror, the orchestration of diplomacy and violence, and the potential of intermediate compromise. For
all, the selection of the guerrilla option has usually been a
result not of careful strategic planning but of desperation.
The final strand of the Myth is that the option for a
guerrilla-revolution is a cold, rational selection, balancing
assets and delineating contradictions—and it is the one
aspect of the Myth that can lead to fantasy. The need to
act without the capacity to do so determines the decision
—the need overpowering, undeniable—and forces the
choice. Limited to tactics, the guerrilla-revolutionaries
often insist these are a strategy.

Far from the frustrated agony of the desperate men
rushing into the armed struggle, the attractions of guerrilla-revolution—low initial investment and high yield
—have caught the eye of the major players on the international field. The Myth has been manipulated for major-
power aims or magnified or distorted to secure aims far
different and often opposed to those of the men in the
field. Consciously or unconsciously, those in the seats of
power have added luster to the Myth by their enthusiastic
endorsements or by their professed concern. Whether the
revolutionary-guerrilla strategy is based on illusions or
whether the means are appropriate to the end has counted
little, against the possibilities for national gain or loss on
the bigger board of world politics.

The revolutionary centers of the world cannot in all
conscience deny the immutable laws, often so disruptive

of rational planning, but they can manipulate the idealists. With guerrillas Moscow can, for example, create a zone of chaotic stability in Africa, disrupting by proxy avowed enemies, harvesting friendship and advantage from new client-allies with considerable assurance that time will reveal neither victory nor defeat but only an aggrandizement of influence. With a guerrilla-strategy the provocation is too slight and the potential for serious change in the world balance too small to escalate, as a more conventional intervention might, into a serious confrontation. The Chinese, with fewer international responsibilities, can afford even to be provocative. Advantages can be acquired on the cheap; revolution, so difficult to achieve in reality, so impossible to deny ideologically, so potentially dangerous strategically, can be fostered without risk. The Chinese can achieve a sense of revolutionary well-being for a system isolated and torn by obscure internal rifts. For the revolutionaries in power, the guerrilla-revolution as the standard of the masses can be waved fraternally over a cynical policy of national gain. Even the pure of heart but limited of purse can pursue revolutionary politics by acquiring at little cost a guerrilla client, thereby providing ideological circuses for a people with little bread and fewer prospects. In southern Yemen, a land of rocks, desert, and desperation, the government can back the Gulf Liberation Front not for sullied gain, strategic advantage, or cynical hope of future oil rights, but out of the purity of fraternal feelings, associating the regime with the great international struggle against imperialism. For all the revolutionary regimes—the great and cynical or the small and idealistic —the guerrilla-strategy can be employed without an expensive ticket of entrance, and with a near-guarantee against unfortunate results, and, beyond the inevitable ideological spin-off benefits, with a possibility of pure advantage. No wonder the guerrilla has been raised into the pantheon of revolutionary heroes, exalted in the literature of ideology, and has seemingly found a place amid the mighty.

On the other side of the hill, the overt forces of order have marshaled in the face of the threat trumpeted from Moscow and Peking, not to mention from Hanoi and Havana. The threat posed by the guerrilla-revolution often seems more real the farther removed the observer is from the scene of battle. On the ground in Vietnam, the American military recognizes its difficulties but can respond in traditional ways. In Washington, the immense commitment of resources, military, financial, and intellectual, was first invested in the early Sixties with enthusiasm if later with despair. This was a result not entirely of actual American strategic concerns in Southeast Asia but in part because, however unconventional guerrilla-revolution, the American response had to be traditional. The guerrilla idea was not alien to the American mind. The theory of the guerrilla was simple and elegant and far more malleable than the complicated mathematical theories and war games of nuclear strategy. The practice of guerrilla-warfare could be grasped by the military mind without long training in formal logic, computer technology, and applied physics. Vietnam was a *real* war, whereas potential nuclear war, second strikes, and the dynamics of mutual alarm remained alien. The threat of the men in the jungle was a threat that could be met on a military level with comfortable, if ineffectual, responses. On the other hand, for the American intellectual theoreticians of order, the nature of the appropriate response—intricate and highly calculated reforms to transform Vietnamese society—fit the prejudices and aspirations of the moment. The oppressing and desperately real challenge of the nuclear threat could only conjure up vast, incredibly expensive systems of hardware and technological triumphs without human compensations, while the guerrilla could be met by using the advanced tools of social science for the betterment of man. Vietnam, where pacification and agricultural innovation could transform combat, was an arena of *real* scope and the logic of ABM and MIRV was not.

For the military mind, the guerrilla threat was magnified because its "unconventionality" must be countered conventionally, using familiar weapons and orthodox tactics in a massive commitment. For the civilians, the threat was magnified because it was unconventional, requiring revolutionary reforms usually so difficult to force on static societies. The result has been that the guerrilla-revolutionary has become for many the anti-hero, the great threat which must be met in comfortable ways or by cherished means. As the centers of revolution have embellished the Myth by necessity and cunning, so have the men of order by elaborating and extending their response out of proportion to the reality of the threat. Even before Vietnam justifiably absorbed the attention of America, guerrilla-revolution had become a fashionable challenge to be met in elegant and complex ways but ways which needed the talents, the scope, the capacities, and the experience of various available careerists. Just as the French in Algeria sought to create a counter-myth, the Americans, until Tet at least, felt they had erected a counter-technique. The Vietnam challenge proved very real indeed and quite intractable, so that the special and highly unpleasant American experience was generalized. Washington believed as deeply in Guevara's Second and Third Vietnams as had the originator. Guerrilla-revolution attracted unwarranted attention at first because it presented an attractive challenge and then because the response in particular circumstances had been ineffectual and therefore, it was assumed, any response in all circumstances would be as ineffectual. The revolutionaries were caught up in the Myth for ideological reasons, manipulating it for limited local advantage; but the men of order had largely saddled themselves with the Myth as a result of specific and painful experience.

The impact of the guerrilla-revolutionary theory on distant friends and present or potential opponents, warped by transmission, distorted by manipulation, and magnified by different illusions, has added a patina of international recognition to the Myth, unwittingly or maliciously. The Myth has been imbued with the legitimacy of recognition that still fails to explain repeated failures. Yet the repeated selection of a guerrilla-revolution can be explained fully neither as a result solely of international admiration nor of specific strategical choice. The backing of Moscow or the opposition of Washington might be a consideration but not the determining one. The lack of other options may be a valid reason in some cases but surely not in all. Basically, the attraction of the theory seems to be not that it is a formula to secure professed goals—the fruits of victory—but that the struggle itself is worth the cost. The price of admission is often low, the excitement of the combat deeply satisfying and indefinitely prolonged, and the final results unimportant since the rules have determined them before action began. From afar the guerrilla loses time after time, but down in the jungle it is not who wins or loses, now, but that the struggle continues, that men persist. Some may stay the course for pay or for shallower and more transient motives, but many love the action of revolution. The satisfaction of the life of the jungles has proven capable of export to farther and often less violent terrain. The way of the guerrilla represents a highly exciting mode of change within a world that increasingly seems immobile, intractable, overweeningly secure, immune to the existence of oppression, exploitation, hunger, misery, and mass murder. The cold, gray power of success, the vast repressive resources of the system, the isolation and impregnability of the establishment have demonstratively frustrated, time after time, the efforts of the most dedicated. Change, when and if it does come, creeps along almost imperceptibly. Even the slightest movement apparently can only be secured by vast and disproportionate expenditures of time, energy, blood, and money. While the way of the guerrilla can rarely produce movement, it can satisfy often inarticulated needs, political as well as psychic.

For a decade in Africa, all the movement has been the wrong way for the nationalists. The great tide of liberation has ebbed; the winds of change blow from south to north. There has been no powerful united Black Africa but only wrangling and fragile mini-states. Parochial politics, narrow self-interest, jealousy, pique, egotism, and corruption have played as great a part in Black Africa as they have in other places at other times. Black Africa has had no monopoly on morality, has had no striking successes in rapid development, has found no means to unity, no great international role to play, and, most significant, has not created out of the early idealism any visible power to act on the white bastion. The liberation movements have not become the point of the lance, for there is no lance except in the *pro forma* communiqués of offices and institutions caught up in other, seemingly more vital, activities. That the liberation movements persist, however, supplies Black Africa with a needed dose of idealism although even then the intensity of concern diminishes rapidly with the distance from the front. Still, if the guerrilla-revolutionaries to the south did not exist, Black Africa would have to invent a substitute. For Black Africans they are an outward symbol of the supposedly inward drive and purpose which seemed so real a decade ago. They supply a political cement, albeit shallow, and a moral example, albeit dim and distant, for the continent. For those involved, the guerrilla campaign itself stands as witness to their dedication and determination to continue the just struggle. For these men to resign themselves to what appears to many inevitable—the hegemony of the white man over southern Africa—would not only be too frustrating personally—all the long sacrifices in vain, all the martyrs futile, all the hopes chimeras—but, more important, would be concession not compromise, recognition not toleration, of what appears to many men institutionalized evil. If ANC or ZANU, now or in the foreseeable future, cannot by force of arms win justice, they can, by acting in the field, by further sacrifice, by new martyrs, by persisting beyond reason, keep lit the glittering torch of liberation. They are now the real heroes of Africa, not the previous generation of liberators, now fat men in government limousines. If they resign, failures in the field, and withdraw into the limited comforts of exile, there is no guarantee that a new generation will grasp the torch at a time and place of their choosing. Perhaps such an inchoate generation does in fact exist in the Bantustans of South Africa or the small shops of Luanda or the Tribal Trust Lands of Rhodesia, but there is no guarantee; therefore, if for no other reason than this, the campaign continues. In so doing, this generation of freedom fighters, building on the myth of the guerrilla, fashions a Black magic to counter the white myth of the Afrikaner and the Briton that embodied their "right" to rule. When in time the black myth matures on the foundation of the revolutionary-guerrilla, then too may the power of the white bastion to impose *its* myth or reality have faded. Then the new myth may supplant the old, as the black freedom fighters will triumph over the white regimes. Until that time, the campaign soothes the larger anxiety of Black Africa, maintains the cause of liberation as a fact, and on a narrower level gives meaning and justification to men on the edge of despair. To desist might save a few lives but would deny justice, deny the past, compromise the future, and forego what might, just might, yet be a winning hand —in return for the deepest humiliation, racial, national, and personal.

For the fedayeen of Palestine the guerrilla-revolution, a disaster area on the field of battle, has been a remarkable political success within the Arab World. The humiliation in the face of Israeli power, particularly among those with interests and desires beyond the normal daily rounds, has been very great indeed. The Palestinian has been the man without a country in the Arab World, dependent on his cousins for subsistence, tolerated if productive, interned if disorderly, denied his history, his heritage, his very status as a free man. For years dependent on promises of others, whose own needs were always more pressing, he has lived on the bitter bread of charity even in the high-rise apartments of Beirut. The immense attraction of the fedayeen philosophy for many was the opportunity to act, to determine history instead of being molded by past errors, to expurgate shame through participation in a high and noble deed, to find a vehicle for idealism. That the guerrilla-act was bad war and dubious politics was not as important as its return in pride. Whatever specific psychological hungers the guerrilla-philosophy fed—and they must surely have been more than superficial pangs —as a revolutionary strategy guaranteeing not so much ultimate victory as an avenue of action, the way of the guerrilla proved tactically sound. There now are such Arabs as Palestinians even if the entity of Palestine re-mains vague. Palestinians can be proud that they act while the other Arabs repeat the old words patience, prudence, and time that emasculated the spirit and denied the prom-ised land. In pure terms of power, for the first time the Palestinians are a factor to be conjured with in Cairo and Amman and Beirut. They can neither be taken for granted nor easily traded for limited national interests. What other policy than the strategy of the guerrilla would have created a new, proud, brave people out of the ashes of defeat, lifted them to a place with the Arab mighty, given them not a home, alas, not the promised land but nevertheless a very real sense of power and control over their destinies so long in alien, if superficially friendly, hands. That the new power could not—has not, they would say—secured the golden fruit of victory palls be-fore the reality of power that does exist, before the deeply felt spiritual transformation.

The changes achieved have been paid for with lost options often offering more real advantages to many Pales-tinians than the more exciting dreams of the fedayeen.

Immediate if humbling negotiations soon after the 1967 debacle might have secured a return to prewar conditions, the recall of the most recent wave of refugees, and perhaps even slight concessions by the Israelis to achieve secure borders. Later the discreet use of terror coupled with serious diplomatic negotiations might still have won back much of what had been so swiftly lost. Such eventualities, however, could only return the Palestinian to the half-life of stateless men moved on the board by other players, could only have brought a *hegira* to the refugee camps, could only offer what for a generation had almost destroyed the Palestinian spirit. The way of the fedayeen instead denied the validity of the route back, of the grinding reality of the past, and held out the high road to total victory. As long as the present illusion persists that the fedayeen, and with them the Palestinians, are moving down that high road, then the Palestinian life is lived on a higher and better plane of good works in the cause of the true faith.

That the good works have not succeeded in the field, have brought extensive suffering to the Arab population, have pushed two Arab governments to the point of collapse, have apparently largely eliminated a diplomatic solution which would ease the physical tribulations of many, and have frozen the cease-fire lines in frontiers advantageous to Israel pales in the minds of the fedayeen before what the war of national liberation *has* achieved. A Palestine entity exists where none did before; a Palestine power is present where none was before; a spirit of determination exists in the Arab Nation, where only resignation reigned before. Moreover, for the fedayeen these visible transformations are shadowed by the victories on the battlefield, invisible yet to other eyes. Even if the scales of illusion do in time fall from Arab eyes, the net gain in pride may compensate for the shattering of the illusion of certain victory over Zionism.

For the Palestinians the guerrilla-revolution has already succeeded by creating a Palestine of the spirit if not of the flesh. Just as in South Africa, where the white myth has attracted slowly and haltingly a like black myth, opposite but yet not equal, so too have the Palestinians found an alternative to the myth of Zionism. Unlike the Palestinians, the state of Israel has had for twenty-five years the military capacity to mold objective reality to fit the myth of Zionism. That very military capacity is an outward symbol of the strength, and it will water further the Zionist myth. The Israelis have made their myth reality, have not been led into the way of fantasy, have turned dreams into concrete and steel, Sabras and soldiers. And across the border wire, the Palestinians too have a new dream buttressed by the myth of the guerrilla, but it is a dream beyond the techniques of achievement that the way of the guerrilla offers. Perhaps, if they are fortunate, the dream will be transformed into reality, perhaps not into the reality of the fedayeen's Palestine state but into a lesser reality, a Palestine Nation no longer seized on the question of specific boundaries but rather content with the possible in a less than perfect world and aware that the proud as well as the powerful can find a place to breathe free—a place, however, narrower in scope, ample for the new spirit. If so, the myth of inevitable victory may not attract the new generation; if not, the rasp of despair may shred the still frail Palestine spirit.

Che's doom-laden journey into Bolivia has become, as he intended, a blood sacrifice in the cause of revolution. The odds against success for Guevara were not material but were only the desperate need to act against injustice. If sacrifice brought victory, then nothing would have been in vain. If it did not, then an example had been raised for others to emulate and all would not have been in vain. The blood sacrifice was made, the symbol perceived, his epitaph written, and the *foco* justified. At the time, the alternatives for Che and for revolution in Latin America were all too pedestrian, all too slow, too vulnerable to corruption, too limited in the past, and too often open to manipulation. The conventional, mature revolution lacked real immediate promise. Latin America seemed to groan under oppression, the people exploited beyond bearing, and yet the self-professed revolutionaries went their narrow party ways bearing petitions instead of rifles. Guevara felt as a political man, a revolutionary, that someone must act to open a crevice in the wall of oppression, to open a way for the silent and despondent to pour out. Che gave the silent ones a myth, not unwittingly, which as a political act was the most he had to offer. He did not succeed in the *foco*, but he had in life, and most particularly in death. The subsequent deification of the Che-the-Guerrilla, Peerless Leader of the Wretched, exploited by song writers, beret manufacturers, bad poets, poster salesmen, and the movie industry, as a romantic rebel against the times and fate should not obscure the fact that if Guevara did not grasp political power—supposedly his indispensable and unavoidable purpose—he did vividly and dramatically show others the necessity of so doing, even if they discarded his tactics. Guevara supplied an ideal for many of the desperate and frustrated. Freed of the responsibilities of narrow politics, alone in the face of danger, master of his destiny, beyond the endless constraints of society, he acted in the true cause, offered his life to the ideal, and accepted the consequences of present failure, sure of the verdict of the future.

More than the Palestinian fedayeen or the African liberation fighters, Che Guevara represented the Myth distilled to pure fantasy, tactics as strategy, the word as the deed. The burden of the message was that to be a revolutionary one must revolt, act without endless planning, without sterile preparation, without waiting for the "mature" situation, and without consideration for the wishes of the prudent or the advice of the wise. This may not have been exactly the signal Guevara meant to send but this is what much of the world received: to act was to

live. If the jungles of Bolivia were too distant to supply a
stage, there were other jungles of political oppression,
spiritual bondage, and racial intolerance. Far away from
the failed *foco*, the students of Paris sealed into an archaic
and unresponsive educational system under a less than
benevolent despotism, the new American Left trapped and
frustrated in the face of the naked power of the huge,
immobile majority of the comfortable when America's
ills cried out for radical change, the young intellectuals in
Caracas or Buenos Aires who saw "democratic" change
hailed and the oligarchs shift musical chairs while the
peasants lived, as had their ancestors, lives of desperate
deprivation—these idealists saw at once, intuitively and
without need of poring over the history of the *foco*, that
Che had found a way out of their own tangled jungle. For
them, Che proved the raw materials of a spiritual revival.
His name was to be exploited, it is true, by all those who
make conventional capital of art, for his life was an art
work; but his name and his act went marching on before
the newly dedicated, as he had intended.

Che's "myth" is unlike that of the Africans and Palestinians. They incorporated the revolutionary myth of the
guerrilla into their own dreams and aspirations, countering
the existing myths of their oppressors. Che rather acted out
the new myth of revolution in a fantasy world, hardly
interested in the location of the stage or the names of the
players. He fashioned his life and his death as a symbolic
act, but an act far beyond the intent of revolutionary
theory or the revolution myth. Both the Africans and the
Palestinians have attempted to apply the strictures of the
revolutionary theory and have been strengthened by
the Myth in the process. Che ignored the very theory he
had sought to amplify, acted as if to accept the myth of
guerrilla-revolution as objective reality should be sufficient
to assure triumph, and perhaps realized that it would not.
Other guerrilla-revolutionaries have drawn back from
Guevara's luminous fantasies. Some few have not. And the

projection into the real world of myths that have decayed
into fantasies has not been limited to guerrillas. The same
phenomenon can be discovered in the students of industrial societies, but that phenomenon falls beyond the scope
of revolutionary theory and malpractice. In any case, the
guerrilla fashion is world-wide, the rhetoric in whatever
language recognizable, the uniforms of insurrection copied
from copies, the songs learned from newsreels or docu-
mentaries. The pure coinage that Che sought to mint has
been debased. When the Pakistani radical Tariq Ali in
London says that "We are all Guevarists," he is largely
right in that the power of the myth of the guerrilla
strengthens the revolutionaries but, perhaps, unwittingly
also largely right in that the example of Che's last fantasy
has by many been accepted as reality.

For those immune to the fantasies of the Guevarists,
the way of the guerrilla can and does offer a means to
evade bleak reality by permitting a course of action that
consoles the wretched, the damned, the humiliated, and
the miserable while holding out if not the certainty at
least the hope of victory—a victory not only in the field
but of the spirit. Such a course may be futile, may be self-
defeating of the high purpose of the cause, may lead but
to the grave, but most assuredly does raise men from the
quicksand of resignation to the hilltops of pride. Often
debased or warped by commercial exploitation, by mindless activists, or by the desperate needs of the foolish or
frantic, the way of the guerrilla still maintains a certain
nobility and high adventure. The vision of the free, proud
man on the hillside—beyond restraint, beyond petty compromise, bearded, brave, and bold in his sacrifice—holds
as much attraction for stifled bureaucrats as it does for the
young men trapped under old institutions. Alas, the slim,
proud man on the hill—his rifle at ease, his soul at rest,
bathed in an aura of justice—is more likely to be a desperate, fleeing, frightened boy, wet, dirty, cold, hungry,
tired, panting his uncertain way through a real but un-

familiar jungle ahead of police dogs, beneath helicopters, a few minutes away from swift death or long years in prison. He for one short span, however, lives as a man —and by so doing so inspires others. This is what the Myth can grant, and it is no mean gift.

Notes

PART I

1. Karl Marx and Friedrich Engels: *Revolution in Spain* (New York, 1939), p. 55.
2. V. I. Lenin: "Discussion on Self-Determination Summed Up," in William J. Pomeroy, ed.: *Guerrilla Warfare and Marxism* (New York, 1968), p. 106.
3. V. I. Lenin: "Guerrilla Warfare," in Pomeroy: *Guerrilla Warfare and Marxism*, p. 90.
4. See Barton Whaley: *Guerrillas in the Spanish Civil War* (Cambridge, Mass., 1969).
5. Kuomintang's First National Congress, January 30, 1925, "Manifesto," quoted in Dun J. Li: *The Road to Communism: China Since 1912* (New York, 1969), p. 25.
6. Samuel B. Griffith II: *The Chinese People's Liberation Army* (London, 1968), pp. 22–3 (quoting Yeh T'ing).
7. Mao Tse-tung: *Selected Military Writings* (Peking, 1963), p. 228.
8. Mao Tse-tung: "Primer on Guerrilla Warfare," in Donald Robinson and S. L. A. Marshall, eds.: *The Dirty Wars* (New York, 1968), p. 283.
9. Griffith: *The Chinese People's Liberation Army*, p. 55.
10. Mao Tse-tung: *On Guerrilla Warfare* (New York, 1961), p. 65.
11. Mao Tse-tung: *Problems of Strategy in China's Revolutionary War* (Peking, 1965), p. 4.
12. Geoffrey Fairbairn: *Revolutionary Warfare and Communist Strategy* (London, 1968), p. 139 (quoting Chinese Defense Minister Marshall Lin Piao in September 1965).

13. Che Guevara: *Guerrilla Warfare* (New York, 1961), p. 3.
14. Mao Tse-tung: "Primer on Guerrilla Warfare," in Robinson and Marshall: *The Dirty Wars*, p. 284.
15. Michael Elliott-Bateman: *Defeat in the East, The Mark of Mao Tse-tung on War* (London, 1967), p. 139.
16. Vo Nguyên Giap: *People's War People's Army* (New York, 1967), p. 56. He did add "as the saying goes" to avoid rank plagiarism.
17. Vo Nguyên Giap: "The Anti-French Resistance War," in Pomeroy: *Guerrilla Warfare and Marxism*, p. 213.
18. Ibid., p. 217.
19. Fairbairn: *Revolutionary Warfare and Communist Strategy*, p. 188.
20. Vo Nguyên Giap: "The General Insurrection of August 1945," in Pomeroy: *Guerrilla Warfare and Marxism*, p. 217.
21. Fidel Castro: "Speech to the OLAS Conference," in ibid., pp. 294, 296.
22. Brian Crozier: "The Strategic Uses of Revolutionary War," in *Problems of Modern Strategy*, Part Two, Adelphi Papers (London), No. 55 (March 1969), p. 46.
23. Fairbairn: *Revolutionary Warfare and Communist Strategy*, p. 141.
24. Castro: "Speech to the OLAS Conference," in Pomeroy: *Guerrilla Warfare and Marxism*, p. 296.
25. Fidel Castro: "A Necessary Introduction," in Ernesto Che Guevara: *Bolivian Diary* (London, 1968), p. 18.
26. George Grivas: *Guerrilla Warfare and EOKA's Struggle* (London, 1964), p. 4.
27. Walt Whitman Rostow: "The Grand Area of Revolutionary Change," a speech delivered at the United States Army Special Warfare School, Fort Bragg, North Carolina, June 1961, in Robinson and Marshall: *The Dirty Wars*, p. 337.
28. John Gerassi: *The Great Fear in Latin America* (New York, 1967), p. 13.
29. Amilcar Cabral: "National Liberation and the Social Structure," speech to the Tri-Continental Congress, January 1966, in Pomeroy: *Guerrilla Warfare and Marxism*, p. 263.
30. Ghassan Rifa'i: "Joseph Alsop and the Political Bomb," *Arab Palestine Resistance*, No. 9 (June 1969), p. 37.

PART II

1. See Barton Whaley: *Guerrillas in the Spanish Civil War* (Cambridge, Mass., 1969).
2. See Enrique Lister: "Lessons of the Spanish Guerrilla War (1939–1951)," *World Marxist Review,* February 1965, pp. 35–9.
3. See Zizis Zografos: "Lessons of the Greek Civil War," *World Marxist Review,* November 1967, pp. 42–5.
4. Ferhat Abbas: "Editorial," from *Réalités Algériennes et Marxisme,* No. 1 (November–December 1956), in William J. Pomeroy, ed.: *Guerrilla Warfare and Marxism* (New York, 1968), p. 250.
5. These particular official figures were given by Gloria Emerson in "Vietcong Terror Works in Village," *The New York Times,* November 26, 1970.
6. Instructions issued to party committees of two Delta provinces in mid-1969 are quoted in Robert Shaplen: "Letter from Saigon," *The New Yorker,* January 31, 1970, p. 46.
7. Ibid.

PART III:
Case Study Two

1. Y. Harkabi: *Fedayeen Action and Arab Strategy,* Adelphi Papers (London), No. 53 (December 1968), p. 4.
2. Ibid. The quote is from Naji 'Alush, in *The Road to Palestine* (Beirut, 1964).
3. Walter Laqueur: *The Road to War, The Origin and Aftermath of the Arab–Israeli Conflict 1967–8* (Baltimore, 1968).
4. Ibid., p. 116.
5. Ibid.
6. The Palestine National Liberation Movement: *Our Revolution* (n.p., n.d.), p. 2.
7. Ibid.
8. *Free Palestine,* Vol. 2, No. 1 (June 1969).
9. Harkabi: *Fedayeen Action and Arab Strategy,* p. 11.
10. Ibid., pp. 14–15.
11. Karameh Reconstruction Society: *Remember Karameh* (Beirut, n.d.), p. 33.

12. *Our Revolution*, p. 8.
13. Ibid., p. 7.
14. Ibid.
15. Ibid.
16. *Free Palestine*, Vol. 2, No. 1 (June 1969).

PART III:
Case Study Three

1. Che Guevara: "Interview," Havana, April 18, 1959, in Rolondo
   E. Bonachea and Nelson P. Valdes: *Che: Selected Works of
   Ernesto Guevara* (Cambridge, Mass.), 1969.
2. Che Guevara: *Guerrilla Warfare* (New York, 1961), p. 15.
3. Che Guevara: "Interview," April 28, 1959, in Bonachea and
   Valdes: *Che: Selected Works of Ernesto Guevara*, p. 378.
4. Che Guevara: "Political Sovereignty and Economic Independence" (speech), in ibid., p. 226.
5. Interview in *Liberation* (Casablanca), March 17–23, 1965,
   quoted in *Che Guevara Speaks* (New York, 1967), p. 120.
6. Ricardo Rojo: *My Friend Che* (New York, 1968), p. 169.
7. John Gerassi, ed.: *Venceremos! The Speeches and Writings of
   Ernesto Che Guevara* (New York, 1968), p. 424.
8. Ibid., p. 420.
9. Ibid., p. 422.
10. Ibid., p. 422.
11. From an article published in *Verde Olivo*, translated and
    quoted by Daniel James: *Che Guevara* (New York, 1969), p.
    347.
12. Gerassi: *Venceremos!* . . . p. 271. Cf. Rojo: *My Friend Che*, p.
    153.
13. Gerassi: *Venceremos!* . . . p. 415.
14. Ibid., p. 412.
15. Ibid., p. 424.
16. Interview with Régis Debray in *Ramparts*, August 24, 1968.
17. Guevara: *Guerrilla Warfare*, pp. 73–4.
18. Ernesto Che Guevara: *Bolivian Diary* (London, 1968), p. 54.
19. James: *Che Guevara*, p. 277.
20. Guevara: *Bolivian Diary*, p. 77.
21. Ibid., p. 88.
22. Ibid., p. 136.
23. Gerassi: *Venceremos!* . . . p. 424.

24. Guevara: *Guerrilla Warfare*, p. 17.
25. Gerassi: *Venceremos!* . . . p. 412.
26. Ibid., p. 411.
27. Ibid., p. 412.
28. Rojo: *My Friend Che*, p. 153.
29. Guevara: *Guerrilla Warfare*, p. 22.
30. Ibid., p. 48.
31. Ibid.
32. Ibid., p. 47.
33. Ibid., p. 45.
34. Ibid., p. 24.
35. Ibid., p. 29.
36. Ibid., pp. 38–9.
37. Ibid., p. 43.
38. Ibid., p. 17.
39. Gerassi: *Venceremos!* . . . p. 412.
40. Guevara: *Bolivian Diary*, p. 127.
41. Gerassi: *Venceremos!* . . . p. 266.

Bibliography

PART I

GIVEN the all but appalling number of works on the guerrilla in his various facets, it is shocking to discover that there is no real work on the development of guerrilla-theory. By far the great majority of works are limited to specific examples and are sufficiently numerous that a "Counterinsurgency Bibliography" for the United States Defense Documentation Center runs into numerous volumes without ever nearing completion. A somewhat more malleable bibliography in Franklin Mark Osanka, ed.: *Modern Guerrilla Warfare* (New York, 1962) runs to thirty-one pages. All bibliographies are usually swiftly outdated because of the unabated stream of material. A great number of these books and articles, many quite astute, cover the theory and practice of irregular warfare in its finished stages or from a specific angle, but the evolution of the theory is ordinarily crammed into a few opening references to T. E. Lawrence or the Spanish campaign of 1808–12. In addition, a substantial portion of Western comment is directed toward revealing the limitations and fallacies of Communist revolutionary warfare and suggesting a variety of specific or general alternatives to disaster. Two books on French reactions to people's wars are the justly famous Roger Trinquier: *Modern Warfare, A French View of Counterinsurgency* (New York, 1964); and Peter Paret's analysis of *La guerre révolutionnaire*, in *French Revolutionary Warfare from Indochina to Algeria* (London, 1964). Communist studies are largely involved in claiming or denying credit for success, illuminating heresy, and propagating the gospel. A good, if orthodox, collection of Marxist theory is William J. Pomeroy: *Guerrilla Warfare & Marxism* (New

York, 1968), which stresses theory over practice. Perhaps, in any case, it is preferable to go to the sources, now generally correlated from the pamphlets and polemics of the past into tidy compendiums. The basic works (T. E. Lawrence aside) are:

Menachem Begin: *The Revolt*. London, 1951.
Régis Debray: *Revolution in the Revolution*. New York, 1967.
Vo Nguyên Giap: *People's War People's Army*. New York, 1967. Also, *Big Victory Great Task*. New York, 1968.
General Grivas: *Guerrilla Warfare and EOKA's Struggle*. London, 1964.
Che Guevara: *Guerrilla Warfare*. New York, 1961.
Ho Chi Minh: *On Revolution*. New York, 1967.
Mao Tse-tung: *Selected Military Writing*. Peking, 1963.
Abdul Haris Nasution: *Fundamentals of Guerrilla Warfare*. New York, 1965.
Troung Chinh: *Primer for Revolt*. New York, 1963.

Two of the most interesting firsthand books on anti-insurgency are:

Sir Robert Thompson: *Defeating Communist Insurgency*. London, 1966.
Colonel Napoleon D. Valeriano and Lieutenant-Colonel Charles T. R. Bohannan: *Counterguerrilla Operations, The Philippine Experience*. New York, 1966.

There are several solid works on Communist theory and practice in Asia; for example:

J. L. S. Girling: *People's War, Conditions and Consequences in China and South East Asia*. New York, 1969.
Michael Elliott-Bateman: *Defeat in the East, The Mark of Mao Tse-tung on War*. London, 1967.
Geoffrey Fairbairn: *Revolutionary Warfare and Communist Strategy, The Threat to South-East Asia*. London, 1968.

Scholarly coverage of Latin America (except for Castro's Cuba) and Africa is more scanty—particularly in the area of theory.

There is ample theoretical writing from the more contemporary movements, but ordinarily it is not readily available. For example, "Theoretical Armament in the Battle of Liberation," by George Habash, leader of the Popular Front for the Liberation of Palestine, can be found, if at all, in a blurred pamphlet. The most extensive

Arab work, *Guerrilla Warfare,* by General Talas of Syria, remains untranslated. The intricate arguments of Latin American revolutionaries appear in obscure and ephemeral reviews. Amilcar Cabral, the most interesting of the African leaders, writes, if not in Portuguese, then in isolated journals. For the Palestinians, Y. Harkabi, former head of Israeli intelligence and not a disinterested source, has included a summary of their ideas in *Fedayeen Action and Arab Strategy,* Adelphi Papers (London), No. 53 (December 1968). For the Africans, the late Eduardo Mondlane's *The Struggle for Mozambique* (Harmondsworth, 1969), gives a fair indication of African ideas in practice, and Kwamé Nkrumah's *Handbook of Revolutionary Warfare* (London, 1968) details the theory. For Latin America, although there are several works on revolutionaries (see Luis Mercier Vega: *Guerrillas in Latin America* [New York, 1969] and Richard Gott: *Guerrilla Movements in Latin America* [London, 1970]), much of the post-Debray generation is still buried in radical broadsheets and theoretical journals.

PART II

Even the most voracious would choke on the mounds of material directly concerned with the practice of contemporary guerrilla-warfare, much less the extensive and often vital literature of politics, sociology, psychology, even psychiatry, relevant to the subject. The United States government and its various agencies alone have produced a considerable library. The Special Operations Research Office (SORO) has issued not only extensive bibliographies but items of relatively limited interest such as Harley F. Dame, Curtis Brooks, and Curtin Winsor, Jr.: *Research Notes Related to the Utility of Horse Cavalry and Pack Animals in Counterinsurgency Operations in the Latin American Environment* (Washington, 1965). One of the most imposing studies is the three-volume study by the Center for Research in Social Systems: *Challenge and Response in Internal Conflict,* completed in 1968. Then there are the endless professional articles in the military journals (see Colonel T. N. Greene, ed.: *The Guerrilla and How to Fight Him, Selections from the Marine Corps Gazette* [New York, 1962]). Two handy anthologies largely concerned with practice are:

Franklin Mark Osanka: *Modern Guerrilla Warfare.* New York, 1962.
Donald Robinson and S. L. A. Marshall: *The Dirty Wars.* New York, 1968.

Three other anthologies somewhat broader in scope are:

Cyril E. Black and Thomas P. Thornton: *Communism and Revolution: The Strategic Uses of Political Violence*. Princeton, 1964.
Harry Eckstein: *Internal War, Problems and Approaches*. New York, 1964.
Carl J. Friedrich: *Revolution*. New York, 1966.

Four general books on the guerrilla are:

David Galula, *Counter-Insurgency Warfare, Theory and Practice*. New York, 1964.
Peter Paret and John W. Shy: *Guerrillas in the 1960's*. New York, 1965.
Robert Taber: *The War of the Flea: A Study of Guerrilla Warfare Theory and Practice*. New York, 1965.
Charles W. Thayer: *Guerrilla*. New York, 1963.

But there are a great many more. Three books not in the general canon are most interesting, if not directly relevant:

Ted Robert Gurr: *Why Men Revolt*. Princeton, 1969.
E. J. Hobshawn: *Primitive Rebels*. New York, 1963.
E. V. Walter: *Terror and Resistance: A Study of Political Violence*. New York, 1969.

Gurr's work includes an excellent selective bibliography, pp. 369–407, listing much of the work done in the social sciences on political violence.

Even the most cursory list of works basic to the various guerrilla-revolutions of contemporary times would be a substantial task to complete, uninformative to the specialist and intimidating to the vaguely concerned. Instead of five books on China, three on Algeria, and the odd volume on the Congo, the following brief list of a dozen works consists of nothing more than a sampling—personal—of the kind of material available.

Gil Carl Alroy: "The Peasantry in the Cuban Revolution," *Review of Politics*, XIX (January 1967), pp. 87–99.
Aubry Dixon and Otto Helibrunn: *Communist Guerrilla Warfare*. London, 1954.
Harry Eckstein: "On the Etiology of Internal War," *History and Theory*, Vol. IV, No. 2 (1965), pp. 133–63.

John L. Enos: *An Analytic Model of Political Allegiance and Its Application to the Cuban Revolution.* RAND Publication 3197, August 1965.

E. Feit: "Insurgency in Organizations: A Theoretical Analysis," *General Systems,* Vol. XIV (1969), pp. 157–68.

Emmanuel J. Hevi: *The Dragon's Embrace, The Chinese Communists and Africa.* London, 1967.

Chalmers Johnson: "Civilian Loyalties and Guerrilla Conflict," *World Politics,* Vol. XIV (July 1962), pp. 646–61.

Douglas Pike: *Viet Cong: The Organization and Techniques of the National Liberation Front of South Vietnam.* Cambridge, Mass., 1967.

Lucian W. Pye: *Guerrilla Communism in Malaya, Its Social and Political Meaning.* Princeton, 1956.

Carl G. Rotberg, Jr., and John Nottingham: *The Myth of "Mau Mau" Nationalism in Kenya.* New York, 1966.

Stephen G. Xydia: *Cyprus, Conflict and Conciliation, 1954–1958.* Columus, Ohio, 1967.

Calton Younger: *Ireland's Civil War.* New York, 1968.

PART III:
Case Study One

The documentation available for the analysis of southern Africa is most substantial, ranging from the seemingly endless United Nations reports through extensive surveys made by various institutes to the transcripts of the South African treason trials. Placing to one side the massive primary documentation, the scholarly studies of the southern African confrontation are alone sufficiently numerous to repel all but the dedicated, covering as they do not only politics but economics, sociology, and anthropology. Particularly well covered are South African politics until the early Sixties, Rhodesia in relation to Britain, and the earlier period of insurrection in Angola, although less so for Mozambique. Although there is much highly partisan work (cf. various volumes in the Penquin African Library), much remains quite useful. The nearer to the present the interest is focused, the more important becomes the available primary material, increasingly laced with propaganda and vague in detail, particularly as the investigation touches on the various revolutionary movements and their opponents, secretive by necessity. The background and foundations of the present, however, have received ample if often slanted coverage, for few—even among the ranks of disinterested scholars—approach the area with fully open minds.

For South Africa there is an extensive, often critical, literature which would require a lengthy bibliographical section even if the vital periodical literature were ignored. The list here is simply an indication of the variety of material readily available:

Mary Benson: *South Africa, The Struggle for a Birthright.* Harmondsworth, Eng., 1966.

Gwendolen M. Carter: *The Politics of Inequality: South Africa Since 1948.* New York, 1959.

Edward Feit: *South Africa—The Dynamics of the African National Congress.* London, 1962.

————: *African Opposition in South Africa, The Failure of Passive Resistance.* Stanford, 1967.

Leon Marquard: *A Short History of South Africa.* New York, 1968.

Anthony Sampson: *The Treason Cage: The Opposition on Trial in South Africa.* London, 1958.

William Henry Vatcher: *White Laager: The Rise of Afrikaner Nationalism.* New York, 1965.

Three additional works written directly out of the struggle are:

Albert John Luthuli: *Let My People Go: An Autobiography.* Johannesburg, 1962.

Nelson Mandela: *No Easy Walk To Freedom.* London, 1965.

Bloke Modisane: *Blame Me on History.* London, 1963.

Once the period of exile or covert politics has been reached, sound scholarly work faces a severe shortage of valid sources. For any indication of the course of events, reliance has to be placed on primary sources, often propaganda but hopefully with a germ of content. Both ANC (*Sechaba*) and PAC (*Anzania News*) publish journals as well as battle communiqués, manifestoes, records of conferences, and position statements. The South African government has its own publicity services, but the most useful material is usually to be found in the transcripts of the various trials. Much of the secondary work based on these primary sources and a variety of interviews is seriously marred by uncritical sympathy for the African nationalist, particularly ANC, or for the South African defense, as Pretoria sees it, against world communism.

Most of the material available on South-West Africa has arisen from the complicated judicial dispute over the nature of the mandate and usually contains a highly recognizable bias (cf. Ronald Segal and Ruth First: *South West Africa: Travesty of Trust* [London, 1967]). SWAPO publishes *Namib Today* and occasionally speeches and communiqués.

Given that the wars in the Portuguese colonies are year after year rediscovered as "forgotten wars," the material available, although not necessarily in English, is extensive and as often biased as that on South Africa (cf. Father Robert Davezies: *Les Angolais* [Paris, 1965], and Amandio Cesar: *Angola 1961* [Lisbon, 1962]), although *Angola, A Symposium, Views of a Revolt* (London, 1962) is an early exception. A brief general book is Ronald H. Chilcote: *Portuguese Africa* (Englewood Cliffs, N.J., 1967), which contains a fair sampling of the works available on the nationalist movements in the bibliography. In the case of Angola, John Marcum: *The Angolan Revolution, The Anatomy of an Explosion (1950–1962)* (Cambridge, Mass., 1969), is a landmark, and probably a definitive one. For Mozambique, Eduardo Mondlane: *The Struggle for Mozambique* (Harmondsworth, 1969), despite being written by the leader of FRELIMO, is a judicious survey of the armed struggle from the nationalist side. No one like Marcum has as yet appeared on the Mozambique scene, and much of the Portuguese material is not too revealing about the nature of the counterinsurrectionary campaign in either Mozambique or Angola (cf. Al J. Venter: *The Terror Fighters, A Profile of Guerrilla Warfare in Southern Africa* [Cape Town, 1969]). At the present most of the nationalist organizations publish journals: UPA, *A vos da nação Angolana;* MPLA, *Angola in Arms;* UNITA, *Kwacha-Angola;* FRELIMO, *Mozambique Revolution;* COREMO, *The Valliant Hero,* erratically, and *O Combatente,* usually, as well as the usual other material (see CONCP: *La lutte de libération nationale dans les colonies portugaises* [Algiers, 1967]).

A substantial portion of the material available concerning Rhodesian politics involves either the collapse of the Federation (see Patrick Keatley: *The Politics of Partnership, The Federation of Rhodesia and Nyasaland* [Harmondsworth, 1963]) or the constitutional issue (see Kenneth Young: *Rhodesia and Independence* [London, 1967]). Several of the nationalists have, however, published their views:

B. Vulindela Mitshali: *Rhodesia: Background to Conflict.* London, 1968.

Nathan Shamuyarira: *Crisis in Rhodesia.* London, 1967.

Ndabaningi Sithole: *African Nationalism.* Cape Town, 1959.

For the early exile-base period, see John Day: *International National-ism, The Extra-territorial Relations of Southern Rhodesian African Nationalists* (London, 1967). For more recent events, there are *Zimbabwe Review* (ZAPU) and *Zimbabwe News* (ZANU) and journalism. The Rhodesians, like the Portuguese and South Africans, publish very little material and exterior work is often deeply biased (cf. Daniel T. Brigham: *Blueprint for Conflict* [New York, 1969]) or not really revealing (cf. Walter D. Jacobs: "Guerrilla Activity in Rhodesia," in *The Science of Defense* [Munich, July 1969]).

PART III:
Case Study Two

Libraries abound with material on the Arab–Israeli conflict. There are more than seven hundred titles in Arabic alone. Once attention is focused on the Palestinian fedayeen, the interested reader is limited, with one or two exceptions, to journalism, at times quite good, to propaganda, at times quite revealing, and to various of-ficial or semi-official communications, rarely of great value. The problem quite simply is that the fedayeen are revolutionaries fight-ing an active war and are understandably security-conscious. The Israelis have always been security-conscious, seldom even formally revealing what everyone had known informally. On the Israeli side, by and large, beyond the casualty figures, substantially accurate, and the press releases on incidents and intrusions, substantially ac-curate but hardly analytical, the most interesting material remains in intelligence files and will probably do so for the foreseeable fu-ture. Dr. Shimon Shmit and General Mattityahu Peled have written perceptively on the fedayeen, but there has as yet been no transla-tion into English. On the fedayeen side, the communiqués are hope-less, the interviews to journalists not necessarily representative of policy, motivated often by politeness and studded with spur-of-the-moment policy "revelations." Much of the fedayeen philosophy, con-stantly evolving and often contradictory, can be disinterred either from interviews or from the pages of a variety of publications (in particular, *Free Palestine!*). Very little can be found concerning the internal dynamics of the fedayeen, the nature of their divisions, even the size of their parade strength. In some degree, these are not even clear to the involved; and even if they were, publication would hardly be in the fedayeen interest. Consequently, an examina-tion of the fedayeen, particularly in recent years, must be based on hints or guesses unless, as is all too often the case, the investigator is interested mainly in eulogy or obloquy. The first real attempt at a scholarly approach to fedayeen philosophy in English was Harkabi's *Fedayeen Action and Arab Strategy*. Somewhat more sympathetic analyses are Hisham Sharabi: *Palestine Guerrillas, Their Credibility and Effectiveness* (Supplementary Papers, The Center for Strategic and International Studies, Georgetown University, Washington, 1970) and Michael Hudson: "The Palestine Arab Resistance Movement," *Middle East Journal*, Vol. 23, No. 3, pp. 291–307. For background, the Palestine Liberation Organization Research Center and the Institute for Palestine Studies, both in Beirut, have in recent years published a series of pamphlets far more substantial than the usual run of Palestinian propaganda (cf. the monthly *Arab Palestine Resistance*, which does on occasion have a good contributor). There is also Ania Franco: *Les Palestiniens* (Paris, 1968). For a variety of the most recent selections, see:

J. Bowyer Bell: *The Long War, Israel and the Arabs Since 1946.* Englewood Cliffs, 1969.

Fred J. Khouri: *The Arab Israeli Dilemma.* Syracuse, 1968.

Walter Laqueur: *The Road to War, The Origins and Aftermath of the Arab-Israel Conflict 1967–1968.* Harmondsworth, 1969.

Maxime Rodinson: *Israel and the Arabs.* Harmondsworth, 1969.

Nadav Safran: *From War to War: The Arab-Israeli Confrontation, 1948–1967.* New York, 1969.

Hishom Sharabi: *Palestine and Israel, The Lethal Dilemma.* New York, 1969.

PART III:
Case Study Three

As befitting a man who was a myth in his own time, Guevara has inspired a veritable flood of articles, instant books, lay analyses, and journalistic interpretation. Benjamin Ortega, in *El Che Guevara, Reacción de la prensa del Continente American con motivo de su muerte octubre–noviembre 1967* (Cuernavaca, Mexico, 1968), has listed literally thousands upon thousands of items drawn solely from a two-month period; and if newspaper interest slackened somewhat after 1967, the same has not been true of printed analyses in general. It is difficult to discover a single journal of repute or of name that has not published at least one Che article. Out of all this has come very little more than can be found in Guevara's own works, with the addition of one or two other memoirs or documents. In reality there are great stretches of Guevara's life that remain blanks for all but those involved. Even a reasonably accurate chronology of his travels does not exist, much less accurate insight into all the back-stage negotiations in Havana and Moscow or his motives or his Congo experience or the Bolivian revolutionary world. As a result, the basic material on Che is Che—and all that means.

There are now several substantial anthologies of Che in English, which collectively contain nearly every scrap of published material:

Roland E. Bonachea, and Nelson P. Valdes, eds.: *Che: Selected Works of Ernesto Guevara*. Cambridge, Mass., 1969.

John Gerassi: *Venceremos! The Speeches and Writings of Ernesto Che Guevara*. New York, 1968.

George Levan: *Che Guevara Speaks*. New York, 1967.

Jay Mallin: *"Che" Guevara on Revolution*. Miami, 1969.

The central works of Guevara have also been published separately in various editions, with minor differences:

Guerrilla Warfare. New York, 1961.

Episodes of the Revolutionary War. Havana, 1963.

The Bolivian Diaries (ed. Robert Scheer). New York, 1967. (Third World Series, London, 1968; ed. Daniel James, New York, 1968.)

There have been a rash of biographies, but Ricardo Rojo's *My Friend Che* (New York, 1968) contains the most novel information. The most substantial life to date in English is Daniel James's *Che Guevara* (New York, 1969); in Spanish there are two: Horacio Daniel Rodriguez: *"Che" Guevara* (Barcelona, 1968) and Hugo Gambini: *El Che Guevara* (Buenos Aires, 1968). For the Bolivian experience alone, see Luis J. Gonzáles and Gustavo A. Sánchez Salazar: *The Great Rebel, Che Guevara in Bolivia* (New York, 1969); for those interested in the relation of asthma to charisma, see Martin Ebon: *Che, The Making of a Legend* (New York, 1969). Marvin D. Resnick: *The Black Beret, the Life and Memory of Che Guevara* (New York, 1970) and R. L. Harris: *The Death of a Revolutionary, Che Guevara's Last Mission* (New York, 1970) are the two most recent additions in English. These have generally incorporated whatever new information appeared in periodicals after Guevara's death.

For Debray, there is his own *Revolution in the Revolution?* (New York, 1967), which includes his ideas previously published in journals; and his statement at his trial, in *On Trial, Fidel Castro/ Régis Debray* (London, 1968), and his collected articles in *A Strategy for Revolution* (New York, 1970). For revolutionary reaction to the Guevara-Debray thesis, see "Régis Debray and the Latin American Revolution" (special issue), *Monthly Review*, Vol. 20, No. 3 (July–August 1968).

Index

Guide to Alphabet Organizations

ANC — African National Congress

ANM — Arab National Movement

CONCP — Conferência das Organizações Nacionalistas das Colónias Portuguêsas

COREMO — Comité Revolucionário de Moçambique

DPFLP — Democratic Popular Front

ELAS — Popular Liberation Army

FRELIMO — Frente de Libertação de Moçambique

GRAE — Govêrno Revolucionário de Angola no Exílio

IRA — Irish Republican Army

MNR — Movimiento Nacionalista Revolucionario

MPLA — Movimento Popular de Libertação Angola

NATO — North Atlantic Treaty Organization

NLC — National Liberation Committee

OAS — Organization of American States

OAU — Organization of African Unity

PAC — Pan-African Congress

PAIGC — Partido Africano da Independência da Guiné e Cabo Verde

PCC — People's Caretaker Council

PFLP — Popular Front for the Liberation of Palestine

PIDE — Polícia Internacional e de Defesa do Estado

PLA — Palestine Liberation Army

PLO — Palestine Liberation Organization

SWAPO — Southwest African People's Organization

UNITA — União Nacional para a Independência Total de Angola

UPA — União das Populações de Angola

ZANU — Zimbabwe African National Union

ZAPU — Zimbabwe African People's Union

A Note on the Author

J. Bowyer Bell was educated at Washington and Lee University and Duke University, and received a Fulbright fellowship in 1956–7. Since 1956, he has been engaged in full-time research, dealing variously with the Spanish Civil War, modern Italian politics, the Irish Republican Army, and the tactics of political violence. He has published widely in political and scholarly journals, and is the author of three books.

Since 1968, Dr. Bell has been a research associate with The Center for International Affairs at Harvard University. He lives with his wife and children in Waban, Massachusetts.

A NOTE ON THE TYPE

The text of this book is set in CALEDONIA, *a Linotype face designed by W. A. Dwiggins. It belongs to the family of printing types called "modern face" by printers —a term used to mark the change in style of type-letters that occurred about 1800. Caledonia borders on the general design of Scotch Modern, but is more freely drawn than that letter.*

This book was composed, printed, and bound by Haddon Craftsmen, Scranton, Pa.

Typography and binding design by Constance T. Doyle.